Praise for
Untrapping Produ

"This is my new favorite book on product managem   vers everything you need to know to lead a product team an   .uuct manager. Author David Pereira does an excellent job of pointing ou ___ and thinking traps that doom products. The book is full of many insights and tools that will be useful for years to come."

—Mike Cohn, Co-founder, Agile Alliance

"David's book shares several hard-earned lessons of what happens when product leaders, product managers, and especially product owners are not trained to succeed in their jobs, and they go on to make predictable and avoidable mistakes. This book can help you avoid some of these pitfalls."

—Marty Cagan, Partner, Silicon Valley Product Group

"This book touches on all the daily essentials for a product person. It's a practical guide and a meta-analysis rolled into one, serving as the 'Greatest Hits' album of product management. Ideal for newcomers and an excellent refresher for those already immersed in the field."

—Petra Wille, author of *Strong Product People*

"David's brilliant book will help you decipher the chaos of product management and show how to escape all the traps that may condemn your product teams to mediocrity."

—Maarten Dalmijn, author of *Driving Value with Sprint Goals*

"*Untrapping Product Teams* is the best way to transition your teams from delivery to empowered. Help your product teams break free of constraints and change the trajectory of your business with David's book. He speaks not just theory, but from experience."

—Aakash Gupta, author of *Product Growth*

"David wrote the book I wish I had read 20 years ago. Instead, I faced these common product team traps without a map of how to practically navigate them. This book is full of wisdom and inspiration for new and experienced product professionals alike. It will save you a lot of time and energy!"

—Simonetta Batteiger, CEO, Inclusive Leaders

"David's book is an antidote to bullshit management, and at the same time, it's so much more than that. It's a wake-up call for product teams to regain clarity and focus. It's a survival kit for every PM in the trenches facing a reality that other product books fail to acknowledge. There is no fluff, no ideal-world scenarios, only experience-based learnings and a generous amount of eye-opening honesty."

—Ioana Ognibeni, Product Lead and Coach

UNTRAPPING PRODUCT TEAMS

SIMPLIFY THE COMPLEXITY OF CREATING DIGITAL PRODUCTS

DAVID PEREIRA

♦ Addison-Wesley

Hoboken, New Jersey

Cover images: yod 67/Shutterstock; Ihnatovich Maryia/Shutterstock.
Author photo: Courtesy of David Pereira. Photo by Anna Hermann.
Multiple figures created by the author with the help of Canva. Go to https://www.canva.com/ to learn more.

For information about buying this title in bulk quantities, or for special sales opportunities (which may include electronic versions; custom cover designs; and content particular to your business, training goals, marketing focus, or branding interests), please contact our corporate sales department at corpsales@pearsoned.com or (800) 382-3419.

For government sales inquiries, please contact governmentsales@pearsoned.com.

For questions about sales outside the U.S., please contact intlcs@pearson.com.

Please contact us with concerns about any potential bias at pearson.com/report-bias.html.

Visit us on the Web: informit.com/aw

Library of Congress Control Number: 2024933282

ISBN-13: 978-0-13-533538-3
ISBN-10: 0-13-533538-8

4 2024

To the most important people in my life:

Maria, my mom, who raised me with unconditional love.

José Antônio, my dad, who always encouraged me to follow my dreams.

Kevin, my brother and best friend, who has always been by my side no matter what.

Anastasia, my wife, who truly understands me and supports all my wild ideas.

Contents

Foreword by Ash Maurya

Untrapping product teams. When I first ran into those words on David's blog, I knew he had something unique to say. David has been on a mission to hone the art of product management—not simply to crank out more products, but to build products that customers truly love.

As products have gone from being delivered in a box to being delivered over the internet, there's been a dramatic shift in how customers consume, demand, and interact with products. Customers no longer want to wait for long release cycles. They want value delivered to them continuously. This fundamentally changes how products need to be built.

It is no longer enough to simply throw more features at customers. That way of building products used to work at a time when there were huge barriers to entry and few competitors. Even if you got the product completely wrong, you had time to course correct and get back on track.

But fast forward to today. . . . With the internet, open source, and cloud computing, it has become cheaper and faster than ever to introduce new products, which means there is a lot more competition than before—both from incumbents and from new companies starting up all over the world.

In the old world, failing to deliver what customers wanted led to failed projects. But in the new world, continuously failing to deliver what customers want can lead to total business model failure. This is because customers today have many more choices than before. If they don't get what they want from your product, they'll simply switch to something else.

Delivering better customer outcomes in the new world requires rethinking traditional product planning, prioritization, and delivery processes. You can't afford to spend long cycles analyzing, planning, and executing your idea. Speed of learning is key. You need a more iterative approach that replaces top-down planning with continuous discovery and validation.

This is the essence of continuous innovation.

When companies learn fast, they outlearn their competition and get to build what customers truly want. When you outlearn your competitors once, you stand ready to launch a new innovative product and capture market share. But whatever is worth copying will eventually be copied. Only by continuously outlearning your competition can you stay relevant to your customers and see your business model continuously thrive and grow.

The good news is that over the last decade, we've pushed the envelope to define better processes, strategies, and techniques for doing all of the above. Now, for the bad news: **Every process works in theory until you add people**.

And therein lies the heart of the challenge David set out to address with this book. Whenever we've switched from an old way of working to a new one, the journey has always required challenging the status quo and has been riddled with many little traps that can derail even the best-intentioned teams. This time is no different.

While many books tell you what to do, David takes a refreshing approach by telling you what *not* to do—informed by his 15-year journey as a product manager at start-ups and giant corporations. He starts by identifying the most common product traps in the first part of his book, then shows you practical steps for avoiding them—all illustrated with numerous real-world examples.

Untrapping Product Teams is a guidebook for anyone charged with building the next generation of digital products that matter.

We are living in a new era of product management, and David is one of the leading voices showing us the way. I hope you'll implement his practical guidance and help pave the way to a world with better products for all.

Welcome to the new era of product management.

—Ash Maurya, author, *Running Lean* and *Scaling Lean*
December 23, 2023
Austin, TX

Foreword by Jim Highsmith

The internet and graphical user interfaces (GUIs) transformed the software product landscape in the mid-1990s as IT applications transitioned from automating internal business processes to engaging external customers—a change that was obvious to everyone but whose implications were not always appreciated. Users then interacted with character-based, monochrome terminals; devices and computers were connected via wire; and internal operations software ran on a mainframe. The switch to customer-facing applications and technologies created a large demand for extra, specially educated product people and teams.

The game changed again in 2007 with the introduction of cloud computing, big data, iPhones, and social media. In the years 2022–2023, we were flooded with news of increased AI capabilities and the possibility of genuine quantum computing. So, interface design has evolved over the course of more than 30 years, from "green screens" to UI, UX, conversational AI, and driverless cars. At each juncture we needed more—a lot more—product people who understood the software development process and could integrate technological advances into effective product designs.

The fundamental competencies required to thrive in product development both now and in the uncertain times ahead are outlined in David Pereira's book *Untrapping Product Teams*. Whereas others approach complexity with complex solutions, this book's subtitle, "Simplify the Complexity of Creating Digital Products," captures David's basic idea. This is exemplified by his backlog management recommendation, which suggests most backlog items should be eliminated. This type of simplification shows up repeatedly in his book.

My all-time favorite quote comes from Dee Hock, former CEO of VISA:

> "Simple, clear purpose and principles give rise to complex, intelligent behavior. Complex rules and regulations give rise to simple, stupid behavior."

David rails against what he refers to as "bullshit management," which arises from complex rules and regulations that are often the product of a "fixed mindset." If you want a prescription to follow, find another product management book. But if you want clarity of purpose and excellent practices that you can evolve supported by reality-based feedback, stick with David. He makes things "simple"—powerful and easy to understand—without descending into "simplistic" in a way that misleads.

One of the current issues that David addresses is the proliferation of "feature factories," often fueled by the terribly misused "velocity" metric. In their drive to pump out features, delivery teams often put on blinders that shield them from anything beyond stripping the next stories off the backlog and hustling them through to completion. DevOps has exacerbated this trend. It's like driving a car faster and faster down a freeway: "We've increased our speed (velocity) three-fold in the last 50 miles; too bad we don't yet know our destination." The antidote to a feature factory is to concentrate on customer value, as David repeatedly reminds us. But is this really a problem? One research study indicated 80% of software features were rarely or never used, wasting nearly $30 billion, according to a *Forbes* online article in 2019.

David's approach to generating customer value is multidimensional, from creating a value-oriented roadmap rather than one based on epics/features, to collaborating on defining release/sprint goals, to serious backlog pruning, to proposing a set of value-oriented rather than productivity-oriented metrics.

There are two fundamental approaches to product development: the prescriptive "plan–do" versus the adaptive "envision–explore." Subscribers to the fixed mindset think they can plan away uncertainty, whereas those who subscribe to a growth mindset understand uncertainty only yields to action through an exploratory process. David repeatedly charges in with ideas advocating a growth, or adaptive, mindset, particularly when describing the product discovery process. He starts off by saying, "It's tough to accept our ideas are mainly flawed," and then adds "I concluded what product discovery is: It's about the journey and not the plan." Fixed mindsets have a difficult time with flawed ideas and bumpy journeys.

Untrapping Product Teams contains a wealth of practical, usable ideas, in the form of narratives, checklists, outstanding questions, and solid principles. In addition, David's use of stories, experiences, and a conversational, first-person writing style engages the reader. While the primary audience for this book will be anyone with the word "product" in their job title, I think a much wider range of readers—from executives to software engineers—will benefit from David's ideas on product management.

—Jim Highsmith, author, storyteller,
and co-author of the Agile Manifesto
Lafayette, CO, 2023

Preface

This is the place where I openly share how *Untrapping Product Teams* came to exist. It gets personal. I give full credit to the many people who inspired me and helped bring this book to life.

Life has been generous to me. I come from a middle-class family in a small village in Brazil. My parents didn't finish high school but gave me the best education I could wish for. I got where I got not because I'm good, but because many people saw potential in me that I couldn't see myself.

I got my first job when I was 17 because Romero Silva, a computer store owner, believed I could learn to assemble computers. When I turned 24, I moved to São Paulo because Leandro Silveira, an experienced executive, perceived my communication skills as sharp enough to transform me into a product manager. Carlos Locoselli, a professor and mentor, invited me to give MBA lessons when I was 29 because he believed I had stories worth sharing. I moved to Germany because Emmanuel Wintzer (product lead) and Raimund Rix (chief product officer) bet on my potential.

How I came to write is another episode of unexpected opportunities.

Julio de Lima is a highly regarded influencer in the field of software quality assurance for me and many others. He inspired me to write my first post: "7 Key Points to Succeed as a Product Owner."[1] It took me hours, but I finally put the post out. Yet, I would not publish anything else for the next two years.

Anastasia, my wife, convinced me to try writing again. She told me on a walk in Gorky Park in Moscow, "You have a burning passion. You need to do something about it." That touched me, and I committed to writing one blog a month. Three years later, I had written more than 300 posts.

Product management is my passion, and I am especially inspired by three people: Marty Cagan, Melissa Perri, and Ash Maurya. After reading Marty Cagan's masterpiece, *Inspired*, my views on product management were transformed. Melissa Perri's book *Escaping the Build Trap* deeply spoke to me. Ash Maurya greatly impacted how I tackle ideas, prioritizing learning over delivery.

Why do I care so much about writing when you can find great material out there?

My epiphany came during the walk at Nymphenburg Park in Munich with Emmanuel, my first team lead in Germany. We talked about my recent blog, and I shared how much I enjoyed it, but I lacked ideas for new posts, which worried me.

---

1. You can read the original version in case you're curious. I've never edited this article to remind me how I started writing. It can be found at https://medium.com/@davidavpereira/key-points-to-succeed-as-a-product-owner-e7643e3edf9e.

Emmanuel untied the knot: "Have you considered writing about the don'ts? Most people write about what you should do, but only a few share what you shouldn't."

That was it! I didn't want people to face the blows I had to take. I wanted to share what I did wrong and what I learned.

As my blog grew, I met many people who helped me become a better writer. A key person was and still is Maarten Dalmijn. He took time to review my rough drafts, challenged me, made suggestions, and helped me evolve. I owe him much for his genuine intention of helping.

Every person on stage has a strong team behind the curtains. I have someone who has always been by my side—Kevin, my brother. He is probably the only person on Earth who reads all my blog posts. He reviewed this book multiple times and was courageous enough to speak his mind and help me make the content sharper. I cannot find words to express my gratitude to him.

I danced around the book idea for a long time but didn't feel ready to commit. April 20, 2023, was the day that changed. I gave a keynote speech, "Untrapping Product Teams," at the Product Tank Munich. After my address, Ioana Ognibeni, one of the best product managers I know, insisted I had to write a book. She said that I had something to say that people needed to know. Her words got to me. Three days later, I started writing the book.

Ioana and I worked together for a year. Her passion for product management amazed me. She said, "The world needs a book talking about reality, and you know how to talk about it in a way that makes people listen." This sentence inspired me to write the book you're reading now.

After talking to Ioana, I wanted to share what I had learned throughout my career. I often learned lessons the hard way. I faced traps and didn't know how to overcome them, or even worse, I was unaware I was trapped. I thought more people could benefit from my experience. However, writing a book is no easy task. It goes way beyond blogging.

I was lucky to find amazing people to help me sharpen the book. Special thanks go to Maria Chec, who encouraged me to keep my authenticity. Simonetta Batteiger, who read the manuscript on a flight from Germany to Boston, helped me identify confusing content and simplify the message.

I'm tremendously grateful for Ash Maurya, who wrote a generous foreword and took the time to encourage me to keep my original title and shared the behind-the-scenes stories of his own book, *Running Lean*. Beyond that, his approach to treating learning as an unfair advantage drove me to craft this book differently, learning from the beta readers since the early book stages.

I must give a massive special thanks to Jim Highsmith, co-author of the Agile Manifesto, who invested significant time reviewing the content, helping me improve it, and doing me the honor of writing a wonderful foreword for this book.

Mike Cohn encouraged me to push this book forward, which boosted my energy to go the extra mile. Having his support supercharged my inspiration.

Special thanks to the beta readers who spent their time reading early versions of the book. I owe you a lot: Sandra Hinz, Stefan Wolpers, Alexej Antropov, Jennifer Forbes, Si Chen, Nuno Santos, Atanas Kostadinov, Corinna Hammersting, Sebastian Borggrewe, Emiliano Saad, Irene Liakos, Felipe Borgonovi, Mike Berman, and Vira Chesnokova.

Of course, I could not forget the outstanding editorial team behind the production of this book. I wholeheartedly thank Haze Humbert for her strong support from end to end, Menka Mehta for all the assistance provided, Julie Nahil and Jill Hobbs for improving the book's readability and flow, and Jayaprakash P. for coordinating the book project.

This book wouldn't exist without all these people. I hope *Untrapping Product Teams* empowers you to rock the world!

Register your copy of *Untrapping Product Teams* on the InformIT site for convenient access to updates and/or corrections as they become available. To start the registration process, go to informit.com/register and log in or create an account. Enter the product ISBN (9780135335383) and click Submit. If you would like to be notified of exclusive offers on new editions and updates, please check the box to receive email from us.

About the Author

David Pereira is a product leader with more than 15 years of experience. He's sharpened his skills by leading diverse teams, from start-ups to giant corporations. Since 2020, he has openly shared his mistakes, failures, and insights on product management, reaching more than 10 million readers worldwide. His thought-provoking courses had 15,000-plus satisfied students across more than 120 countries.

The numbers don't drive David, but the outcomes do. He often receives messages from people worldwide sharing stories on how his content helped them overcome a challenge, get a new job, receive a promotion, or even start a business. Such messages touch and inspire him.

Let his unique expertise inspire your journey.

Feel free to drop a message at contact@d-pereira.com.

Introduction

When I started my career in 2008 as a software engineer, it didn't take long to receive a nickname, *Mr. Why*. Every day, I'd get a list of requirements to implement without the faintest idea about their purpose. Trying to understand, I asked many questions but rarely got answers. When I did get something, it was pretty unconvincing. Here are some examples: "Because the business said so," "Sales promised it to our customers," or the classic, "My boss's boss wants it." Chasing unsatisfactory answers was my life, but something was about to change.

In 2012, I received the opportunity to become a product manager. Although I had no idea what it entailed, I got excited about one particular aspect: to be in a better position to obtain satisfying answers. As a product manager, I could ensure teams would receive problems to solve instead of solutions to implement. I thought this would be easy to achieve. Well, I was naïve. Most business stakeholders would tell me precisely what they wanted, yet only a few would share why it was necessary. I learned the hard way that what business wants doesn't always match what customers need. And then, unexpectedly, life surprised me with another opportunity.

In 2016, I got my first chance to act as the head of product management. Now, instead of hitting the wall and getting unsatisfactory answers, I would be the one giving the answers. At that time, I wanted to solve the digital product management equation once and for all. I envisioned creating outcome roadmaps, empowering teams to uncover opportunities worth pursuing, and crafting meaningful solutions. I wish life would be that easy. Day in and day out, I fought against the corporate firewall. Top management wanted predictability in outputs and commitment to timelines. I had to battle to protect teams from the feature factory.[1] Sometimes, I led them to successful outcomes; at other times, I had to digest the bitter taste of failure.

For 15 years, I've been part of the same complex equation. It's called digital product management. If you're working in an organization developing digital products, you're also part of this equation, directly or indirectly.

After all these years, I recognize that no matter which part of the equation you are, common challenges lie ahead of you. The diversity and complexity of those challenges don't matter. What matters is how you deal with them. You'll face complex ways of working, which many around you will contribute to making even more complex. However, you'll have a better chance of standing out once you simplify the game.

Everyone has a different understanding of product management. My simple explanation is the art of uncovering opportunities to create customer and business value. Good product management results in products customers love, enabling the business to thrive.

---

1. The term "feature factory" was popularized by John Cutler in 2016 when he wrote "12 Signs You're Working in a Feature Factory" (https://cutle.fish/blog/12-signs-youre-working-in-a-feature-factory).

I've been wondering for a long time about the real challenge of digital product management. After a lengthy reflection, I concluded collaboration is the most arduous challenge. Almost everyone around you will push off in different directions, and only a few people will support you in doing what you have to do. It's easy to end up in a situation where you're doing anything but product management.

The more complex collaboration becomes, the less value you can create. Trying to simplify how teams work isn't natural for most people, but simple ways of working enable teams to progress instead of getting twisted up with processes.

For many years, I struggled because I didn't know how to deal with the challenges I faced. Sadly, I was often unaware when something was wrong. For example, I thought that feature roadmaps were normal, so I created more of them. I believed I was the bridge between the business and tech teams, so I wrote precise requirements. It took me a while to realize the problem was me: Because I was often unprepared for the job, I made things more complicated than necessary. As a result, I led teams straight into traps.

I wrote this book to equip you to overcome the inevitable challenges you will face with digital products. This book will also help you recognize problems you're possibly unaware of. The digital product world is full of traps, and that's the reality whether you like it or not. The main point is that you need to know how to recognize and overcome dangerous traps.

Untrapping Product Teams guides you from complexity to simplicity. You will learn where a pinch of simplicity enables better results, and I will help you understand how to do it step by step. It's not a sprint but a marathon, which can be tiring. Yet, the results are worthwhile if you're willing to embark on the journey. Shall we?

Who Can Benefit from This Book

I've read hundreds of books throughout my life, hoping to evolve my knowledge and become a better professional. That did happen to a certain extent, but I often felt stupid because I didn't know how to apply the insights to my reality. I made this book as actionable as possible because I want you to feel powerful!

This book is for anyone working with product teams. By product teams, I mean a team of cross-functional professionals working on a digital product. Product teams come with many different labels attached to them. Essentially, they're other words for the same thing: teams empowered to deliver value.

You will relate to the content in this book and identify applicable insights if you're part of the product team, lead such a team, or work directly with one. Product managers will benefit the most from this book, as I share many stories from this perspective. Overall, you will learn what makes or breaks product management, and I will take you on a journey from strategy to delivery.

This book also serves founders who want to create organizations where great ideas can flourish. Throughout the book, I will elaborate on the necessary aspects of creating valuable products while decreasing the odds of creating bad ones.

If you're searching for practical content, this book's for you because I wrote the content based on my 15 years of experience working with product teams worldwide. I've been part of start-ups, well-established organizations, consulting groups, and the public sector during this time. The stories in this book relate to my real-world practice.

How to Read This Book

I tried to write this book as if we were having a conversation over a cup of coffee. During this chat, I'm not ashamed to share my biggest mistakes because I care about you, and I want you to avoid the painful blows I had to take.

You can approach this book in two ways: as a five-course meal, moving from start to finish, or as a buffet, where you pick up whatever chapter you want to read. The first option will help you have a better overview of dangerous traps and how to overcome or avoid them. This story aims to engage you and encourage you to take action while empowering you for change. If you prefer the buffet style, you can reflect on what interests you now and read whatever chapter speaks to you the most. You can gain value from each chapter even when not reading the previous and subsequent chapters.

What to Expect from *Untrapping Product Teams*

I aim for this book to be similar to my blog[2]—thought-provoking, practical, and honest. I will expose dangerous traps, explain their impacts, and explore alternatives to overcome them. You can expect tangible stories because I don't want to leave you wondering about real-world situations.

I strived to maximize insights per minute because I value your time.

The content is structured into three parts:

- **Part I: Facing Dangerous Traps.** This part helps you analyze your situation and understand which action to take. We will detail the differences between coordinative and collaborative flow. You will learn to evaluate the big picture, mindset, and what complicates value creation. Then, I will help you recognize the dangerous traps and their impacts while

---

2. I started blogging in 2020, first on Medium.com (https://davidavpereira.medium.com/). Then I migrated to Substack to get closer to my audience. You can find my updated blog at https://dpereira.substack.com/.

gradually preparing you to overcome them. By the end of this part, you will have plenty of insights to boost value creation and simplify unnecessary complexities.

- **Part II: Overcoming Dangerous Traps.** The chapters in Part II focus on equipping you to break free from the traps exposed in Part I. You'll learn the fundamentals of product management combined with simple techniques. Then, we'll embark on the product journey. We'll clarify how to create a strategy simplifying decision making, apply mindful product discovery, use delivery to accelerate value, and measure results beyond outputs. Part II concludes by exploring traps associated with people and collaboration, first by understanding what makes or breaks product teams and then by clarifying how to build stakeholder relationships.

- **Part III: Remaining Untrapped.** Falling back on common patterns is a natural instinct, but you cannot sit back and relax unless you want to get trapped. Part III clarifies how you can craft product principles and use them to set the foundations to keep your teams untrapped. Then, I will equip you with qualitative health checks to help you step back and recognize the status quo, empowering you to improve your situation.

By the end of this book, you will have a solid set of tools in your personal toolbox—from product strategy to product delivery—that prepares you to simplify complexity while driving value. I can't promise you a bulletproof recipe for success, because I don't have one. But I can share what works with hundreds of other teams worldwide.

I'm on a mission to empower product professionals to simplify the product world. This book aims to help everyone who reads it join this mission and battle the overwhelming complexity, ultimately solving the digital product equation. What people call impossible, we make possible.

Let's rock the product world together.

PART I

FACING DANGEROUS TRAPS

"Pain + Reflection = Progress"
—Ray Dalio

In the first part of this book, we will explore what reality looks like for different product teams. The ultimate goal is to expose dangerous traps and understand their impacts. I will walk you through common ways of creating digital products that trap or untrap teams. Then, we will explore the differences between growth and fixed mindsets and how they contribute to results. To close this part, we will paint the real enemy as vividly as possible. I will help you identify detrimental aspects to product teams and gradually equip you to overcome them.

PART I

FACING DANGEROUS TRAPS

1

How Common Ways of Working Trap or Untrap Teams

Expectations and reality tend to diverge in the realm of digital product management. Let us imagine a few scenarios to compare expectations with reality.

Suppose you become a product manager and are excited to create products customers love and help your business thrive. With such a motivation, nothing can stop you. But suddenly, you bump into the corporate firewall. When you face prescriptive roadmaps, extensive timelines, and output commitment, you get sucked into backlog management, quickly getting demoted to a backlog manager.

This kind of disappointment isn't exclusive to product managers. Imagine you're a software engineer. You're passionate about crafting clean code and building scalable solutions. You want to bring your best to the team, but then you realize that shipping features at the speed of light matters most. Pressured, you cut quality to meet deadlines. Now, you're no longer a software engineer. Without realizing it, you've become a coder. Your code stinks and your solutions aren't scalable. Despite initially delivering on time and budget, you're surprised because nobody uses the shiny features you gave your heart and soul to create.

What would happen if you were a product designer? You'd also get a gold pass to the club of frustrated people. You aim to create intuitive designs and outstanding user experiences, but your motivation lasts only until reality hits you. Astounded, you realize that success means creating pixel-perfect prototypes that business stakeholders love and approve, even though they don't represent your customers.

Do any of these situations ring a bell to you? If not, we may live in different worlds, because I've been part of them from South America to Europe, from start-ups to well-established corporations. The question is, what do you do when you face such situations?

When people lack skills, some may complain and do nothing about it. This attitude is what I call becoming the victim of the circumstances.[1] In contrast, with the proper skill set, you can challenge the status quo and transform your situation by engaging in a step-by-step journey.

Simple actions can help you overcome the common traps described earlier. To equip you with the skills to make that possible, I invite you to join me in a conversation about how teams typically work, because that reality has a tremendous impact on what they can achieve.

Let's explore the dynamics frequently present in feature factory companies.

How Feature Factory Companies Work

Not every company is the same. Every organization has its particularities and dynamics, though they all share some common traits. Understanding your company's unique dynamics enables you to identify opportunities to simplify how its product teams work.

First, let's look at companies' typical structure. Companies have multiple departments—for example, management, marketing, operations, customer service, product, and so on. Sometimes, these departments are called teams or areas. What separates departments from one another are their responsibilities and way of working. Departments often work inside their bubble and coordinate tasks with other departments when necessary.

In larger companies, the complexity increases with divisions and units under different leaderships. The relationship between such divisions may be quite distant, and collaboration becomes daunting. For our analysis, we'll stick with a small company. Figure 1.1 depicts some typical departments.

What all departments have in common are ideas, and each department often perceives its ideas as important and urgent. Some ideas relate to their work, others to the company's core product or service.

The more unclear the company's vision and strategy are, the harder it becomes to decide what to do with endless ideas.

---

1. Scientifically, being a "victim of the circumstances" relates to the person's locus of control. Having an internal locus of control means that the person thinks they control their own life and the outcomes of events, while having an external locus of control means embracing the opposite view. Julian B. Rotter developed this concept in 1954, and it has since become a key aspect of personality psychology.

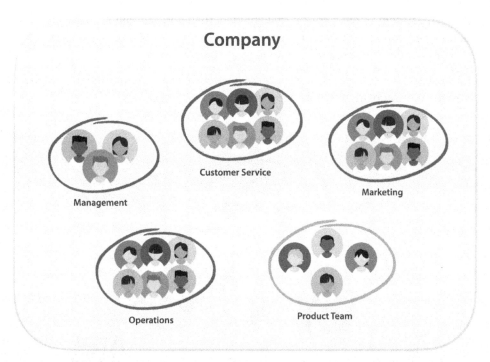

Figure 1.1
Example of company departments

This situation is overwhelming because ideas have different objectives and, in most cases, have no connection with each other. In turn, the excess of ideas and pressure for delivery challenge product teams. Meeting expectations requires interactions with all departments, understanding their wishes, and doing something about them.

Collaboration between Product Teams and Business Stakeholders

Creating a backlog is a common way of dealing with the ideas suggested by the business stakeholders (i.e., the business members interested in your product or service). This method represents a dangerous trap for product teams. Collecting ideas and adding them mindlessly to a backlog is easy—but having a gigantic list of unrelated ideas creates unbearable expectations.

The depth of ideas varies significantly. Sometimes, they are on a milestone level, such as "Expand our product to a new audience." At other times, ideas are related to specific wishes, such as "Allow customers to export their orders of last 90 days." This diversity complicates prioritization. Yet, the typical approach is to put everything in the same bucket and have long discussions until everyone agrees on what comes first.

With extensive backlogs, more business stakeholders than you can handle will knock on your door, asking when you plan to deliver on their ideas. That forces you to coordinate tasks with everyone, complicating collaboration as you juggle multiple topics.

Figure 1.2 illustrates the complex dynamics between product teams, departments, and the backlog. The bigger the company, the more complex this situation becomes.

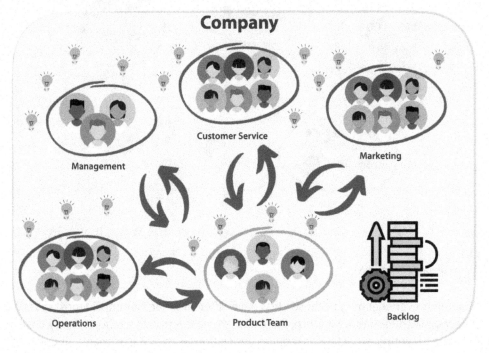

Figure 1.2
Product teams' interactions with business stakeholders and the backlog

When you look at Figure 1.2, what's wrong with it? Take a minute to reflect on it.

Products exist to serve customers, not business stakeholders. When the people creating the product don't interact with customers, creating useless products is the potential result.

It shocks me how often companies develop solutions for their customers without interacting with them. It's easy for us to fall in love with ideas, become blind to reality, or, even worse, forget about it. The results are often undesired.

Releasing New Features Nobody Cares About

How's your experience releasing new features? Maybe it's a hit or miss. Let's continue our conversation about the sad reality of feature factory teams.

After months of hard work and exhaustive coordination, the product team got a new feature out of the backlog. Everyone from the team and business loves it. The new shiny feature is ready for customers, but something unexpected happens. Customers who interact with the new feature don't understand its purpose and cannot benefit from it. Confused, customers reject the new shiny feature beloved by business stakeholders, and inevitably everyone becomes frustrated (Figure 1.3).

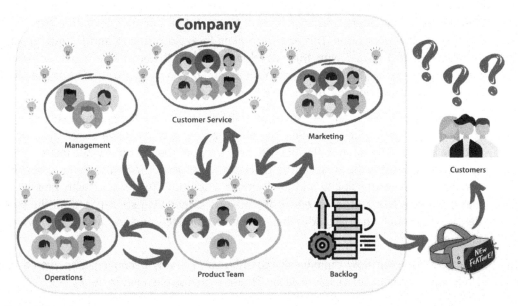

Figure 1.3
Building features customers don't need

Creating solutions companies love, but customers couldn't care less about, isn't why product teams exist. Yet, that happens more often than it should. I call it a bug, not a feature. As with all critical bugs, it requires a hotfix.

If the feature factory is a bug, what would fix that? You cannot expect a simple fix, but fostering empowered teams with collaborative flows will transform the situation. Marty Cagan, SVPG Partner, wrote a blog post defining empowered teams[2]:

> Great teams are comprised of ordinary people that are empowered and inspired. They are empowered to solve hard problems in ways their customers love, yet work for their business. They are inspired with ideas and techniques for quickly evaluating those ideas to discover solutions that work: they are valuable, usable, feasible and viable.

---

2. Marty Cagan, "Empowered Teams," www.svpg.com/empowered-product-teams/.

Empowered teams have significantly higher chances than feature factory teams to create value. Yet, enabling empowered teams isn't trivial. We will discuss what it takes to get there in Chapter 10. For now, let's focus on the collaboration challenges.

Over the years, I've noticed two standard product development flows spread across companies regardless of their framework:

1. **Coordinative** → Team members spend significant time coordinating activities among themselves, stakeholders, and other teams. Most of their energy goes into organizing how to get the work done. This approach aims to avoid mistakes and failures, which forces teams to be rigid with their development flow. It becomes a "strict" contract because someone gets the blame when something goes wrong. Plans become the ultimate goals because nobody knows what they are fighting for.

2. **Collaborative** → Team members focus on collaborating to use their current knowledge to uncover promising opportunities. The ultimate goal is to create value for customers and the business. The team is flexible with how they get the job done while focusing on driving value. Trust is the basis for the collaborative approach. When something derails, the team takes responsibility and jointly finds a solution. Teams start with simplified plans, progress toward the *unknown*, and adapt the following steps based on the evidence. An overarching goal guides their decisions, ultimately creating value for everyone involved.

The product development flow dramatically contributes to teams becoming empowered or trapped in feature factories. Let's explore each of these two possible flows in detail.

Coordinative Flow: A Logical Way of Working with Unexpected Results

How do you transform an idea into something valuable?

That's one of the most important questions for companies. A poor answer leads to waste and demotivation.

The beginning of most product development flows is almost always the same. You probably have several ideas and a limited capacity to transform them into reality. The question is, how do you progress?

A coordinative flow aims to carry out ideas from beginning to end, treating each step as a strictly different phase. Figure 1.4 depicts this approach.

Coordinative Development Flow

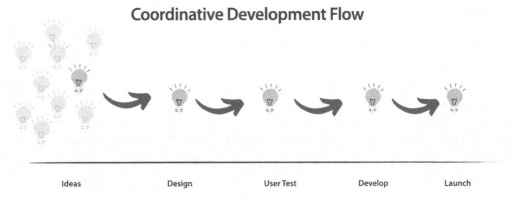

| Ideas | Design | User Test | Develop | Launch |

Figure 1.4
How an idea moves from beginning to launch with a coordinative flow

The coordinative flow starts with prioritization, aiming to find the most *promising* idea. However, that's easier said than done because several discussion rounds will occur. When you say *yes* to an idea, you're saying *no* to numerous others, and almost no business stakeholder accepts that answer easily.

Prioritization is one of the reasons product managers struggle to sleep. Getting everyone committed to one objective is tough. In a coordinative flow, prioritization will take weeks, if not months.

Design

The design phase starts once you define what the team will work on. The result is often a high-fidelity prototype that business stakeholders approve. This approach is dangerous because software engineers and customers tend to be left out of it. Sadly, the solution becomes the focus, not the outcome.

You may assimilate the design phase as a traditional waterfall process. Yet, having extensive design phases happens with agile methodologies as well. Whether you work with Scrum, Kanban, Scrumban, or something else, it doesn't matter: The result can be the same. Often, product designers aren't part of the product team, and teams receive detailed solutions to implement instead of opportunities to explore.

Designing solutions outside the product team is another disturbing bug that requires a hotfix. We will address that later in this book (see Chapter 4).

User Test

After much coordination, business stakeholders finally approve the design, and it's time to test it with potential customers.

The results are probably compromised because everyone already loves the solution. Sadly, falling prey to confirmation bias isn't the exception, but rather the typical outcome. Given their passion for the solution, product designers search for positive signs—and unsurprisingly, they find them. They may accept minor solution tweaks, but no solution pivot or drop will happen in this phase.

Develop

After product designers *confirm* the high-fidelity prototype makes sense to end users, it's time to develop the solution. Product designers throw the specs over the fence and hope software engineers do the job right. Of course, software engineers aren't likely to welcome the solution with wide-open arms because they weren't part of the previous steps. Even so, it becomes their job to transform the high-fidelity prototype into a working solution.

During the development phase, product designers and software engineers often come in conflict. Software engineers challenge the design as they see potential alternatives, and product designers want the implementation to follow the high-fidelity prototype strictly. Together, they find compromises, and none of them are happy about it.

The sad part is the extreme focus on the output. Nobody talks about the customer at this stage. Yet, they keep working on it until the solution is ready for the big moment.

Launch

Given the amount of coordination needed, it takes months to transform an idea into a solution. You shouldn't be surprised when something takes half a year. Each phase is strictly defined and has many steps to ensure a perfect solution by the end of it. Yet, something unexpected happens when you launch the solution.

Despite all of the internal enthusiasm and love for the newest fancy solution, customers don't engage with it—and you have no idea why.

You're sure the design went through rigid feedback loops, the color tonalities are correct, and management approved. The user test took place with at least ten potential customers, and they *confirmed* they would use the solution because it looked nice to them. Moving from prototype to solution was challenging, but you did it. You're clueless about what went wrong.

You wanted to celebrate the feature launch. After all, getting to this point required many exhausting discussions and took a toll on your nerves. Inexplicably, you ended with the fanciest piece of crap ever created (Figure 1.5). Sorry about my vocabulary, but recognizing reality requires facing it as harshly as possible.

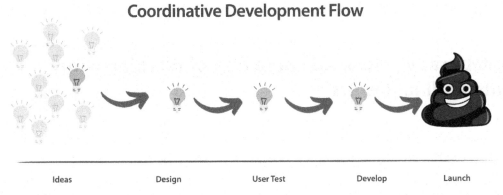

Figure 1.5
Launching something and getting disappointed with a coordinative flow

What shocks me isn't winding up in this tragic situation. I ended there more times than I can count, but I learned my lesson. The question is, what do you do after you face an undesired outcome?

The most common answer makes little sense to me. Go back to prioritization, pick another idea, and do it all over again. When you follow the same approach, chances are high that you will face the same results again.

The coordinative flow forces teams to focus on outputs over outcomes, diminishing them to feature factories.

Nine Out of Ten Ideas Will Fail

Our success rate is worse than we can imagine. Look at start-ups. Ninety percent of them don't last more than five years.[3] Ideas suffer much the same fate. Curiously, that goes unnoticed as teams invest much time figuring out how to reduce development time. I see value in this matter, though I perceive another question as more pressing: *How fast can you drop bad ideas?*

We assume our ideas are good, but reality shows us otherwise. Yet, we insist on following the same approach repeatedly. No wonder we face undesired results.

---

3. "90% of Startups Fail: Here's What You Need to Know about the 10%," *Forbes*, www.forbes.com/sites/neilpatel/2015/01/16/90-of-startups-will-fail-heres-what-you-need-to-know-about-the-10/.

Sound product management requires adapting based on learning. It's fine to get things wrong. It's not fine to ignore reality.

Collaboration over coordination is the principle that can get you out of this trap. Instead of making your development flow rigid and complex, you will benefit by making it simple and flexible.

Let's explore a different way of working that increases the odds of driving value faster.

Collaborative Flow: A Simple Way of Working with Outstanding Results

Nobody deserves to waste time. I know how much it hurts to see your work leading nowhere. After many years on the road, I learned that failures are inevitable. Instead of adding steps to prevent failures, identifying and quickly dropping flawed ideas make more sense.

Everything I share in this book is simple because I'm not good at dealing with complexity. Day in and day out, I strive to remove complexity by adding simplicity. That's how I uncovered ways of working that increase the chances of creating value sooner.

The more you simplify, the sooner you can move from a feature factory to an empowered team.

Unlike the coordinative flow, the collaborative flow focuses on iterations instead of phases. Each iteration enhances learning, empowering teams to choose between investing further or dropping the idea.

Figure 1.5 illustrates how teams start with several ideas and collaborate to identify what drives value while dropping what doesn't.

Collaborative Development Flow

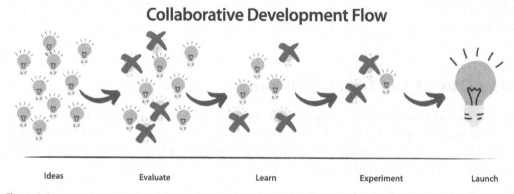

| Ideas | Evaluate | Learn | Experiment | Launch |

Figure 1.6
Dropping bad ideas fast enough and focusing on promising ones with a collaborative flow

Let's understand the different iterations of a collaborative flow and how that leads to empowerment.

Evaluate

The beginning of a collaborative flow is the same as for a coordinative flow. You've got plenty of ideas, and everyone wants everything done by yesterday. The trick isn't to identify the most *promising* ideas upfront, but rather to evaluate all of them and drop the misfitting ones. *Dropping ideas gives you freedom because you've got fewer expectations to manage.*

To drop ideas, confront them with your strategy. Here are the questions you should ask:

- How does it get us closer to our product vision?
- How does it relate to our product strategy?
- How does it contribute to our current objectives?
- How does it deliver on our value proposition?

Drop the idea if you lack answers to any of these questions. You may miss some of the attributes I mentioned (vision, strategy, objectives, value proposition) and struggle to assess your idea against them. You've got to do your homework (read Chapter 5 to set your product strategy).

Don't invest time in ideas unrelated to your strategy. By that, I mean don't increase the size of your backlog, but instead make your trash bin bigger.

You'll be tempted to park your idea somewhere and eventually return to it. Don't do that, because it will distract you. Whatever is relevant to your customers and business will return to you.

Idea evaluation should take a couple of hours, not more than that. Collaboration is essential, so get key business stakeholders to do this exercise with the product team. It's not about defending ideas, but rather about checking how they fit your strategy.

Strive to identify fitting ideas and drop unrelated ones pragmatically.

Learn

The learning iteration starts with ideas fitting your strategy, but that doesn't mean jumping straight to implementation. You should drop ideas your customers don't desire, the business cannot support, you don't have the technology to develop, or it's unethical to pursue. Keep it simple, and ask the following questions about each remaining idea:

- How much do customers want it? (Desirability)
- How does the business benefit? (Viability)

- How well can we deliver it? (Feasibility)

- How right is doing it? (Ethics)

Figure 1.7 represents an adapted version of the Innovation Trinity popularized by IDEO,[4] also known as a product Venn diagram. The overlapping areas highlight the sweet spot of promising ideas based on the preceding questions.

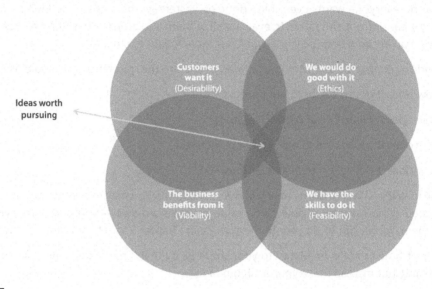

Figure 1.7
An adaption of the Innovation Trinity showing the sweet spot of promising ideas

The sooner you drop bad ideas, the sooner you can focus on the promising ones. Answering critical questions will help you with that. I like how Marty Cagan (2018) approaches this issue. He uses the following questions to address critical risks:

- Will the customers buy this or choose to use it? (Value risk)

- Can the user figure out how to use it? (Usability risk)

- Can we build it? (Feasibility risk)

- Does this solution work for our business? (Business viability risk)

You may not find answers to each of these questions, but you will have assumptions. Invest some time testing the critical assumptions (business critical and weak evidence), and decide which ideas are worth pursuing.

---

4. IDEO popularized the Innovation Trinity, also known as a product Venn diagram. I adapted this version to add ethics, as I see the importance of taking this factor into account. See https://blog.leanstack.com/lean-startup-or-business-model-design-or-design-thinking-is-the-wrong-question/.

This iteration should take a few days, but not more than that. Use qualitative information to determine how to progress. You can do interviews with customers and business stakeholders, low-fidelity prototype testing, and quick technical experiments as needed.

The goal is to find evidence confirming ideas are desirable, feasible, and viable (refer to Chapter 7 for more information on how to do this). If one of these characteristics is missing, drop the idea and move on.

A common trap is focusing on viability and feasibility. Just because you can do something, that doesn't mean you should do it. Investing in an idea without evidence of desirability is no more than a bet. The result is often a feature nobody uses. Proceed only with the ideas that have evidence strong enough to justify the investment you're about to make.

It's fundamental to collaborate with business stakeholders and customers. Otherwise, you will end up with undesired results.

You'll drop 30% to 50% of the remaining ideas.[5] If your numbers are out of this range, either you're too strict or you're too loose. I'd recommend reviewing your evidence and decisions.

Experiment

After learning about the key aspects of your ideas, it's time to run more robust experiments. You want to test which solutions can deliver the potential results. Exploring a few alternatives and sticking with the most promising ones is essential.

It's all too common to pick one solution and go all in with it. I discourage you from following this path, because it quickly leads to commitment escalation. As humans, the more invested we are in something, the more willingly we invest in it.

You need to choose which experiment makes more sense to you. Your ultimate objective is to have solid information that justifies investing further. For that, you will need a combination of qualitative and quantitative data.

It's not within the scope of this book to cover the diverse product experiments you can apply. I recommend reading *Testing Business Ideas* by David Bland to learn more about this topic.

Here's my secret: I like using tech debt (software quality compromises requiring future rework) as a tool to accelerate learning. The goal is to hack a quick and dirty solution, get it live to a small portion of your audience, and gather evidence on how that helps them get the job done. I must warn you, though, software engineers are often opposed to increasing tech debt. They tend to be strict about creating this kind of tech debt, because many product managers do not support them in paying it off on time.

---

5. It's hard to accept that. But over time, I learned that many ideas cannot resist an encounter with reality. When I tested ideas with an open mind, I ended up dropping almost half of my ideas. Yet, when I neglected evidence, I ended up creating something that nobody needed.

Prudent use of tech debt is a tool[6] (more on that in Chapter 8). It's like getting a mortgage. You go to the bank, get a mortgage, and acquire your dream house. You collected the desired value fast, but then you owe the bank and should pay the debt off. If you accumulate more debt, you may go bankrupt. The same thing happens with tech debt. It enables you to reduce the time to collect value, but whenever it's proven worthwhile, you must pay the debt off before getting a new loan.

You will drop another 30% to 50% of the remaining ideas during the experiment iteration. The reasons will vary, but it turns out that customers often show unexpected behaviors, which enables you to review how worthy your idea is. Not all ideas justify the investment despite being desirable, feasible, and viable at first glance.

The critical part of experimentation is to drop solutions that don't work. Feature factory teams can't do that because delivering the output is their goal. But empowered teams can because achieving the outcome is their success metric.

Whenever you want to drop an idea, involve your business stakeholders to reach this conclusion collaboratively. Evidence will support your decision, and involving business stakeholders will get their buy-in (read the discussion of "opinions over evidence" in Chapter 2).

Launch

Ideas that survive the experiment iteration are the prominent ones. In the previous iteration, you built to learn. Now, you build to scale. Paying the tech debt off before you make the solution available to your whole audience or jump to your next opportunity is fundamental.

Unlike with a coordinative flow, applying a collaborative flow will help you drop bad ideas faster. This method benefits from the power of collaboration over coordination.

Be aware that not all companies are comfortable with a highly collaborative flow. For example, in Germany, many companies long for yearly plans with feature roadmaps and prescriptive timelines. Sadly, those plans create an exhaustive need for coordination to get everything progressing. Yet, you can foster change gradually. When facing such situations, you could take a step-by-step journey to help companies uncover better ways of creating value (read Chapter 4 to get insights on how to act).

I have one thought about teams that are able to create value faster than others, and it's a rather obvious one: You have to do what most teams don't do to achieve the results most teams don't get. Move away from coordinative flows, and do your best to focus on collaborative flows instead.

The more coordination you have to endure, the less time you have to focus on uncovering what creates value. Don't force your teams to behave as feature factories.

---

6. Martin Fowler categorizes technical debt into four quadrants. The one I'm recommending relates to deliberate and prudent use. See https://martinfowler.com/bliki/TechnicalDebtQuadrant.html.

The more effectively your teams can collaborate, the faster they can adapt, learn, drop bad ideas, and focus on promising ones. That's the power of enabling empowered teams.

Key Takeaways

- The first step to untrapping your team is reviewing your current situation. Understanding the dynamics can reveal opportunities to simplify your development flow.

- Symptoms of a feature factory include a lack of goals, output obsession, delivering solutions that solve no problem, unclear direction, unwillingness to drop ideas, and inattention to results. The opposite of a feature factory is an empowered team that focuses on outcomes and is eager to inspect and adapt continuously.

- The closer you are to a coordinative development flow, the longer it takes to deliver value and the more waste you create. Coordinative flows unwittingly transform plans into goals.

- The closer you are to a collaborative development flow, the sooner you create value and the less waste you produce. Collaboration helps you adapt plans to reach your goals when reality makes your plan obsolete.

- When you fully understand the product development flow, you can foster changes step by step. The first step is collaborating with business stakeholders and team members to recognize what's unnecessarily complex. Equipped with that knowledge, you can gain support and collaborate to simplify your work.

In this chapter, we discussed how teams commonly work. That's a critical piece of the puzzle, but it isn't the only reason teams struggle to deliver value. Chapter 2 covers another fundamental aspect: how the mindset affects digital product creation.

2

The Mindset Impacts on Dangerous Traps

In Chapter 1, we discussed different ways of working. We explored how a collaborative flow facilitates value creation and how a coordinative one complicates it. You might think changing the flow would be enough, but you'd be missing a critical aspect. You need to understand the predominant mindset[1] spread over the company because that will equip you better for any changes you want to foster.

Comprehending the mindset driving product decisions is crucial to understanding its impacts on your daily business. What surprises me are the similarities I observe in many companies worldwide. It's common to see an extreme focus on predictability, detailed plans, and change aversion. A common fallacy is "That's how we've been working for years."

In *Mindset: The New Psychology of Success*, Carol Dweck (2007) described the two types of mindset—growth and fixed—and their impacts. A growth mindset shows curiosity and eagerness to learn. A fixed mindset searches for stability and predictability. One works well for digital products; the other limits the potential.

Although mindset relates to individuals and not to companies, it is critical to understand the common mindset that permeates the organization. Once that's clear to you, taking action becomes smoother.

---

1. "Mindset" refers to a set of beliefs or attitudes that determine one's behavior, outlook, and mental attitude. It shapes how individuals interpret and respond to situations and challenges (Dweck 2007).

This chapter covers how growth and fixed mindsets influence product teams. In addition, I'll elaborate on how you can foster change by simplifying unwelcome complexities. This discussion won't be extensive but rather is geared toward equipping you to recognize dangerous anti-patterns and ways to overcome them.

Let's start our conversation with a high-level definition of growth and fixed mindsets for digital products. The *growth mindset* focuses on uncovering the unknowns. It uses available knowledge as the starting point and searches for opportunities to broaden perspectives. Curiosity encourages discovering the new. In contrast, the *fixed mindset* focuses on resisting changes because it perceives them as dangerous. It takes the current knowledge as enough, and as a result, it blocks the unknown. It strives to comfort its owner by creating the illusion of being in control. Fear stops discovering the new.

It's common to find more people with a fixed mindset. That's a natural defense and survival mechanism to prevent undesired experiences and protect ourselves from danger. Unexpectedly, it blocks threats and opportunities altogether, proving unfit for our innovative world. Conversely, a growth mindset goes beyond surviving; it's about thriving.

Figure 2.1 summarizes the core differences in mindset for product teams.

Figure 2.1
Growth mindset versus fixed mindset

What's a Growth Mindset?

When growth drives you, you accept that what you know today will change, given what you learn tomorrow. You embrace the unknown to reinvent the future. Yet, this mindset creates a certain stress level because you've got to get comfortable with the uncomfortable.

You need to remain open to continuously changing your perception because it's never final. Our nature is a considerable challenge to us. As humans, we fear the unknown.

When I started my product management career, I was sure my primary responsibility was to bridge communication between business and tech. That's how I explained my job to everyone.

After a few years, I realized something was wrong and adapted my perception. I started picturing myself as an orchestra conductor. Although I played no instrument, I had to ensure the music created was outstanding. I kept that vision for a year until I noticed I had positioned myself at a higher level than the team, which I didn't mean.

Once again, my product management perception evolved. I started seeing myself as a jazz player. I'd start the music, and the others would join me, bringing their most creative aspects. Together, we'd create something none of us could do alone.

I don't dare say that's my final perception, but it's my current view of a good product manager. Time may show me another perspective, encouraging me to evolve.

What's a Fixed Mindset?

When you fear the unknown, you find ways to protect yourself from it. Predictability is a driving principle for a fixed mindset. That's why detailed plans give you what you want. You get the comfort you're searching for.

During my first job as a product manager, I was responsible for an internal product used by thousands of employees. It was a tool to help store owners accelerate their tasks and become more productive. Despite having no customer pressure, I spent more than 20% of my time working on timelines, feature roadmaps, and negotiating deadlines. Such aspects relate to a fixed mindset because predictability drives decisions.

Another aspect I struggled with was stability. Four times a year, I had to present reports to top management showing the team's output speed. I had to explain why sometimes we delivered fewer story points. Even though almost nobody understood their meaning, almost everybody appreciated it when the reports showed stable numbers.

The fixed mindset got me searching for answers to use available knowledge to help me make peace with the unknown. The problem was that I spent too much time planning and speculating and too little time learning from reality.

Identifying the Mindset's Impacts

I give talks at conferences worldwide, remotely and on site. I like understanding the audience's challenges at the beginning of my presentations. That helps me bring the most suitable examples for them. I often ask the participants to complete a survey so I can get a glimpse into their reality. The survey results are alike no matter where I give the keynote, which astonishes me.

In 2023, I gave the keynote at the Agile Swarming Conference[2] in Poland. During my presentation, I asked participants to fill out the reality check survey, the results of which you can see in Figure 2.2. It astounded me to see how hundreds of participants face dangerous product anti-patterns.

I conduct the same survey when I'm consulting with companies. I ask product teams, business stakeholders, and management to rate how often they experience the five dangerous anti-patterns listed in Figure 2.2. Then, I discuss each aspect with the leaders. The ultimate goal of this survey is to understand how ready teams are to step into the unknown.

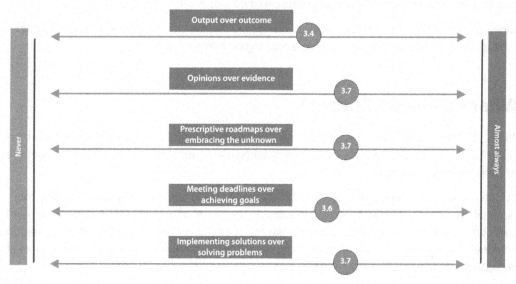

Figure 2.2
Reality check survey, Agile Swarming 2023

---

2. Agile Swarming is an event sponsored by Motorola at which attendees can share agile practices. The event is free, and professionals can learn from other practitioners. Find more about it here: https://agileswarming.com/edition-2023/.

Before deep diving, I'd encourage you to take a few minutes and reflect on your reality. Fill in the scale in Figure 2.3 with what you observe regarding these dangerous anti-patterns.

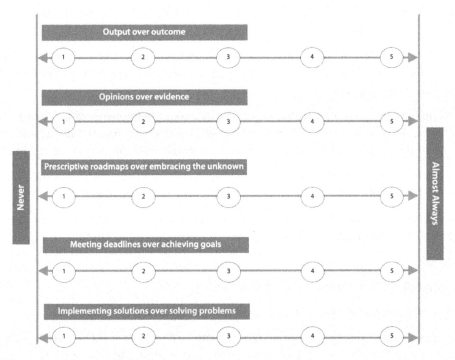

Figure 2.3
Reality check survey

Output over Outcome

Delivering features without knowing what they are for is one of the most common traps teams face. Defining a solution, working on it, and shipping it is easy. But then what happens next? The team jumps to the next item on the list because they have a colossal backlog, yet nobody measures how the features drive value to customers and the business.

When guided by a fixed mindset, team members focus on outputs because that's known to them. Sadly, this approach often results in useless features because the outcomes are ignored. In contrast, when a growth mindset drives decisions, teams are curious to find ways to deliver desired outcomes. They try different solutions, learn, and then commit to one that works.

Following the principle "outcome over output" can lead to a growth mindset attitude, but sadly, it has become jargon. Product professionals struggle to bring it to life. Let me simplify the understanding behind outcome over output.

To illustrate the connection between outputs and outcomes, picture a car. Which security features does it have? Some examples are seat belts, airbags, and emergency brake assistance. All of these are outputs. What they enable are outcomes. Seat belts and airbags reduce the chances of injuries in case of accidents, while the antilock braking system (ABS) reduces crashes.

An output is a means to an end, while the outcome is the end. Output is what you create, and the outcome is what the output enables.

You can reach the same outcome with different outputs. Continuing with the car example, minimizing injuries during an accident is the outcome, and a seat belt is an output that drives it. The same would go for an airbag.

Focusing on outputs is normal because we can jump straight to implementation, which sounds efficient. In contrast, outcomes are abstract and leave us with empty hands. One depends on the other. The critical aspect is where you start because it significantly affects the result you create.

When the output comes first, delivering what's defined matters more than reaching goals. The issue is that teams have only a single chance of succeeding. The bet is too high.

When the outcome comes first, achieving the desired result matters most. Teams can explore different solutions, drop bad ones, and stick with the most promising ones.

In a nutshell:

- Output obsession creates a team of executors.
- Outcome empowerment establishes a team of achievers.

Unfortunately, you're likely to face output requests more often than you'd like. Use the power of questions in your favor. Whenever you receive an output request, step back and ask:

- What does that enable our users to achieve?
- Which business value does it drive?
- What does success look like?

Such simple questions help you understand desired outcomes and focus on what matters. Don't be surprised if you don't get answers to all questions, but don't proceed until you have them. You can help your business stakeholders identify the answers but should not commit to outputs without knowing the outcome.

Opinions over Evidence

Everyone has an opinion about something, but only a few have evidence supporting their opinion. One common situation in the business world strikes me as sadly misguided: Opinions without evidence drive product decisions. This situation is like playing with fire. You will eventually burn yourself.

With a fixed mindset, you can expect opinions to drive actions. However, a growth mindset will use opinions as the beginning instead of the end.

Let's explore a hypothetical situation. A business stakeholder learned about ChatGPT and concluded that having a chatbot would be a killer feature. The next day, she presented it to her boss, who immediately fell in love. Immediately, they called the product manager and asked her to stop everything and start working on the chatbot.

What's wrong with this situation? Both business stakeholders have only opinions to support their decision making, but they are treating them as reason enough to build a solution. Their excitement obfuscates the risk of creating something nobody will use.

I don't recommend ignoring opinions, but they shouldn't drive you. To drive value, you should gather evidence and gradually increase commitment.

Getting evidence is just the start. Be careful about how fast you commit to solutions. Another all-too-common pitfall is weak evidence leading to solid commitment.

For example, suppose that after several interviews, product managers get excited because the users said they'd *pay* for a specific feature. Such evidence leads to backlog items and commitment to developing the whole feature. This behavior is dangerous. It's crucial to understand the evidence's strength.

A statement is weak evidence, which shouldn't encourage a high investment but does justify exploring the idea. A meaningful step is to make a small investment to create stronger evidence. For example, you could build a landing page and ask users to leave their email addresses so they can receive a notification once the new feature is available. Alternatively, you could be more extreme and ask users to pay in advance for the feature. That would certainly be strong evidence they want it. Yet, you may be surprised to find that no more than half of users who showed *buying intentions* will actually buy the feature.

From Opinions to Evidence

It's inevitable that you'll face opinions. People love sharing their thoughts even when you don't ask for them. The magic lies in moving from opinions to evidence. Once again, questions will give you better results than jumping into action. When presented with opinions, ask a few simple questions:

- Which evidence supports your idea?
- What gives you the confidence this is the right thing to do?
- How did you come to this conclusion?

Such questions reveal the evidence you have or lack, enabling you to make a better-informed decision. The equation is simple: The weaker the evidence, the smaller the investment you should make.

Let me walk you through an exchange between a person with a fixed mindset and me.

Helping Others Step Back

Once, a senior manager asked me to completely change how we presented our delivery time. I asked him what he wanted to achieve with that. He confidently said that showing the delivery time the way he mentioned would drive conversion up. Then, I said, "You're very convinced about it, which makes me curious. Could you share which evidence you have about it?"

He looked me in the eyes and, with an aggressive tone, said, "I'm a senior manager. That's enough evidence."

I knew the ego got in the way. I needed to get him to reflect.

I said, "I'm not challenging your expertise. I respect that, and I'm sure you know what you say, but as a product manager, I need to understand how you came to this conclusion. Let's say we implement the change you mentioned, and it rocks. Then we're all happy. But it can go wrong, and then we're all mad. Changing the delivery time will impact 400,000 customers, who are sensitive to this information. Do you want to make a change endangering our conversion rate?"

He got thoughtful and said he didn't want to endanger anything but had strong feelings about it; he thought the change could strengthen the business. He finally said that he might not have any evidence, but he believed the change would make sense.

As he stepped back, I told him we could run a test with a small percentage of our audience and compare results. After that, we could make an informed decision. He agreed. In a few hours, we could hack a solution, run A/B tests, and then realize the solution didn't bring any improvement. In fact, it lowered the conversion rate.

Untrapping Lesson: Ask questions leading to a "no" answer because it relates to loss aversion and triggers reflection.

When you ask someone if they want to succeed, they'll promptly say yes while not considering the question. But when you question them about whether failure is their wish, they'll reflect.

To help a person with a fixed mindset be curious, you need to foster reflection.

Prescriptive Roadmaps over Embracing the Unknown

The end of a fiscal quarter is a stressful time for most product teams. It's time to speed up, deliver the roadmap promises, and plan the next quarter. Software engineers search for opportunities to cut corners, product managers negotiate scope with business stakeholders, and product designers make usability compromises. At the end of this chaos, everyone suffers, and nobody is happy.

At the beginning of my career, I didn't challenge prescriptive roadmaps (detailed plans with predefined features). I used to like them because I knew what I had to do. But I learned the hard way that no plan survives contact with end users. Whenever I talked to end users, I had "a-ha" moments, which made prescriptive roadmaps obsolete.

Embracing the unknown is daunting because it leaves us anxious. We wonder what the next steps are, and we have no answer. Such discomfort is disturbing. Yet, failing to embrace the unknown limits opportunities because teams focus on what's planned instead of learning from reality.

The Birth of Prescriptive Roadmaps and Its Consequences

Prescriptive roadmaps aren't evil by design. Top management is pressured to deliver results, and they fear their people being idle. Crafting a detailed roadmap ensures everyone has work to do, but the question is, what do people do when reality proves the roadmap wrong? The mindset has a strong influence on the reaction to this question.

A fixed mindset will ensure teams continue to follow the plan. Even if that contradicts reality, the plan becomes the goal. A growth mindset cannot neglect learning. As a result, teams fight for change, leading to higher chances of creating value. Sadly, prescriptive roadmaps will encourage a fixed mindset behavior and make it harder to embrace the unknown.

What disturbs me about prescriptive roadmaps is the vicious circle they create. Everyone invests time in pointless estimates, squeezes items into the roadmap, and throws plans over the fence, and then teams receive the pressure. Unsurprisingly, teams almost never deliver everything from the roadmap, which frustrates them and annoys management. Next quarter, the same nonsense repeats, and working isn't fun anymore.

I learned that simple roadmaps lead to extraordinary results, whereas prescriptive roadmaps lead to mediocrity. A simple roadmap will tell teams where they need to arrive and give them key milestones. Teams have decision-making power and can determine suitable alternatives to reach the agreed milestones. On the way, teams learn what doesn't work and adapt the course of action.

Moving Away from Prescriptive Roadmaps

You may wonder where to start. If you have a prescriptive roadmap, you're not alone. Many companies haven't experienced any other way of working. You can view this status quo as a chance to transform it gradually.

Moving from a prescriptive roadmap to a simple one is a journey. I don't know any top managers who would support a complete replacement from day to night. However, I know many executives who would support experiments to increase value creation.

Results talk louder than words.

Don't waste energy lecturing executives on why feature roadmaps aren't helpful. Suggest an experiment with 20% of the team's capacity. Commit to an outcome and do your best to deliver it. Once you get it right, you'll gain support to scale.

A prescriptive roadmap describes outputs, while an empowering roadmap describes outcomes. Let me give you some examples:

- **Output:** Show product recommendations during check-out.

- **Outcome:** Increase basket size by 10%.

- **Output:** Implement a chatbot to address delivery issues.

- **Outcome:** Reduce customer service requests related to delivery by 50%.

Output forces execution, while outcome opens up to explore different solutions. Chapter 5 explores ways to nail roadmaps.

Meeting Deadlines over Achieving Goals

Most deadlines are arbitrary, and only a few are strict.

Launching a product at a conference, regulatory changes, and legal enforcement can require you to adapt your actions to meet deadlines. Yet, delivering a feature by the end of the quarter is arbitrary, and you won't get in significant trouble by missing this deadline.

Leaders often set deadlines to gain commitment to results and work backward to achieve them. Deadlines aren't bad per se, because they force people to prioritize. Yet, misusing deadlines is a problem.

Deadlines have advantages and disadvantages. A clear advantage is that they force teams to decide what not to do. A significant drawback is that teams sometimes see no choice but to compromise on quality. Additionally, they quickly lose the drive to create value.

With strict deadlines, it becomes a rat race to make the impossible possible. Meanwhile, everybody forgets which outcome they're fighting for.

You need to reflect on whether meeting deadlines or reaching goals is more important. The first option tends to hit hard on quality, while the second helps teams focus on results.

The mindset plays a critical role in how teams deal with deadlines. A fixed mindset will result in a complex plan replete with detailed steps that lead up to the deadline. There won't be any room for learning, and a rigid timeline will be imposed. Meanwhile, a growth mindset will reflect on the goal behind the deadline; it will start with small steps to discover the unknown and adapt the plan gradually.

One of the biggest challenges of deadlines is how they are set. Often, someone outside the team defines a deadline and informs them. Consequently, the team struggles to commit to it without understanding why the deadline matters.

A better way to drive commitment is by sharing the context and desired outcomes. Then, craft a potential delivery window with the team. This attitude gets team members on board and gives them constraints to deliver results instead of compromising to meet arbitrary deadlines.

A common question I face is, "Should we ditch deadlines?" I discourage organizations from doing that. Leaving the team with an open-ended date leads to analysis paralysis, and nothing gets done. A deadline or, even better, a delivery window forces teams to be mindful and prioritize what drives expected results.

Focus on reaching goals and agree on a delivery window with the team. This attitude will maximize the odds of driving desired outcomes.

Implementing Solutions over Solving Problems

It's shocking how often teams work on solutions without knowing which problem they are solving.

For many years, I thought I was a good product manager because I could quickly come up with solutions. I would then present my sketches to product teams in a simple way so they could implement those solutions. What I didn't realize was how much I limited teams.

It's hard to navigate between the solution and problem spaces. We usually get busy implementing solutions, and the ultimate goal becomes finalizing it instead of solving problems. Dan Olsen (2015) explains the differences between the problem and solution spaces well:

> Solution space includes any product or representation of a product that is used by or intended for use by a customer. Problem space is where all the customer needs that you'd like your product to deliver live. Customers are also not likely to serve you their problem space needs on a silver platter.

An extreme focus on solutions leads to features that solve no real problem. Curiosity is the best remedy to avoid building useless solutions. Don't jump into implementing solutions when you lack understanding of the problem. Start with what you know so you can learn what you don't.

No team can craft a meaningful solution without a deep understanding of the problem. Before designing solutions, you need to answer some questions:

- Which problem are we trying to solve?
- Who experiences this problem?
- How does the problem get solved right now?
- How often does it happen?

- How many users share the pain?
- How much do they care about it?

Let me give you an example from a marketplace I worked for.

- **Problem:** It takes over three months to onboard partners, which frustrates them.
- **Who:** Partners and account managers.
- **Current solution:** Manual onboarding process done by software engineers.
- **Frequency:** 8 new partners per month.
- **How many users experience the problem**: All new partners.
- **Importance:** Partners cancel contracts because our onboarding is too slow for them.

Knowing the problem space enables you to craft meaningful solutions. Not knowing it is the same as relying on luck, which is a poor business choice. It takes some time to learn the problem space, but investing this time is better than building a solution that solves nobody's problems.

Let me share a tragic story to help you understand the importance of knowing the problem space before implementing a solution.

The Painful Cost of Misunderstanding the Problem Space

A business analyst joined the company, and as part of onboarding, we had lunch together. She had an idea to create a solution to replace the manual spreadsheets used by our trainers.

Back then, we had hundreds of trainers traveling all over Brazil. They used Excel to store the training information, which business analysts later consolidated to create reports for our customers.

The idea was simple: Create a student training platform. It would reduce the manual workload from trainers and business analysts while being more engaging for students. I had no reason to believe the idea would fail, so I led the team to implement it.

The business analyst and I flew to Porto Alegre three months later to present our solution. We were excited about what we created. I saw everyone was curious as we arrived, so I went straight to the point and presented the solution we were so proud of.

It didn't take long before a bucket of cold water hit our faces.

A trainer asked how she'd use the web platform in the airplane because that was the only time she could prepare for the training. At that moment, I realized I missed the mark. I failed to understand the problem space. Brazilian flights had no internet connection.

We built a misfitting platform because I fell in love with the solution and ignored the problem. I lacked the curiosity to understand the problem because I was too busy planning the solution.

Untrapping Lesson: Understand the problem before you implement the solution.

Key Takeaways

- A fixed mindset reduces the chances of creating valuable solutions because changes are unwelcome. In contrast, a growth mindset maximizes your chances of delivering value because you embrace changes instead of resisting them.

- When opinions drive decisions, frustrations become unavoidable. Using the power of questions enables you to move from opinions to evidence.

- Prescriptive roadmaps will limit teams' potential. Take small steps to move toward outcome-oriented roadmaps. For example, agree with management to experiment with 20% of your roadmap focused on outcomes.

- Before implementing solutions, ensure you know the problem they solve. Otherwise, you will end up creating something that solves no problem.

- Don't panic if you face the anti-patterns mentioned throughout the chapter. You can take action and drive change. The critical attitude is to address one point at a time.

In this chapter, we explored the five dangerous anti-patterns that tend to affect all kinds of companies. Overcoming them is vital to creating value steadily. Yet, that won't be enough to unleash your team's full potential. A relentless enemy is ahead, complicating your life and extinguishing your ability to drive value.

The next chapter introduces the real enemy and clarifies how simplicity can defeat this horrific villain.

3

What Distracts Teams from Creating Value

By now, you understand that a coordinative flow combined with a fixed mindset will dramatically slow teams down. You're also aware that a collaborative flow is a light way of working, and when you combine it with a growth mindset, teams are better equipped to deal with the unknown. Yet, we didn't explore how a busy routine blended with hidden traps can distract you.

Let me ask you an important question:

How busy are you?

I wouldn't be surprised if you're busier than you'd like, and your routine sucks your energy.

Getting your day packed with requests, meetings, reports, etc., doesn't take long. Then, you realize that working 40 hours a week isn't enough. So you go the extra mile and give more time to your company. Yet, the results don't improve. You get more tasks done, but creating value remains unchangeable.

Why does this happen when working with digital products?

Dealing with complexity isn't natural to most of us. We want to be in control and feel safe. As a defensive mechanism, we create methods to make us feel in control. Often, such methods deal with complexity by making it even more complex.

I see two ways of dealing with such a challenging reality. The first is becoming passive and accepting reality even when you dislike it. The other is taking an active role, where you don't perceive the status quo as final. I call the first the passenger and the second the driver. Let's understand how it looks:

- **Passenger:** You let someone take you on a ride and embrace the journey however it is. It's a choice to prioritize harmony and avoid conflicts. You may detest how the journey evolves, but you accept the driver's decisions even when you know better ways to reach the desired destination.

- **Driver:** You know where to go, so you take the steering wheel, focusing on your objective while enjoying the journey. You strive to reach the desired destination and deal with road-blocks as they appear. You aim to create value instead of wasting time.

In this chapter, we will discuss the usual situations that distract you from creating value. Then, we will explore how you could take the driver's seat and foster change.

Facing the Real Enemy: Bullshit Management

I assume you're surprised by the term I started using some years ago, "bullshit management."[1] I wrote a blog[2] that reflected what I've observed in dozens of companies and wanted to give it a proper name. You may wonder what this phrase means. Let me define it:

> Bullshit management is the art of spending time doing things that bring no value but drain your energy.

Whenever you don't understand why you're doing something or don't see how that creates value, you're probably doing bullshit management.

Don't panic; you're not alone. I will help you defeat this villain!

The first step in the battle is understanding the impact of this enemy. The more bullshit you handle, the less value you create.

I confess that I did more bullshit management than product management. It took me years to learn how to differentiate between the two. Many times, I thought that was my work. But now, it's clear what contributes to and distracts from value creation.

The more present the following ten items are in your reality, the more distractions you'll have:

1. Gathering requirements

2. Extensive product backlog

---

1. The term "bullshit management" isn't new. It's been used for decades with different meanings. For example, in 2009, Henry Frankfurt wrote the best-seller book, *On Bullshit*. Two years later, Jos Verveen wrote the book *Bullshit Management*. In 2022, I started applying this term specifically for misinterpretations of product management.

2. "Are You Doing Product Management or Bullshit Management," https://medium.com/serious-scrum/are-you-doing-product-management-or-bullshit-management-3055e875eb69.

3. Output reports

4. Consensus-driven decisions

5. Output approval

6. Meeting marathon

7. Fear of saying no

8. Bridging communication

9. Opinion-driven decisions

10. Failure avoidance

Let's detail each item and discuss its impacts and how to identify and overcome them.

Gathering Requirements: A Distraction to Value Creation

Suppose you want to eat a burger, so you go to a restaurant. As you arrive there, the waiter comes to you and asks, "What would you like to have?" You promptly say, "A cola and the chef's burger without onions, please." The waiter takes your order and asks, "Would you like french fries, too?" You agree, and the waiter notes it and asks, "Anything else?" You say, "That's it." The waiter walks away and hangs the order in the kitchen. If you're lucky, they cook the burger without onions.

How similar is this situation to creating digital products?

In 2012, that was how I worked as a product manager. I went to business stakeholders, asked what they wanted, took notes, made a few suggestions, and adapted my notes to ensure I took the requirements correctly. After that, I'd hand them over to software engineers, and they'd deliver something based on what I wrote down.

The waiter focused on the wants but didn't know the actual needs. The burger combined with a cola wouldn't match the needs if the client had high cholesterol or diabetes. Like the waiter, I focused on what the business stakeholders wanted but didn't uncover their real needs. I didn't even bother asking that. I thought they'd know best, and I shouldn't dare to ask such stupid questions.

I took the passenger's seat and let business stakeholders be the drivers. They came with requirements, and I found solutions to them. Yet, I didn't know what those requirements were for.

The word *requirement* is dangerous because it's final. We assume we have to do it that way. But is that our real job? Jeff Patton (2014), author of *User Story Mapping*, would disagree:

> Remember: at the end of the day, your job isn't to get the requirements right—your job is to change the world.

You cannot change the world by just taking requirements.

The real job is tough. You need to uncover the needs beyond the wants. On top of that, you should accept that wants from business stakeholders often don't match the needs of end users.

To escape from this common trap, slow down and ask questions. Don't be an order taker; be like Sherlock Holmes. It's a lot about investigating and deciding what's a signal and what's noise. It's not because a business stakeholder tells you to do something you must do; your real job requires decision making and separating good ideas from bad ones.

Extensive Product Backlog: When the Past Limits the Future

The longer the product backlog, the more expectations business stakeholders will have. Here are some questions for your reflection:

- Do you have more than a few dozen backlog items?

- Do you fear deleting backlog items because of the repercussions?

- Does your backlog look like a wish list?

The more times you've answered yes to the previous questions, the more your backlog distracts you.

Managing your backlog requires being the driver, not the passenger. You cannot let someone else decide how you do it because that will lead to a convoluted backlog, which will quickly drain your energy and contributes very little to value. Keeping an extensive backlog to tell business stakeholders their requests are registered instead of removing items unrelated to your current goals isn't mindful.

The extensive backlog trap is a worldwide problem. You can wind up in this situation by following either of two paths. First, you inherit an extensive backlog. Second, you flood your backlog with requests. No matter how you get there, though, it doesn't justify remaining there.

Some people disagree when I talk about this trap. They tell me you can keep unimportant items at the bottom of your backlog and ignore them. That's possible, but what's the value in it? People expect you to deliver once it's there, and you should know why the items matter.

A cluttered backlog traps you in the past, whereas a decluttered one forces you to continuously explore the future. Treating your backlog as a vehicle to create value is paramount because it's not a bucket to throw all requests into.

When you take the driver's seat, you align your backlog items to the utmost goal and remove whatever distracts you from that. Chapter 8 explores how to mindfully manage your backlog and set routines to keep it lean and valuable. As with everything in life, it's about choices and consequences.

Extensive product backlogs drive teams, which should never be the case. Teams should drive the backlog.

You can be the driver and develop a backlog that accelerates value creation, or you can be the passenger with a distracting wish list. Think about the outcome you want and pick the best choice for you.

Let me share a story about dealing with a cluttered backlog.

The Inherited Mess

When I started a new job as a product manager, my manager asked me to go through the product backlog as my first task. I was astonished when I faced a mountain with 1762 items.

I did my best to go through the inherited mess for one week. I talked to software engineers, business stakeholders, designers, customers, management, and other product managers. I was hitting the wall. Some people told me not to worry about some items as they were low priority, and most didn't even remember what those requests were for.

I couldn't continue working that way.

My inner rebel spirit pushed me to take the driver's seat. I did what made sense to me. First, I deleted everything untouched for six months, around 800 backlog items. We used Jira, meaning those who created the ticket received an email. Guess what happened? I got two emails back. One, from a quality assurance engineer, said, "We solved it already." The other, from a business stakeholder, admitted, "I don't remember creating this ticket."

I got excited by cleaning up the messy backlog, so I did it again. I deleted all items untouched for three months. Then, the backlog shrank to 117 items. This time, I got no emails. Within this backlog size, I could work. I reflected on our goal and curated the backlog, ultimately leaving only 63 items.

None of the removed items caused any trouble. Nobody cared about them. But some magic happened afterward. As a team, we became more collaborative. Instead of asking what we could take from the backlog, we explored what we could do to reach our goals.

Untrapping Lesson: Do what's necessary to focus on progress, even if that frightens you.

Output Reports: Wasting Time

How do you know you're on the right track?

Simple. Look at your velocity[3] and ensure it's constant or growing. Great product teams produce output steadily. They work like machines, solid, stable, and predictable.

How does the previous paragraph speak to you? If you believe that's 100% correct, the feature factory is hitting you. Let me help you escape it because I've been there for years.

Output metrics are more distracting than you imagine. Obsession with velocity diminishes your team's potential and sets the wrong direction.

Once, I was part of an extraordinary team. We crafted solutions users loved and delivered high business value. Yet, we weren't like most teams. Sometimes, we over-delivered; other times, we created no output because we were busy running experiments with customers. However, that was about to change. Our CEO read about Scrum and decided to hire a Scrum Master.

My life dramatically changed as the Scrum Master introduced velocity and the burndown chart (neither is part of Scrum). The Scrum Master told us that we had to estimate with story points, monitor daily progress, and take action when derailed.

After two months following this approach, we didn't create anything close to what we had in the past. Management started measuring our success by how stable our velocity was, and we got distracted by talking about outputs while ignoring outcomes.

Output metrics like velocity tell you how fast you can deliver. But they reveal nothing about how much value you create for customers and the business.

Looking back at this story, it's clear we moved from driver to passenger. Before the velocity and burndown chart, we focused on outcomes. We made decisions based on creating desired results and didn't let others tell us what to do. But after the Scrum Master arrived, we accepted someone else driving and became passengers. As a result, we forgot what we wanted to reach and focused on the process.

When your attention goes to outputs, you end up with loads of live features, yet little value created. But when your attention goes to outcomes, you reduce output speed but maximize value creation.

> **Note:** I'm not claiming Scrum is bad. Nor do Scrum Masters necessarily lead to poor results. I'm not against Scrum, but I despise implementations that focus on the process while ignoring learning and collaboration.

---

3. *Velocity* is a term commonly used by agile teams; it refers to the number of story points delivered by the end of each development cycle. Story points are a common way of estimating tasks. They're based on complexity, and not time as most methods are.

Consensus-Driven Decisions: Slowing Down Progress

What's consensus to you? For most people, consensus is about getting everyone on board with decisions before progressing. Everyone is happy because they give their perspectives.

My view of consensus is different. It's the slowest decision-making method combined with the art of creating the worst possible option by watering down ideas. The result of consensus-driven decisions is often a horrible alternative that wasn't even on the table. To illustrate that, let me share a story with you.

> My wife and I were getting ready for a friend's wedding. She couldn't decide between high heels and flat shoes, so she asked my opinion. Trying to help, I asked her what was more comfortable, and she pointed to the flats. I said, then you've got your answer. But she argued, saying high heels would be fancier. I wanted her to be comfortable, but she wanted to be fancy, so I suggested a third alternative, combining both options. Right foot high heel and left foot flat shoe. That way, it would be fancy *and* comfortable.

This situation sounds like nonsense because it is nonsense. Now, let's look at a business situation. A product designer researched customers, the pains they face, and the gains they pursue.

After understanding the customers, the product designer sketched a user journey and a prototype. When she presented her solution to software engineers, they challenged her, and business stakeholders did the same. Curiously, neither the software engineers nor the business stakeholders talked to any customers, but behaved as if they knew what customers wanted. Tired of discussing the matter, the designer adapted the prototype, leading to a version nobody (including customers) liked but they all committed to.

Is that the best way of creating digital products?

The question is, who should be the driver? In the previous example, everyone acted as the driver, and the designer accepted their suggestions and amended the solution. A better way would be for the designer to be the driver and mindfully decide which recommendations to take and which to reject.

Moving from consensus to consent can help you avoid getting stuck. Consensus blocks progress until everyone agrees on the decision, whereas consent accelerates progress because people accept it to move forward, even if they don't love the solution. I recommend the following principles to battle with consensus:

- Establish alignment instead of pleasing everyone.
- Evidence talks louder than opinions.

These principles may sound strict and as if I'm encouraging teams to work in silos. But that's not what I'm really recommending. Going back to the example, instead of challenging the designer, understanding the decisions would be a better start. For example, a software engineer could ask which other options the designer considered or which problem the prototype is trying to solve. A conversation would lead to a better result than throwing empty opinions on the table.

In high-performing teams, members trust each other's expertise and complement one another. The team is bigger than the sum of its individuals. Each individual knows when to take the driver's seat and when to enjoy the journey as a passenger.

Output Approval: Limiting Team's Accountability

How easy is it for software engineers to release software to the hands of end users?

A friend, Rainer Collet, a savvy chief product officer, claims the organization has a reliable release process when the most junior staff can release software to users. Before listening to this thought, I had never considered this aspect. The simpler it is to get changes to end users, the quicker we can learn what drives value.

Have you ever had a step in your workflow called "PM approval" or "PO approval"? If you have that now, remove it immediately. Then, continue to read.

It's common to have a Product Manager (PM) or Product Owner (PO) (read Chapter 10 to clarify this ever-lasting confusion) sign off on deliverables from teams. But that's a massive problem for many reasons:

- The PM/PO becomes a bottleneck.
- Teams have reduced accountability.
- The relationship isn't on the same level.

In a product team, no one is on a higher level than other members. Hierarchy inside product teams hinders the development of outstanding products.

To clarify this point, I need to share an example of when PM approval was required.

The software engineer worked closely with the designer to finalize the feature and then handed it to another engineer for a code review. At this point, a back-and-forth took place, and after that, another team member ran quality assurance tests. Finally, the product manager would review the feature, check the acceptance criteria, and approve or send it back. When the feature was rejected, the whole process happened all over again.

This scenario is an example of a waterfall inside an agile framework. It creates much waste and little value. You could do something simple instead: collaborate closer to your team.

Set the context, determine what's important to solve, and what success looks like. Then, empower teams to be creative and come up with ideas.

I faced the workflow mentioned earlier but decided to remove the "PM approval" step. Curiously, quality increased because software engineers felt a different sense of accountability. And I had more natural exchanges with the team. It was like removing a heavy burden from our shoulders.

Meeting Marathon: Long Days with Little Value Created

How many hours a week do you spend in meetings?

As a software engineer, I had plenty of time to code. I could intensely focus on my work and would quickly get things done. Since I've moved to product management, I've struggled with an extensive meeting routine.

At the beginning of my product journey, I thought I was a meeting manager instead of a product manager. I had to schedule, organize, facilitate, and plan meetings. Sadly, I failed to challenge how such meetings created value. I was on a ride as a passenger with no idea who the driver was and where we were going. It was like being kidnapped with a blindfold and hoping for the best. But nobody kidnapped me; I did it myself.

Until 2020, the meeting marathon was intense. But when the COVID-19 pandemic hit, the marathon suddenly became unbearable. Pre-pandemic, people would go to the office and face physical limits to meeting together. Offices have limited meeting rooms. That meant sometimes you wouldn't find a room, and no meeting would occur. Apart from that, the rooms have limited space.

Today, remote work enables a different level of collaboration but also creates unlimited rooms with endless seats. The result: more meetings with more people.

I often hear software engineers complaining they lack sufficient time to code, and I observe product managers overwhelmed with a daily ultra-meeting marathon. Product designers also join the club and struggle because they have no time to actually design products. Like me, at the beginning of my product journey, they are blindfolded on a ride without knowing the driver or destination.

We land in such dreadful situations because we often enjoy the ride as a passenger, and I speak from experience. I used to accept meeting invitations without reflection because I trusted the organizer needed me. Then, I got trapped in meetings unrelated to what mattered to my teams, and I couldn't add value to the exchange.

You wouldn't accept joining a ride blindfolded without knowing where to go. So why would you accept a meeting without a goal and a clear connection with your objectives?

Don't let others drive your agenda. To thrive, you've got to be the driver of your time, not a passenger.

Take action to escape the meeting marathon:

- Create recurrent blockers for focus time.
- Reject meeting invitations without a clear objective.
- Before accepting a meeting, reflect on how it contributes to your goals. Accept goal-related meetings and reject the others.

Fear of Saying No: The Art of Getting Overwhelmed

How often do you say no?

It's tough to say no because people don't expect it. Yet, every yes you give is a new responsibility you take on.

I used to please business stakeholders. I wanted to help them as much as possible, but quickly became so overloaded that I couldn't deliver on expectations.

When you recklessly answer yes to all requests you receive, you become the stakeholders' puppet. They pull the strings and define where you go. You have no control over your destination and have no idea where you're going. That's not funny. But when you're mindful and master the art of saying no, you break free from the strings and focus on your destination instead of pleasing others.

The ability to say no is one of the most valuable skills outstanding product professionals have. However, it's easier said than done. I've observed many people, including myself, struggling to reject requests. The reasons vary from fear of being impolite to negative repercussions. It's much easier to give a yes than a no.

Let's consider an example from daily life.

How Saying No Prevents Unnecessary Problems

On a sunny day, a young family goes for a walk. Along the way, they pass in front of a store, and the five-year-old kid says, "I want this toy."

The easiest thing to do is to buy the toy. The kid stays quiet and happy for a moment. But what are the consequences? More toys at home and the kid will keep asking for other toys and may not even play with them. What if you dare to say no? The kid may cry, complain, or even shout. You can continuously say no without explanation and get the same behavior or worse.

Maybe you could help the kid opt against that toy, and then the kid doesn't make the request again. You don't want more toys messing up your home, and you save some money. But you know, that's the hardest option.

Untrapping Lesson: Help others say no to themselves instead of bluntly rejecting their requests.

A strategy to say no is essential. My first one was straightforward: I'd say no three times to any request without considering it. If the person returned the fourth time, I'd listen. By doing that, I reduced the number of distractions, but my boss received complaints that I was a business blocker.

Saying no without explaining why is a bad strategy. Nobody appreciates rejection, and sooner than you might imagine, the relationship deteriorates.

The challenge isn't to say no. The real challenge is to say no and keep the relationship sustainable. In the preceding example of the parents, saying no to the kid is easy, but the kid won't digest the answer until the kid accepts why their parents rejected her wish.

Building digital products is a team game, and business stakeholders aren't your enemies. Cultivating a meaningful relationship with them is mandatory. Otherwise, you cannot get their support.

If you want to say no to someone, you better help the person say no to themself first.

My first strategy was faulty because I said no without helping the person accept it. A better approach is to help them understand why the request doesn't relate to your goals. You need to listen to them before you bluntly reject their requests.

For example, name your current goal and connect it to your current strategy and vision. Then ask, "How does your request get us closer to our goal?" Whenever I ask this question, I hear, "Well, it doesn't, but it's important." Then I engage in a conversation to understand how much evidence the person has: "What convinces you about it?" I first value the idea and ultimately make my problem their problem: "If I'm saying yes to your request, what can I say no to?" Such questions often lead to reflection. Surprisingly, business stakeholders usually remove their requests. In short, they say no to themselves.

If you lack a product vision, strategy, or goals, saying no will be daunting because you'll miss something to anchor on. We will cover the right ingredients in Chapter 4.

Saying yes is the same as being a bus passenger, going wherever the bus takes you. Saying no is being the driver, in control of your destination. So, are you riding or driving?

Bridge Communication: Becoming the Bottleneck

What's the job of a product manager?

In 2012, when I got my first job as a product manager, I struggled to tell my family and friends what I did. I found a simple definition of bridging communication between business and tech. I felt honored that I could understand business requirements and translate them into tech specs. What I didn't know was the side effects of it.

The software engineers were clueless about how their work created business value and had no idea why the business stakeholders wanted some features so badly. I didn't know, either. Then, the business couldn't understand why everything took so long. And there I was, bridging the communication between both sides. Even to the best of my abilities, I couldn't avoid creating misunderstandings. It often became "us" versus "them."

On top of that, I became the bottleneck. I didn't want business stakeholders talking directly to tech people because I feared they would load them with requests. That's why I did my best to protect the team. It's embarrassing to share this tale, but I created a bubble and fostered a feature factory due to my lack of skills.

Although this story dates from 2012, when I was in Brazil, I continue to see this situation more often than I'd like. In 2017, I moved to Germany. Since then, I have noticed many product managers with the same flawed perception I had. I took that as a chance to share my own painful experiences with my colleagues, hoping they could move from bridging communication to fostering collaboration. It worked well sometimes, but not always.

The trouble with bridging communication is that it positions the product manager at a different level than the team members. This attitude is frustrating. I've seen organizations that forbid software engineers from engaging with customers. Curiously, software engineers are the people creating solutions for customers. Product managers can solve this puzzle by connecting the dots instead of becoming a bottleneck. Great product managers act like a catalyst[4]: They accelerate change.

In a classic corporate environment, the bridge product manager is typical. Most people perceive it as nothing alarming. However, once they experience fluid collaboration with software engineers, product designers, and others, they notice how they can create value faster and resist the bridge anti-pattern.

Don't limit yourself to being a bridge between tech and business. Creating value requires acting as a catalyst fostering collaboration with multiple parts (more on that in Chapter 11).

It's unimaginable for product managers to drive everything alone. That's why limiting software engineers and designers to being passengers all the time is unwise. When you foster collaboration, you give them a chance to act as the driver of solutions, and together you can all thrive.

Opinion-Driven Decision: Ignoring Evidence, Creating Waste

Digital product management is populated with some dangerous animals. The most dangerous is the HiPPO, the highest paid person opinion. I attended many meetings where the CEO would say something that would become the ultimate truth. People would mindlessly follow the CEO's assertion, and no one would dare to challenge it. Have you ever seen anything like that?

Opinions in product management are often wrong. I may think I know best what works for users, but if I lack evidence, my opinion is no more than an assumption. And creating products based on invalid assumptions is like relying on luck. That's a horrible choice.

---

4. Catalyst definition from the Cambridge Dictionary: "an event or person that causes great change"

Even in the face of all available data, opinions greatly influence decisions. I cannot definitively state how often that happens in the world, but I can speak from my experience: Opinions drive strategy, roadmaps, goals, and features. That scares me. I've coached product managers world-wide, and they face a similar pattern: the opinion-driven decision framework.

The C-suite thinks something is important, so that something becomes the measure of success.

Middle management believes specific features bring value, so those features become priorities.

Product designers believe pixel-perfect design matters greatly, so teams must implement pixel-perfect solutions.

Software engineers are against tech debt, so using tech debt isn't accepted.

Product managers believe that multitasking is the way to go, so that becomes the way of working.

All of these points are opinions. Curiously, they lead to a bizarre reality. A better way is to differentiate opinion from expertise and evidence.

When teams follow opinions, they often hit the wall. When teams listen to experts, they hit the wall less often. But when teams combine expertise with evidence, they have a higher chance of succeeding faster.

It's shocking how much waste companies create. Following opinions leads to features never or rarely used. Suja Thomas, Ph.D., a lead data scientist from Pendo, studied feature usage in publicly traded cloud software companies.[5] The result was frightening:

> 80 percent of features in the average software product are rarely or never used. Publicly-traded cloud software companies collectively invested up to $29.5 billion developing these features, dollars that could have been spent on higher value features and unrealized customer value.

Don't let opinions drive your decisions. Step back and ensure expertise and evidence trump unfounded opinions. In Chapter 7, we will discuss how to run experiments, enabling decisions based on evidence. Before we get there, let me suggest two ways to get HiPPOs to listen to you:

1. **Feature report:** Generate a report with all features created over the last 12 months. Show how often users interact with them and the value created for them and the business. Chances are high that 50% of features are ignored and drive no value. With such a report, you can ask a powerful question, "Is that the way we should be working?"

2. **Observe interviews:** HiPPOs tend to have strong opinions and won't change unless they see something different. Getting them to observe customer interviews can open their eyes, as they will uncover unknowns. As HiPPOs observe customers, you can get them to step back and connect their opinions to evidence.

---

5. 2019 Feature Adoption Report: https://go.pendo.io/rs/185-LQW-370/images/2019%20Feature%20Adoption%20Report%20Digital.pdf.

Failure Avoidance: Killing Innovation Chances

Is reducing mistakes more important than accelerating learning?

When companies fear failure, they create more processes to reduce the chances of making mistakes. It's understandable because failing tastes bitter, and almost no one enjoys it. But creativity vanishes when people have to mind their steps, and that's a major failure. The more processes you have, the less creative your people can be.

What do you do when you face a bitter failure?

- *Leaders with a fixed mindset do not welcome failure.* When someone fails, they ask what they will do to avoid it next time. As a result, people feel ashamed and play it safer next time. They adapt processes or create new ones to prevent failures. Step by step, this approach eliminates creativity.

- *Leaders with a growth mindset foster a learning atmosphere.* They may even celebrate failure. Instead of punishing people, they ask them what they learned from the experience and request them to share their knowledge with more people.

Investing time in justifying failure isn't helpful; it's demotivating. In contrast, learning from mistakes is powerful and motivating. Does that mean you should recklessly try anything you want? Of course not.

My favorite take on failure comes from Alexander Osterwalder et al. (2020), who make it clear why you need to understand the importance of balance:

Avoid big failures, or you're dead.

Embrace small failures, or you're dead.

Companies will evaporate when they face failures more significant than they can take. For example, when someone invests months or years in doing something without evidence, chances are high that you will face a dramatic failure. Such situations are destructive and unforgivable. That's when you lose investors, employees, and customers. Recovering the business becomes an impossible mission.

The transformation happens when companies create a fail-fast culture. A learning attitude lets you adapt your product to what makes sense to customers. It's like an experimentation mindset: You get an idea, then you name the assumptions, prioritize, define experiments, set expected results, run tests, learn, and decide. Sometimes, the evidence suggests pursuing and investing more in your idea. Other times, it is better to drop the initiative or maybe pivot.

Embracing failures fosters growth.

Avoiding failures encourages mediocrity.

Bullshit Management Check

Maybe you strongly connect to some of the points mentioned in this chapter. If they're too present in your scenario, the discussion here may demotivate you. But don't worry, because you're not alone. This situation is more common than you think. I've been mastering bullshit management without knowing it.

Over time, I came to understand the difference between product management and bullshit management. Then, I continuously fostered one change at a time to transform my reality for the better. Sometimes, I could easily take the driver's seat and fight for a change. Other times, I got tired, took the ride as a passenger, and accepted how it was, even though I disagreed.

Many companies will have an imperfect scenario to create outstanding digital products. I like taking that as an opportunity to be a change catalyst.

Facing bullshit management is unavoidable. Dealing with it is a choice.

Here's a simple tip: Reflect on your reality and review how the ten points from this chapter are present in your daily life. Ask your team members and colleagues to do the same. Then, pick one issue at a time and try acting as the driver instead of the passenger. Don't take the status quo as unchangeable. You can make a massive change step by step.

To conclude this chapter, take your time and fill out the bullshit management checklist (Figure 3.1). Use what I shared to reflect on your reality.

Key Takeaways

- Knowing when to enjoy the ride as a passenger and when to take the driver's seat is critical to defeating common challenges.

- It's easy to get busy with too many irrelevant things. Focusing on the few things that matter most is hard.

- Perceiving the status quo as final will prevent teams from growing. Strive to pick one aspect at a time and gradually drive change.

- Bullshit management is present everywhere. Ignoring it isn't helpful, but facing it and doing your best to deal with it mindfully enables you to accelerate value creation.

- Help people around you step back and recognize what drains their energy and contributes to no value creation.

This chapter concludes Part I, Facing Dangerous Traps. We extensively discussed how companies commonly work and their usual challenges. We also got acquainted with the villain distracting you and getting in the way of creating value. Chapter 4 provides an overview of the ingredients that can improve your situation and help you overcome the dangerous traps we explored.

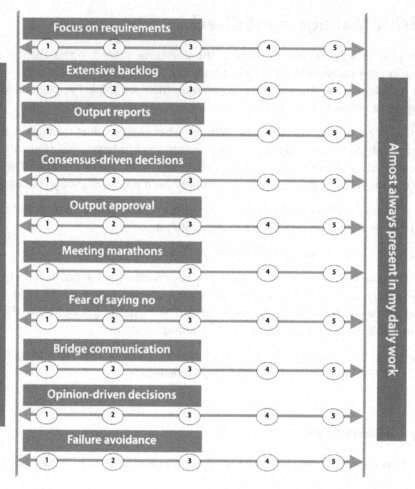

Figure 3.1
Bullshit management checklist

PART II

OVERCOMING DANGEROUS TRAPS

"Always take a chance on better, even if it seems threatening."
—Ed Catmull

In Part II, we explore ways to break free from the dangerous traps discussed in Part I. We start our conversation with an overview of the key ingredients for thriving with digital products. This overview elaborates on the importance of each element and critical aspects but leaves the in-depth exploration to the following chapters. As you get familiar with the key ingredients, we will investigate product strategy, discovery, and delivery in detail. You'll learn about the traits that can make or break product teams and the vital aspects of measuring results. Finally, this part concludes with a discussion of what it takes to create winning product teams.

4

Using the Right Ingredients for Product Teams

Creating digital products is similar to cooking. As a foodie, I casually try my luck following recipes from renowned chefs. Sometimes, I get edible results. Most times, I get something that has nothing to do with the original recipe. Why does that happen to me?

Cooking isn't only about the recipe. It has much to do with how you do it and which ingredients you use. But even when you have everything you need, you may get undesired results because the secret is your take, love, and approach. The chef tremendously impacts the outcome, just as the product manager does with the digital product.

Great chefs can cook great meals even when some of the ingredients are lacking. They use what they have to achieve the best they can.

Product management isn't about deploying frameworks and following processes. It's about being adaptive to create value. How you play the game is as important as which ingredients you use.

The ultimate goal of this chapter is to give you an overview of key ingredients that unlock progress. We will superficially explore each to understand its essence and how it contributes to value creation. Quite intentionally, I leave frameworks out of the discussion here. Over the years, I have observed teams becoming obsessed with frameworks, where implementation by the book becomes more important than collaboration. I want to ensure I don't contribute to this confusion.

Let's start by getting familiar with the key ingredients. To illustrate that, we will explore a case from a hard-to-reach beach bar that became recognized as the best restaurant in the world—five times.

How a Simple Restaurant Became the World's Number One

Can you imagine a restaurant getting more than 2 million reservation requests annually? That was the case for El Bulli when Ferran Adrià ran the restaurant.[1]

What made it so special? El Bulli wasn't like any other restaurant. The kitchen staff wouldn't cook classic recipes but invent their own. They'd try thousands of different dishes before serving a guest. It wasn't about dining; it was about having an unforgettable experience. Every year, millions of people would try booking a table, but only 8000 would be privileged to enjoy the exclusive 5-hour, 30-course dinner. The rest would have to try again in the following year.

Ferran Adrià pioneered experimental cuisine and set new standards for fine dining. For him, it wasn't about creating dishes, but rather about creating experiences. He even partnered with a Swiss company to develop specific cutlery to ensure an exceptional experience.

The critical difference went beyond cooking. The strategy, discovery, and delivery approach of El Bulli was unique in its sector. That's what helped the restaurant to win three Michelin stars and five awards as the best restaurant in the world.

We can take many lessons about El Bulli's strategy, discovery, and delivery, which will help us understand how they interconnect. Another lesson is to analyze the importance of adapting according to your situation. Despite all of its success, El Bulli closed in 2011 due to recurrent financial losses (more on that in a few minutes).

Understanding the Right Ingredients for Product Teams

Coming back to digital products, by now it should be crystal clear how complex this game is. Maybe you're even tired of reading about it. I understand, so let me offer you a deal. From now on, we will talk about simplicity. I will help you simplify the overwhelming complexity.

When you get the three elements of product strategy, discovery, and delivery aligned, the results can be magical. As you can see in Figure 4.1, these three elements are intertwined. Each of them

---

1. Read "The Story of El Bulli" to learn more about this restaurant that transformed the culinary world: https://artsandculture.google.com/story/the-story-of-elbulli-real-academia-de-gastronomia-espa%C3%B1ola/qwURz-FLVhm19LQ.

is vital to enable product teams to thrive. When one is absent or dysfunctional, the team suffers and falls into traps like those discussed in Part I of this book.

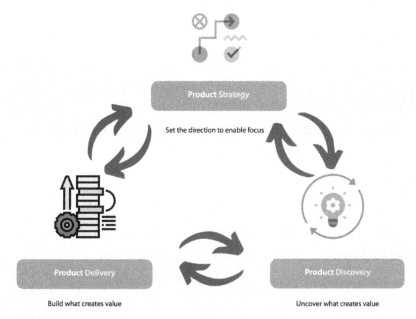

Figure 4.1
The key ingredients of product management

Let's examine each of these ingredients at a high level to build an understanding of what they are for and how you can benefit from them.

What a Solid Product Strategy Enables

Knowing where to focus and what to ignore is vital when developing products. The multitude of choices can overwhelm teams and impede progress. The result of a sound product strategy is smoothing decision making.

I worked for many companies under many different scenarios, but the one aspect that always slowed us down was complex decision making. Working in the e-commerce arena, I remember endless discussions about so many topics that I couldn't focus on anything. I couldn't agree with business stakeholders on what to focus on next because everything was a priority. When every-thing is a priority, nothing gets done.

Product strategy solves this problem. It includes the following key aspects:

- **Why** → Give the context while connecting it with your vision.

- **Who** → Define who you're serving and who you're leaving out.

- **What** → Define what you envision achieving and name what's intentionally left out.
- **How long** → A time frame is necessary to facilitate deciding on suitable options.

Clarifying Product Strategy

I imagine you wonder about the practical aspects of crafting a meaningful product strategy. You could start by clarifying the points I mentioned. The most important aspect isn't how you present your product strategy, but what it constitutes.

Let's return to our example of El Bulli. Which strategy made this restaurant so successful?

- **Focus:** Create memorable experiences for diners.
- **Authenticity:** No à la carte menu; the chef chooses the courses.
- **Differentiation:** Every year has a new menu.
- **Target audience:** Premium audience (400 USD per person[2]).
- **Excluded audience:** Customers searching for traditional dishes.
- **Scarcity:** Opened only six months a year, limited to 8000 diners.

You may read the description of this strategy and think it's too thin, but that's the point. It gives you enough guidance on what to focus on and drop. At El Bulli, they did everything to provide memorable experiences.

El Bulli's authenticity is unquestionable. It was the first restaurant with two Michelin stars to remove its à la carte menu. Ferran Adrià perceived the choice of dishes and sequence as fundamental to providing the best dining experience. El Bulli's staff controlled the experience and served each dish as part of their creation, and diners would never have a repeated dinner.

Product strategy doesn't need to be fancy; it needs to simplify decision making.

Product Strategy Lifespan

It's unlikely your first product strategy will hit the nail on the head. Don't treat your first strategy as final. As you test it, you will quickly realize some tweaks are necessary, if not a significant change.

Setting the strategy in stone is unwise, and changing it every second week is an alarm that something is considerably off. The product strategy starts with a hunch about what will enable you to reach your vision, and combined with discovery, you will understand what works and what doesn't.

---

2. The original price was around 250 USD, but would be around 400 USD in 2023 after adjusting it for inflation.

El Bulli's strategy won it Michelin stars and recognition as the best restaurant worldwide, creating a demand greater than it could fulfill. However, the restaurant's staff didn't adapt the strategy to reflect their new situation. I daresay they missed the opportunity to become even more successful.

Demand was 250 times bigger than supply. El Bulli served 8000 diners and left around 2 million unattended. Yet, the restaurant remained closed for half of the year and didn't increase the price. Unwillingness to adapt the strategy led to its closure in 2011 with a loss of half a million dollars.

The strategy needs to evolve within your situation. As the saying goes, whatever brought you here won't get you further. That happens when your scenario changes, the strategy becomes obsolete, and failure to adapt can be lethal.

Accelerating Learning with Product Discovery

Uncovering unknowns is what you get from product discovery. It empowers you to quickly drop ideas that don't survive a confrontation with reality so you can focus on the remaining ones.

Product discovery isn't a process that guarantees value creation. It's also not a phase after strategy and before delivery. It's the way to learn what drives value and what distracts you from it. Applying product discovery practices will fuel your knowledge, empowering you to adapt your strategy and product delivery.

Let's explore three common scenarios: excessive delivery, excessive discovery, and sustainable balance.

Excessive Delivery

Many companies develop an obsession with maximizing delivery. That can happen due to pressure from the business or a lack of product management expertise. When delivery becomes the focus, success means more features. The result is often a cluttered product with many features that create no value.

When all energy goes to the present, somebody else makes the future.

Excessive Discovery

The other side of the coin is an extreme focus on discovery. The team aims for perfection and struggles to define what's enough. They continuously apply product discovery and test different solutions but struggle to commit to delivering something, ultimately falling into analysis paralysis. The result is dreadful: Nothing gets done, and everyone gets disappointed.

When all energy goes to the future, somebody else creates the present.

Sustainable Balance

A better way is a sustainable balance. Part of the team invests around 80% of its time into discovery and the rest into delivery, while the other members of the team do the opposite. This scenario wisely enables discovery and delivery.

The critical aspect is understanding that it's one team, not micro teams. The people responsible for discovery put effort into uncovering what matters while dropping bad ideas. The people in charge of delivery ensure they drive desired outcomes. The whole team takes ownership of their present and future. Together, they craft meaningful solutions to solve worthwhile problems.

When you balance discovery and delivery, you implement a dual-track agile approach, which means combining present and future. Setting it up is daunting, but the results can be extraordinary.

A common way of solving this puzzle is by defining who will focus on the future versus the present. The product trio[3] fits this definition well. A product manager, designer, and software engineer (the trio can differ depending on your product) work on the problem space and uncover value drivers. The rest of the team focuses on delivering value.

Balancing discovery and delivery is hard, but it gives you a chance to thrive. Teams working with collaborative flows will smoothly reach a sustainable balance, whereas teams with a coordinative flow will probably get trapped with excessive delivery or discovery.

How Did El Bulli Apply Discovery?

Every year, El Bulli would experiment with around 5000 dishes and keep 125, at most, for the upcoming season. Ferran Adrià, El Bulli's chef, perceived the results as 98% learning and 2% success.

A unique characteristic is how El Bulli developed new dishes. The managers would close the restaurant six months a year, and the staff would move to El Bulli Taller (a workshop location in Barcelona), where they relentlessly tried out new dishes. Barely any restaurant can afford to remain closed for such a long time, but that was one of the secrets of El Bulli.

On the one hand, no one can deny how unique El Bulli became. The awards speak for themselves. On the other hand, separating serving guests and creating new dishes limited how much value they could collect.

Strictly separating discovery from delivery will allow you to focus, but it will get in the way of creating value steadily. That's why finding a sustainable balance between both is vital.

---

3. The product trio is a concept defined by Teresa Torres. Generally, it is a team consisting of a product manager, a UX designer, and a software engineer. The trio works on the future aspects, and when it's worth pursuing, they connect with the whole team. Read more about it: www.producttalk.org/2021/05/product-trio/.

Approaching Product Delivery Mindfully

The goal of product delivery is to create outcomes. A team shipping features at lightning speed isn't a sign of delivering value, but simply shows the team is efficient in creating output. What matters is what the output creates. Product delivery isn't about delivering solutions, but rather about driving value.

When I had my first contact with product teams, my responsibility was to ensure the teams delivered as specified and on time. I didn't care about what the features enabled, nor did I check if customers used them. That's an example of product delivery without strategy and discovery.

Without a product strategy, teams struggle to make simple decisions. They become disempowered and depend on others to decide what's critical.

Without product discovery, failures will be costly, leaving teams with low morale. Product discovery acts as the glue between strategy and delivery.

While product discovery lives in the future, product delivery relates to the present. Discovery understands future value drivers, and delivery works on the present to enable the future. But that doesn't mean that product delivery is only about building. On the contrary, it requires a great deal of learning, which is counterintuitive for many people.

It's natural that once a team gets a feature to build, they want to make it right from the beginning. Yet, this attitude creates a problem, because it assumes the feature is correct. Reality is tough; users will surprise you no matter how many experiments you run. That's why the more mindful approach is to start small and learn how users benefit from your solution before you invest in a full-blown implementation.

How El Bulli Created Unforgettable Experiences

After six months of experimenting with different dishes, you might think that El Bulli's chefs strictly followed the menu to perfection. Yet, their goal wasn't to provide the menu but the experience. El Bulli's staff tirelessly adapted the dishes to enhance the experience.

Every day, the staff of around 50 people would get together, and Ferran Adrià ensured everyone was on the same page. As diners arrived, the chefs would observe how they reacted to their dishes, take notes, and share their observations with the other chefs. They'd make adaptions to improve the results continuously.

Clearly, El Bulli was different from other restaurants. Chefs had to remain curious and open to the new. Some of their beloved dishes could cause unexpected reactions, but instead of perceiving them as a failure, they viewed them as learning experiences that enriched the dishes.

Delivery isn't about following a plan, but rather should be perceived as a moment to confront reality, learn, and adapt.

Elements of Meaningful Product Delivery

Learning is a critical part of product delivery. When teams neglect this part, frustrations are inevitable. Great product teams don't overcommit to a solution. They are brave to start with a solution they aren't proud of, which enables them to measure value for a sample audience.

The following elements will increase the odds of driving value:

- Start small and evolve gradually.

- Focus on outcomes.

- Create opportunities to collect feedback.

- Dare to discard a solution when it creates no value.

- Collaborate instead of coordinate.

How you apply product delivery doesn't matter. What matters is what you create from it.

I see many discussions about the "best" agile framework and how one is better. I perceive such conversations as a waste because they distract you from your goal of creating value. You may opt for a framework, but before you do so, consider your challenges and which framework would help you. If you opt to deploy a framework without understanding your current challenges, you will create problems you didn't have and could easily avoid.

Keeping your collaboration simple will help you address issues faster. The more flexible you are, the more quickly you can react.

Finding the Right Ingredients for Your Situation

It's all too common to face a situation where delivering more features is all that matters, strategy is absent, and nobody supports product discovery. The question is, what can you do today to allow for a better tomorrow?

The first step is to understand the cards you have. Then, decide on the best move to make. It's fundamental to recognize you won't have all the cards you wish, but making a move with your cards will enable you to win others.

You have stronger decision-making power when you're a product leader like a chief product officer (CPO), vice president of product, or the equivalent. In that case, I'd encourage you to start crafting a product strategy and build alignment over it. The strategy provides clarity and facilitates decision making. But creating or adapting the strategy isn't something anyone can do. This choice is suitable for leaders but not for those lacking decision-making power.

You might be part of a product team and realize you're missing the ingredients we discussed. Then, your starting point would be different. Applying product discovery would enable you to uncover whether it makes sense to build certain features. Yet, your organization might be resistant to that conclusion. A simple way to start is with assumptions. Pick a feature you will work on, name the assumptions, test them against reality, and share evidence with your team and business stakeholders. It's hard to neglect evidence, which will give you the experimentation card.

The secret lies in starting small. Strive to identify the slightest change you can make today, learn from its result, and progress gradually. Accept your constraints, but don't let them block you.

Key Takeaways

- Strive to "start simple" with your product strategy, discovery, and delivery. You don't need to deploy a framework immediately, because that may shift your focus to implementing the framework instead of progressing.

- Product strategy, discovery, and delivery aren't separate phases of product management. They are highly intertwined, and one fuels the others to enable value creation. When they lack one of the elements, teams struggle, and creating value becomes harder than it should be.

- In a situation where ingredients are missing, act like an experienced chef. Do your best with the available ingredients to create great results.

- To improve your situation, foster small changes. For example, when trapped in a feature factory, start by naming and testing your assumptions. This approach will enable you to help others understand why some features aren't worth building.

- Don't try meeting organizations miles away from where they are. Be one step ahead of them when you meet them, and strive to uncover the smallest action you can take today for a better tomorrow. Know your goal but focus on the journey.

This chapter explored how product strategy, discovery, and delivery contribute to value creation. We also discussed the impacts of misimplementation of these ingredients and the absence of one of them. At this point, though, I imagine you long for more practical guidance. Chapter 5 provides that kind of guidance, equipping you to set a sound product strategy.

5

Crafting a Meaningful Product Strategy

Setting a relevant product strategy is one of the most critical aspects of successful product teams, but it can be overwhelming. A quick internet search will turn up dozens, if not hundreds, of ways to set your product strategy. But how do you select the best-fitting option for your team?

It's not my intention to identify the advantages and disadvantages of each method. First, I don't know all of them. Second, I don't think it matters.

I did try several different strategy techniques. Some helped me, others not so much. Over the years, I found my way of crafting a product strategy that works well across industries and different company sizes. That's what I want to share with you.

Product strategy is a vast subject, a broad-enough topic to fill a whole book.[1] I don't dare to promise a silver bullet. And I don't want you to perceive my suggestions as a recipe for success, but rather as a means to simplify decisions and bring focus to your teams.

I must warn you that product strategy isn't a document you craft and forget. For me, it's a combination of different pieces that solve the puzzle; leave one out, and confusion takes over. We've already pinched some of these pieces in Chapter 4, but now we'll go into more detail. In particular, I will share techniques and examples of how you can apply them in real life.

---

1. Nacho Bassino (2021) wrote a book that aims to clarify how you set product strategy, *Product Direction: How to Build Successful Products at Scale with Strategy, Roadmaps, and Objectives and Key Results*. Read it to explore this challenging part of product management in depth.

Figure 5.1 shows the four key elements needed to solve the product strategy puzzle. Before we examine the product strategy elements in depth, though, we need to discuss who you serve and to clarify the product life cycle. You need to know that information to craft a guiding strategy.

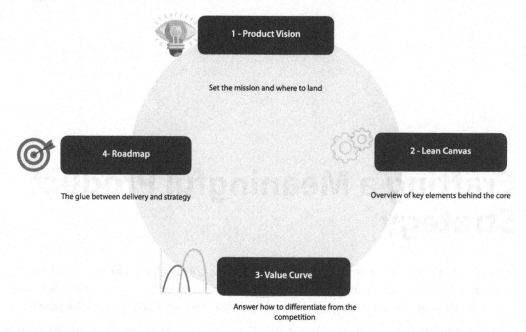

Figure 5.1
Product strategy key elements

Identifying Who You Serve

Products exist to improve people's lives.

The iPhone is one of my favorite products because it makes me more productive, equips me to take eye-catching pictures, and seamlessly integrates with my other devices. I got my first iPhone in 2013; that was the iPhone 5. But there's something curious about that: iPhone has been on the market since 2007. I got my first one six years later.

I'm not an early adopter. I'm more like the early majority. What does that mean? I read reviews before I buy a new product because I want to know that someone has used it and benefited from it. Is that right? That's the point. There's no right or wrong. But you can learn something from this.

You need to know who your target audience is and what stage your product is in (we will cover this topic briefly). Not everyone is the same. For example, when bringing a new product to the market, you should identify the audience willing to use it, even if the product isn't perfect. Failure is unavoidable if you try getting your initial product to an audience that expects a stable version.

In 1962, Everett M. Rogers wrote the first edition of *Diffusion of Innovations*, where he laid out a theory aiming to explain how, why, and at what rate new ideas and technology spread. The book's most recent edition was published in 2003. Although that was decades ago, it's still applicable in the context of digital products.

Figure 5.2 represents the typical adoption curve for technology and new ideas. It includes the following audiences:

- *Innovators care about new technology.* They long for access to early-stage products nobody else has. They are okay with a broken experience because they are primarily interested in the new.

- *Early adopters want to be ahead of the curve.* They seek to experiment with new products and services. These people waited in line at the Apple Store to buy the first-ever iPhone.

- *The early majority only accepts products with solid recommendations.* They are open to trying something different only after many people have tried it and expressed their approval. Getting to them generally takes a couple of years. That's me with the iPhone.

- *The late majority want to use only bulletproof services.* They'll consider a product or service only if it has solid support from beginning to end. Convenience is king.

- *Laggards are change-averse.* They start using something new only if there are no alternatives. In most cases, when current options are deprecated, they move on. That's my mom using smartphones beginning in 2020.

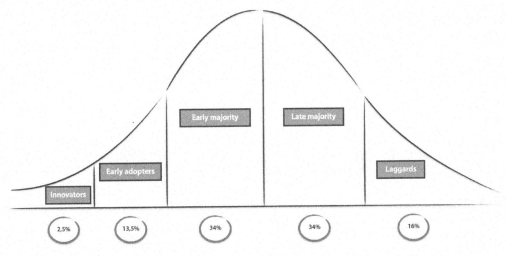

Figure 5.2
Product adoption life cycle adapted by David Pereira

A mistake commonly made by product managers is targeting the early majority without satisfying the early adopters. You cannot thrive with the early majority without early adopters falling in love with your product.

Here's the key lesson: Find your early adopters, get your product in their hands, learn, adapt, and get positive reviews. Then, and only then, are you ready to target the early majority.

If you already have a running product, understand your target audience. When targeting the late majority, the game differs from when you're focusing on the early majority.

I recommend reading *Crossing the Chasm* by Geoffrey Moore to learn more about it. He addressed in detail how to treat each audience and move further. This book was originally published in 1991, but the concept is still valid. The third edition was published in 2014.

Understanding Your Product Stage

At which stage in the life cycle is your product? To answer this question, you need to understand the product life cycle. Thanks to the economist Raymond Vernon,[2] that's a piece of cake. In 1966, he introduced product life cycle theory, defining the four stages of products' lives. Although Vernon's work was done before our digital era, it's still applicable to our reality. Figure 5.3 shows how the product life cycle develops.

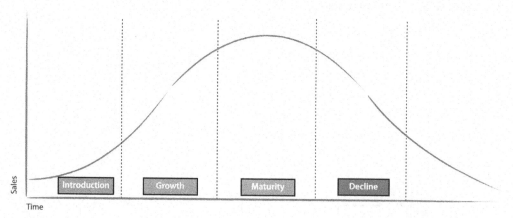

Figure 5.3
Product life cycle

---

2. You can learn more about this theory by reading this blog post: www.toolshero.com/marketing/product-life-cycle-stages.

Let's clarify the meaning of each phase:

- **Introduction:** You're still figuring out how to penetrate the market. You need to craft a solid go-to-market strategy. The chances of pivoting are high because you don't know how the market will react. Your strategy should get your product to innovators and early adopters.

- **Growth:** The market has accepted your product, and demand is increasing. Your strategy should enable you to increase your market share. It's paramount that you understand your adoption cycle and adapt your strategy according to your audience. What works for an early adopter won't work for the early majority.

- **Maturity:** Once your product reaches a certain sales level, you struggle to increase your user base. A sound strategy will address retention to ensure you don't lose customers. You may consider introducing a new product to keep your customers. Sometimes, that means disrupting yourself before somebody else does it.

- **Decline:** Inevitably, your product becomes less relevant due to new options in the market or other aspects. Put simply, your product is losing customers. When you address the maturity phase adequately, this decline won't scare you. It will be a transition from one product you offer to another. But if that's too late, your competitors will be happier than you.

Failing to recognize your product stage and audience will lead to selecting the wrong strategy. Product strategy doesn't have anything similar to "one size fits all." That's why you must understand your situation before reflecting on the strategy.

Now, let's explore the elements of a sound product strategy, know what problems they solve, and see how you can combine them to guide your teams.

Product Vision: Knowing Where to Land

A compelling vision will put your team on a mission by inspiring and motivating them. Without that sense of purpose, teams get lost because they don't know what they're fighting for.

Setting a product vision is daunting because it requires alignment, collaboration, and decisions on where to land and what to leave out. A great vision is memorable, audacious, achievable, and inspiring.

One of my favorite visions comes from John F. Kennedy. On May 25, 1961, he stood before the U.S. Congress[3] and said, "This nation should commit itself to achieve the goal, before this decade is out, of landing a man on the Moon and returning him safely to the Earth."

---

3. Watch the original speech from Kennedy: www.kennedy-center.org/video/center/discussionspoken-word/2019/president-john-f.-kennedy-speech-to-congress-on-space-exploration/.

Why is this vision so compelling? Let's evaluate the attributes:

- **Memorable:** JFK's message was brief yet strong. It was easy for people to keep that in their minds.

- **Timely:** JFK laid out a vision that spanned almost a decade. It was 1961, and he mentioned that the nation should commit to reaching it by the decade's end.

- **Inspiring:** The goal JFK set was novel—"landing a man on the Moon and returning him safely to the Earth." No one has ever done that before. He inspired an entire nation to dream about reaching such an audacious goal.

- **Achievable:** The commitment JFK asked for was daunting, but one could imagine making it possible with the proper resources.

Let's come back to the product management world. Inspiring people to embark on a mission motivates them to bring their best to work. And without that, they will lack the drive to push forward.

I've worked for more than ten companies and consulted for dozens of others. Most of them either lacked a product vision or had something everyone ignored. Yet, the ones with an inspiring vision stood out.

If you're starting the development of a new product, establishing a vision will help you a lot. But like most people, you'll eventually join a running team without a product vision. The question is, how do you set the bloody product vision?

Simple. Get a template, fill it, hang it on the wall, or pin it on a digital board, and that's it. I wish life could be that simple. A product vision requires alignment and buy-in. Otherwise, nobody cares.

Bad Product Vision

Before crafting a product vision, you better understand what a bad one looks like. Here are some examples:

1. Be the number one product in our segment with outstanding execution and winning culture.

2. Our product will revolutionize the market with cutting-edge technology.

3. By leveraging our deep industry expertise, advanced technological infrastructure, and a comprehensive suite of integrated solutions, we aim to develop a revolutionary, all-in-one platform enabling individuals and businesses to achieve unprecedented levels of productivity and efficiency in an increasingly complex and fast-paced digital landscape.

All of these examples miss the core of a great product vision: customer centricity. It's about what we do for the customers, not about how excellent the company is or wants to become.

The first example tells you where to land but misses why it matters. Everyone wants to be number one, but what makes your product different is a fundamental question to answer. The second example is fuzzy, and the third is so wordy that you deserve a free lunch once you memorize it.

Good Product Vision

A product vision is customer-centric, memorable, audacious, and achievable. Of course, you also need to know when you get there. I suggest using an existing format as a starting point to simplify the aspects. My favorite format is an adaption of Geoffrey Moore's (2014) elevator test:

> For (target customer) who (statement of need or opportunity), the (product name) is a (product category) that (key benefit, reason to buy). Unlike (primary competitive alternative), our product (statement of primary differentiation).

Let's take Microsoft Surface as an example:

> For the business user who needs to be productive in the office and on the go, the Surface is a convertible tablet that is easy to carry and gives you full computing productivity no matter where you are. Unlike laptops, Surface serves your on-the-go needs without carrying an extra device.

This template has the required elements to provide guidance, but it's still relatively long to grasp the core.

My tip is to leave only the punch line and delete the rest because that's memorable. For example: *"The Surface is a convertible tablet that is easy to carry and gives you full computing productivity no matter where you are."* With this vision statement, you can make decisions during your day and connect your activities to getting you closer to the product vision; whatever distracts you from it, you can drop it.

Crafting Your Product Vision

Let's start with how *not* to do it. Don't do it alone, and don't strive for perfection. Going it alone will ensure no commitment to the product vision, so that it becomes a useless statement.

The core of developing the product vision is to start with why. Once you know that, crafting the vision will become more natural. Simon Sinek, author of *Start with Why* (2009), said: "People don't buy what you do; they buy why you do it. And what you do simply proves what you believe."[4]

---

4. Simon Sinek, 2009, Ted Talk, www.ted.com/talks/simon_sinek_how_great_leaders_inspire_action.

I've tried different ways of crafting a product vision, but most led me nowhere. Let me suggest an effective approach:

1. *Exchange information with high-level management* or the product sponsor and strive to understand their vision and the why. Show curiosity and learn what matters to them as much as possible.

2. *Talk to customers* and observe how the product helps them. If it's B2B, understand why they chose your product over the competition.

3. *Look at the available options* in the market and clarify what makes yours unique.

4. *Come up with a draft* and invite key business stakeholders to sharpen it with you. Iterate a couple of times, but not more than that.

5. *Commit to it and start using it* as much as possible. Good options are roadmap, planning, and review. Ensure the product vision is alive, and don't hide it. Use it whenever you can.

Once you have a vision, you can challenge roadmap items whenever they're unrelated to the vision. You can also question feature requests that don't help you get closer to your vision. In short, the product vision enables you to say no to distractions.

The vision isn't a sentence that employees memorize and can recite when asked. It's a solid understanding of where the product should land and why that matters. Reaching this level requires constant alignment. Companies can benefit from visuals, picturing customers benefiting from the product and improving their lives.

I suggest you keep the following quote from Marty Cagan in mind: "Admittedly, a good product vision is a bit of an art form, as fundamentally it is a persuasion tool."[5]

Lean Canvas: Defining the Key Aspects to Thrive

After identifying your product vision, you can start imagining the future. Connecting the dots between the target audience, problems, value proposition, and other aspects is essential to creating a meaningful product. The Lean Canvas created by Ash Maurya[6] can do this job well.

The result of crafting a Lean Canvas is an alignment with teams and business stakeholders on the most relevant aspects behind your business idea. Beyond that, you clarify what you don't know and act on it.

Contrary to what many people think, it's not about filling in the blocks and moving on. It's about making decisions on the business fundamentals, iterating, learning, and adapting.

---

5. "Product Vision vs. Mission": www.svpg.com/product-vision-vs-mission/.

6. Learn more about the Lean Canvas: https://leanstack.com/lean-canvas.

The Lean Canvas is extremely simple (hold on for the example; it's coming in about three minutes). Crafting one shouldn't take more than 30 minutes. If you're taking longer than that, you're missing the point. The idea isn't to create a bulletproof plan, but rather to have a starting point that accelerates learning.

Before crafting a Lean Canvas, we need to talk about business models. Many product teams work without understanding how the company creates and delivers value. That surprises me.

Business Model

For many decades, companies crafted extensive business plans that explained how they'd become profitable. Such plans included detailed spreadsheets, forecasts, and more speculation than one can imagine.

I wrote several business plans, and I hated this process every single time because I couldn't see value in them. Yet, I received pressure from everyone to make it available, even though nobody could tell me why the business plan enabled us to create value sooner. Developing a solid business plan would take me weeks, if not months. Unfortunately, I don't recall any business plan that didn't become obsolete after the first customer contact.

Classic business plans drain energy and create false expectations. That should be part of the past, not the present or the future.

A business model is a simplified way to describe how the company collects revenue. Here are five typical business models for digital products:

1. **Subscription:** The user pays a recurrent fee. It's possible to have different tiers differentiating the service offering. For example, Netflix and Amazon Prime use this model.

2. **Freemium:** Users can benefit from the product's value without paying anything, but they face a few limitations that only premium users can get. Dropbox uses this format by offering free storage up to a few gigabytes but requiring users to pay if they want more storage. This approach is a common strategy for product-led growth companies.

3. **Software as a service (SaaS):** Instead of hosting a product on-premises (i.e., in a local data center), companies can hire a SaaS product. For example, Personio reached an 8.5 billion USD valuation in 2022[7] with a full-service human resources solution in Europe based on a SaaS business model.

4. **On-demand:** "Pay for what you use" plans have become increasingly popular, as they reduce friction to hire a service. That's how cloud solutions often work. That's the case for Amazon Web Services (AWS), Google Cloud Platform, and many others. Another example is car sharing, where you pay per minute.

---

7. "Personio Nabs $200M at a $8.5B Valuation as Its HR for Small Businesses Hits the Big Time": https://techcrunch.com/2022/06/21/personio-nabs-200m-at-a-8-5b-valuation-as-its-hr-for-small-businesses-hits-the-big-time/.

5. **Marketplace:** You connect the offer with the demand. If someone wants to sell something and someone wants to buy, you enable that exchange to happen. This business model generally charges one side and makes it free for the other. Airbnb and Uber are marketplaces in which the former charges the buyers (guests), and the latter charges the sellers (drivers).

Now, let me tell you something: When starting with an idea, you don't know which business model will work for you, so you better test multiple models before you try scaling.

> **Note:** There are dozens of business models. You can learn more about them by reading *Business Model Generation: A Handbook for Visionaries, Game Changers, and Challengers* by Alexander Osterwalder and Yves Pigneus (2010). Additionally, you can check the Appendix for extra resources.

Crafting a Lean Canvas

A well-crafted Lean Canvas simplifies decision making and reduces the learning cycle. You can streamline the process of crafting the Lean Canvas by following a specific order. The reason is simple: It will help you build a story around your idea. Figure 5.4 depicts the sequence.

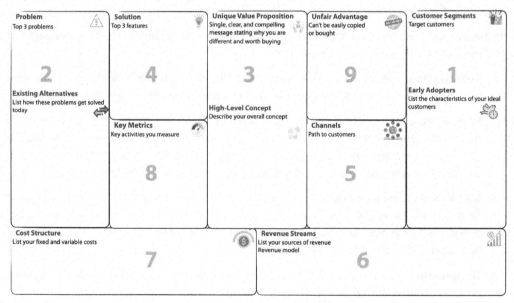

Figure 5.4
Lean Canvas from Ash Maurya, adapted by David Pereira

Right now, you may be thinking, "That's cool, but how do I fill the blocks?" Based on my understanding, I created a Lean Canvas for Substack (the newsletter platform I use), though I don't claim it's precisely Substack's business model. We'll use that example to demonstrate how the Lean Canvas shows the dynamics of a business in a single canvas.

1. Customer Segments

First come your customers. Without them, you have nothing.

Define the target audience you serve as directly as possible. You can have different levels but make them clear. Also, don't forget to mention the early adopters in your market, because starting with them is fundamental. It's important to focus the customer segments fairly narrowly because overloading this part will create confusion instead of guidance.

In our example, Substack is a platform connecting writers with readers. Writers can use the platform to share their content through newsletters, and readers can subscribe to newsletters from writers they relate to. Substack was founded in 2017, and many players were already on the market.

Substack nudged a few influencers to bring their content to the platform to kick off its operations. Among them was Bill Bishop,[8] an influential writer who focuses on China. During the first month, he brought thousands of readers to the platform.

By capitalizing on the early adopter writers, Substack kept growing steadily over the years, doubling the number of its readers year after year.[9]

2. Problem

Name the problems your target audience faces.

Make the problems brief and easy to understand. Make sure you mention the available alternatives to overcome the issues you uncovered. You should define the focus when you have a platform with two or more audiences. For example, Substack has writers and readers. Although one won't use the platform without the other, the organization prioritizes writers over readers.

Substack noticed how hard it is for writers to build and monetize a community. At the same time, readers struggle to connect with writers they relate to.

Medium is an alternative to Substack but fails to help writers get closer to their readers. Medium handles content distribution, making it harder for writers to reach their followers. For example,

---

8. Bill Bishop was one of the first influencers at Substack, bringing six-figure revenues to the platform (https://gettogether.substack.com/p/big-things-start-small-how-substack).

9. Substack user and revenue statistics: https://backlinko.com/substack-users.

when I had 3000-plus followers on Medium, I got more than 100,000 reads per month. But then the algorithm changed, and no matter what I did, I couldn't reach those numbers again, even with 90,000-plus followers. Meanwhile, Substack enables me to reach my audience consistently.

Platforms like Ghost and Patreon deliver a similar value proposition as Substack but don't help writers grow based on recommendations.

3. Unique Value Proposition

Define why customers would come to you. In other words, state how you create value by addressing your audience's problems.

"The home for great writers and readers."[10] That's the value proposition of Substack. Writers help each other grow while connecting readers with those to whom they relate most.

Substack helps writers connect with readers seamlessly. It also helps writers grow through recommendations from other writers, creating an organic growth engine. Readers can consume content without a subscription while subscribing to the newsletters that interest them the most.

4. Solution

Reflect on how you (aim to) solve the problem and describe your high-level solution. It's essential to understand the solution can go beyond a digital product. You may need to include services to make it attractive enough for your audience.

Substack offers a platform where writers can fully manage their newsletters and create premium tiers for fans. The platform is rich with analytics, helping writers understand which content works and which doesn't, enabling them to improve their craft. Readers benefit from an engaging platform with excellent user experiences, while having the chance to get closer to those writers whose thoughts they value.

5. Channels

Knowing how customers get to your product and service is vital. That's what this block is for. Reflect on the question, how do you get to your customer segments?

Substack relies on organic growth engines. Writers collaborate with other writers and recommend the publications they support. Readers can benefit from referring Substack to other readers, creating rewards for all sides.

---

10. The value proposition was found at the Substack website in 2023, https://substack.com/.

6. Revenue Streams

Which revenue sources does your idea create? Typical examples are subscriptions, premium subscribers, ads, and commissions. You can combine multiple revenue streams. Here's where your savvy about business models can help you explore alternatives to realize value from your business.

It's critical to keep the business model simple and understandable. Substack charges writers a percentage of their newsletters' subscription premium, 10% as of this writing.

You may wonder why writers wouldn't bypass Substack and create a newsletter directly on their own website. Substack enables organic growth. For example, my newsletter "Untrapping Product Teams" is recommended by more than 50 publications, enabling it to have steady growth, which I would struggle to achieve alone.

Business models have trade-offs, but users will stay when you offer a great experience.

7. Cost Structure

What are the costs you will incur to deliver on your promises? Some examples are development, marketing, and payroll costs.

Your product strategy has a high impact on the cost structure. For example, when bringing a product to market, chances are high that every new customer is a financial burden because you're still proving your product's market fit. Later, the cost structure will differ when your product is in the growth stage.

Substack invests a lot in high-quality platforms with intuitive design, on top of all the costs it incurs from developing a top-notch platform. Also, Substack has been constantly expanding its offerings worldwide. As of this writing, the company is in the growth stage.

8. Key Metrics

New ideas are fragile, and you may hit the wall. That's why it's crucial to know how you measure success.

Set three to five key metrics to ensure your business is booming. Differentiating actionable metrics from distracting ones is tough. That's why I dedicated Chapter 9 to this topic.

Coming to Substack, I perceive three metrics as critical: free subscriptions, churn rate, and premium subscriptions.

9. Unfair Advantage

The longer companies can protect their unfair advantage, the more prosperity they have. For example, Google has the most advanced web search engine and has protected it for so long that the company's name has become a verb.

The unfair advantage reflects what you have that others cannot easily copy. The more complicated it is to copy, the stronger your unfair advantage will be.

One of the most significant unfair advantages of Substack is the writer community, where each writer helps the other writers grow. It would take years to build a community similar to the one that Substack has been developing since its founding. Public recommendations enable writers to increase authority and strengthen their community. Substack continuously improves its growth engine, enabling writers to make a living out of it.

Figure 5.5 depicts Substack's Lean Canvas.

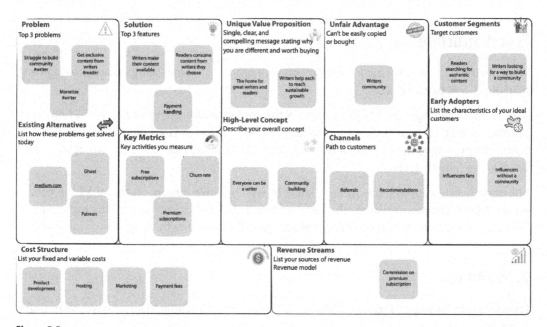

Figure 5.5

Lean Canvas example: Substack

I need to tell you a hard truth: You won't get your Lean Canvas right from the beginning. Along the way, though, you'll learn, and adapting will be inevitable. I recommend going block by block and asking what your assumptions are. Let's take Substack as an example:

- Influencers will create content.
- Readers will convert to subscribers.
- Free subscribers will convert to premium subscribers.

These points represent some of the assumptions behind Lean Canvas. You need to test the most critical ones and collect evidence. Here's a hint to ensure you don't forget the critical assumptions: You can add another box to your Lean Canvas. Figure 5.6 is an example of how I do it.

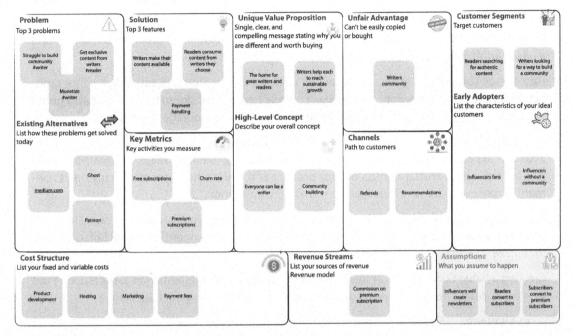

Figure 5.6
Lean Canvas example with assumptions

It's normal to pivot solutions, audiences, and problems. Continuously iterate until you have solid evidence supporting your business model. Here are two examples:

- *From renting DVDs per post to the largest video stream platform.* Netflix started by renting DVDs that were sent to customers by mail, then moved to streaming licensed content, and later started creating content. In 2022, nine out of ten most-watched series on Netflix were Netflix originals.[11]

- *From a failed multiplayer online game to one of the most famous communication tools worldwide.* After failing to attract enough users for its online game, *Glitch*, the team noticed that the internal communication created for its company was more valuable than the game. They pivoted, and that was the birth of Slack.[12]

Successful business models adapt to reality instead of living in a fantasy world.

---

11. Statistics about Netflix: https://truelist.co/blog/netflix-statistics/.

12. The Slack origin story: https://techcrunch.com/2019/05/30/the-slack-origin-story/.

Value Curve: Designing to Differentiate

Clarity about how your product is differentiated from the competition is paramount. Yet, to do that, you need to understand how your competitors position themselves. That's what the Value Curve can do for you. Combined with a Lean Canvas, it becomes even more powerful.

I'm not saying that you should get obsessed with the competition and panic when they release a new feature. You cannot be a better shadow, but you can be different.

I discourage competition obsession because it endangers your product's authenticity. Your product needs to have characteristics that make it unique because if it doesn't, you're probably going to compete on price—and that's a challenging game I don't encourage you to play.

The Blue Ocean strategy, developed by Renée Mauborgne and W. Chan Kim (first published in 2005 and expanded in 2015), can help you understand how to differentiate. This method forces you to think about crucial aspects of your product and make critical decisions early on. Its primary purpose is to create a new market and avoid competition.

You may be in a business where innovation is challenging, and you compete on price, features, or service. Even so, I see incredible value in reflecting on your competition and defining aspects that make you different.

Creating a Value Curve results in the alignment of your crucial differentiation aspects. Don't get stuck with details because that can distract you. Focus on deciding the following:

- **Eliminate** → Define what you don't offer.
- **Reduce** → Select a few attributes to emphasize less.
- **Raise** → Define attributes you want to increase the value.
- **Create** → Start something unavailable in the market.

This exercise can be simple: Look at three or four direct competitors and identify around seven product attributes. Then, on a scale from zero to ten, rate how well they cover each attribute. Zero means they don't have it, and ten means they offer the best option. Chances are high that each competitor will have a similar curve once you plot the result on a graph. Then, it's your chance to position your product for differentiation.

Let's consider a traditional and a digital bank. Table 5.1 reflects the rated attributes.

Table 5.1   Blue Ocean Strategy: Comparison between Traditional and Digital Banks

Attribute	Digital Bank	Traditional Bank
Brick-and-mortar agency	0	7
Account manager	0	8
Speed to open an account	8	4
Flexibility	9	5

Attribute	Digital Bank	Traditional Bank
Fee	2	7
Customer service	3	8
Everything digital	6	0
Multiple free services	5	0

Table 5.2 reflects the differentiation aspects.

Table 5.2   Blue Ocean Strategy: Traditional Bank versus Digital Bank

Eliminate	Raise
Brick-and-mortar agency	Speed to open an account
Account manager	Flexibility
Reduce	**Create**
Fee	Everything digital
Customer service	Multiple free services

Plotting the Value Curve lets you notice that massive difference. If you add multiple traditional banks, they would have similar Value Curves. That's why the digital bank stands out in Figure 5.7.

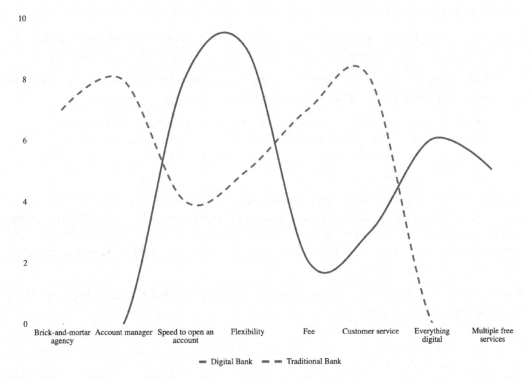

Figure 5.7
Example of a Value Curve

It's fundamental that you stop doing some things your competition is doing and create something they aren't. For that, you must understand your customers in-depth.

Differentiation is daunting, but ignoring it is deadly.

Roadmap: Establishing Clarity on What to Achieve

Connecting the future with the present is tricky. The product vision may inspire you to act, but you don't know where to start. The Lean Canvas brings clarity but may lack a tangible starting point. That's when the roadmap becomes your path from the present to the future. Unfortunately, poorly crafted roadmaps can be your free ticket to the feature factory.

As we discussed in Chapter 2, prescriptive roadmaps trap teams. The key lies in providing directions and not instructions. You can achieve that in multiple ways. A common alternative is using objectives and key results (OKRs). It can point you in the right direction and empower teams. Still, they're not my favorite alternative because it's more complex to help management implement OKRs correctly than to craft an outcome-oriented roadmap.

My favorite roadmap template is an adaption of the Now–Next–Later format created by Janna Bastow.[13] I used this framework for a long time and see much value in it. The simplicity is what strikes me. It works as follows:

- **Now** → Your focus now. This part aims to provide the focus for one to three months. The key is not to commit to individual initiatives but rather to the column called "Now."

- **Next** → Represents relevant aspects that you will potentially work on right after you finish the critical ones. The content evolves based on what you learn.

- **Later** → Digital products are dynamic. You cannot predict their future for more than six months. Whatever enters here means you're considering working on it only after you finish the other parts. You lack evidence to support them and they aren't convincing enough to make you review the previous columns.

I developed solid alignment with management and teams whenever I used this template (more on how that works in a minute). That empowered us to drive business outcomes. But the column "Later" troubled me. It got so big that we couldn't manage it. I eventually concluded we were using "Later" as a way to avoid conflicts. We had different perspectives on some items but would put them aside and not discuss them.

Fake harmony doesn't help create alignment. That's why I decided to add a pinch of salt by including the column "Trash."

---

13. Learn more about the Now–Next–Later roadmap template by Janna Bastow at www.prodpad.com/blog/invented-now-next-later-roadmap/.

- **Trash** → This is the most critical part. You agree on what you won't do, which goes to the trash. Be brave to remove irrelevant ideas to save your energy for the promising ones.

When I first implemented this column, I got into heated arguments. But we finally addressed the conflicts and dropped ideas unrelated to our strategy. That meant we wouldn't come back to them unless something significant changed.

Figure 5.8 shows my Now–Next–Later–Trash template.[14] I assume you're eager to know how to put this template into practice. But first I need to raise a minor concern: The template alone is, by far, not enough. It requires collaboration with high-level management to get their support.

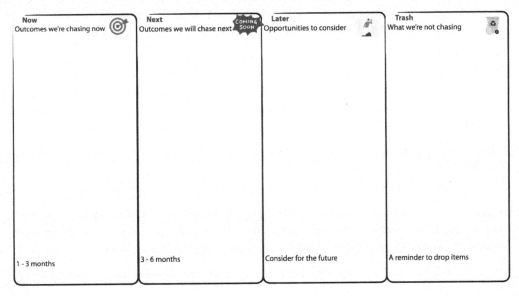

Figure 5.8
Roadmap template

Before I share how you can align with your key business stakeholders, I need to ask you a question: What defines success for your team? If success means delivering features on time, I recommend a gradual approach to what I'm about to share. But, if success relates to reaching goals, you can probably follow everything I'm sharing next. Here are the four steps to craft empowering roadmaps:

1. **Priority:** Product managers align with high-level management on what's most important. For example, that might be growth, retention, or profitability. Agree on the direction.

---

14. You can download all of my templates for free at https://d-pereira.com/templates.

2. **Future:** Which outcomes could your business wait for? This question will give you clarity on what to do next. Explore which initiatives you can drop because they won't be part of your product.

3. **Team:** The whole product team crafts goals they commit to for the upcoming months. This exercise tends to last around two hours.

4. **Agreement:** Product managers present the roadmap suggestion to management to get their buy-in. Naturally, product teams receive pressure to deliver more, but goal alignment is the point. The secret is understanding what matters to management in the short and medium terms, and then adapting the roadmap to reflect that. A common trap is adding something to please management. Don't do that. Stretching the team too thin will quickly backfire. Strive for alignment and not promises.

If your scenario is closer to a feature factory, management won't accept a roadmap focused on outcomes. My recommendation is simple: Agree on a virtual capacity of 20% of the roadmap for outcomes and devote the rest to outputs. I know that's not what you ultimately want, but it will help you build trust with management before they give their full support to your outcome roadmaps.

To help you understand, let me give you an example from an e-commerce enterprise I worked for.

Customer lifetime value was our biggest struggle. Our acquisition costs were growing, and our lifetime value was declining. Quickly, we noticed flaws in our user experience and wanted to address them, hoping to balance customer acquisition costs and lifetime value.

While crafting this roadmap, many feature options came to me. Everyone had a perfect solution. Some examples:

- Redesign the product detail page

- Increase the newsletter frequency

- Present products according to the persona

- Price differentiation per location

What's the issue with these solutions? The truth is that they present no issues, and all of the solutions make sense. The real trap is that they are outputs, not outcomes. This approach would force the team to implement solutions instead of solving problems.

After many discussions, we committed to the following:

- **Now** → Increasing basket size became our ultimate goal. We devised two targets: (1) reduce no-result searches and (2) increase recommended products added during the cart.

- **Next** → Right after this, we wanted to come back to growth while keeping our customers satisfied. We had some ideas, so we clarified them but agreed not to tackle them during the next three months.

- **Later** → Growth would become our focus once we stabilized our acquisition costs and lifetime value. Some aspects immediately came to mind, such as entering new markets and creating new revenue streams, but we all agreed that would be a talk for another coffee get-together.

- **Trash** → During our lengthy exchanges, we agreed on dropping some of our beloved topics to ensure they wouldn't distract us. We concluded that promoted products and free vouchers weren't part of our identity. Combined with that, we agreed that search was our core, and we could not outsource it, so the idea of outsourcing the search engine found its way to the trash bin.

Figure 5.9 shows the resulting roadmap.

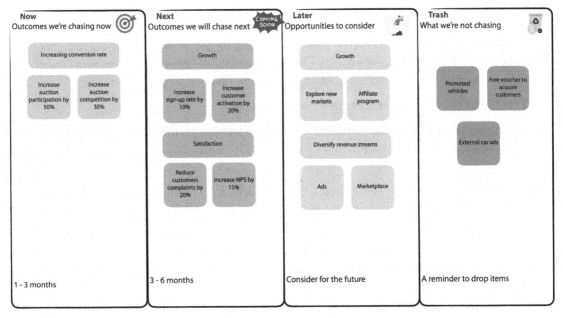

Figure 5.9
Roadmap example

Is this roadmap oversimplified? Yes.

Does it provide focus to the team? Yes.

Do you need a complex roadmap? No.

Often, your job is to simplify what everyone else is complicating. Let me share a story where a complicated prioritization led to a month of work wasted.

Painful Nonsense Prioritization

It was the beginning of Q2, and the product director came to me and said I should start working on the prioritization for Q3. I promptly disagreed, because I thought I should focus on reaching our Q2 goals.

Then the director said, "Let me explain how things work. David, we want to ensure the best time usage from our software engineers. We pay gold for them and cannot afford to waste their time. So please create a product backlog list, and for each item, you need to put the number of customers the initiative reaches, potential impact, confidence level, and high-level effort. Then, we will run some calculations and pick our best choices."

I argued it sounded like a lot of work before we could get hands-on. And the product director confirmed it was time-consuming, so I had to start it.

I invested hours and hours of analysis in this task. It took me many days of work over the quarter to develop a list and all the information. I felt frustrated because we talked much about the work but didn't do anything tangible. And things got even worse.

At the end of Q2, we agreed on a list of priorities based on our scoring system. But, after we presented the list to the C-suite executives, the CEO said that the price strategy mattered most and asked us to find something contributing to it and drop everything else.

We feared we would waste time, and that's what happened.

Untrapping Lesson: Don't make prioritization complex. Simplicity is the key to adapting fast.

Prioritization is a bet on what matters most. Yet, you cannot prioritize without a strategic goal. Trying to do so will lead to painful waste, as in the story I just shared.

Outcome roadmaps define what you want to achieve but not how you should do so. That lets you explore what drives customer value while reaching the desired business results. That's when product discovery plays a critical role, because you can only succeed when both sides of the equation benefit.

Key Takeaways

- A good product strategy will set enough constraints to simplify decision making and enable focus. In contrast, a bad product strategy will create confusion and contribute to analysis paralysis.

- The product strategy should provide enough guidance to create value for customers and the business.

- Product strategy isn't written in stone, but rather evolves as you learn about your target audience, market, product, and opportunities.

- Define assumptions when crafting your product strategy, and test them as quickly as possible before fully committing. Getting your product strategy right from the first attempt is nearly impossible.

- A sound product strategy isn't a document you put in your drawer and forget about. Instead, it's a set of elements that clarify who you serve, where to land, which constraints to follow, and which short-term goals you're focusing on.

This chapter covered the key elements of crafting a meaningful product strategy. Its lessons are intended to create clarity on how to progress and simplify decision making. The next step is identifying how mindful product discovery enables uncovering value drivers. That's the topic we will tackle in Chapter 6.

6

Forget What You Know to Get Ready for the Unknown

Most ideas will fail because we don't know what we don't know. It's hard to swallow that painful fact. I've been chewing on this reality for a long time. Yet, recognizing it enables us to ask questions, learn, and create valuable products instead of useless ones.

Product discovery done right helps you learn when you're wrong. It uncovers unforeseeable opportunities to create value, ultimately enabling you to create the unimaginable. Yet, you can achieve that only when you are comfortable stepping into the unknown.

This chapter equips you to embrace the unknown. We will explore how to move away from dangerous biases and get closer to value drivers.

Let me share the story of my first contact with product discovery.

My Unforgettable First Date with Product Discovery

Sunday, 4:37 p.m.: My phone rings. It's my new boss.

"David. Don't go to the office tomorrow. Come to Albert Einstein Hospital at 08:30 a.m. My wife is sick, and I'm staying in the hospital with her. I need to talk to you before you start. There are some challenges you should be aware of. I will walk you through what you need to know."

That call astonished me. I kept thinking about it for the rest of the day. I was sure my new job wouldn't be like my previous one. That was my first time at a start-up. My head was spinning, and I barely slept that night.

The next day, I met with the start-up CEO. I had imagined the first meeting would last around an hour, but it didn't take longer than 7 minutes. I was speechless after the CEO told me:

"David. Let me be direct with you. Results matter, so you better be fast. We've got 10 million USD cash and burn 1 million USD per month. Raising capital takes from three to six months. So we better prove a market fit, or you start looking for a new job in six months. Let me tell you what you must achieve in three months—a 30% increase in conversion rate. Talk to the tech lead and UX designer to figure out how to redesign our car dealers' app because our customers dislike it. I don't want excuses. Get it done. We will talk again in a month."

As my coffee got cold, I reflected. I honestly didn't know what to do. I truly doubted I could get this right. I took a few minutes to breathe. Then, I started structuring my thoughts, and something clicked. I saw a different way of tackling this challenge—something I had never done.

The CEO gave me a goal and a solution. What if the solution is wrong? I better learn how to confront it with reality as fast as possible. I took a cab and went to the office. On the way, I reflected on what I should do and what I should not.

Once I arrived. I faced another surprise. The UX designer and tech lead were in another country, and neither spoke Portuguese. I wondered, "How can they create something for car dealers without understanding them?" It was clear to me someone had to understand the target audience, and it had to be someone who spoke their language.

Despite my lack of experience talking to customers, I did what I thought I should do. I visited a few car dealers to observe how they worked, their challenges, and how our solution helped them. Such learning ultimately forced me to pivot the solution before we faced an unbearable failure.

Untrapping Lesson: Be brave to do what's necessary, even when you lack support.

It was 2016, and I had gotten involved in a problem I had no idea how to solve. I was used to gathering requirements, writing user stories, estimating, and accelerating delivery. This experience was different. I had a goal and a solution I doubted. Without knowing it, I had started applying product discovery due to my excessive curiosity and unwillingness to mindlessly implement a solution.

That was my first experience with product discovery, which would shape my take on product management forever. Over the years, I evolved and shaped my knowledge with more methods and techniques. But I got my lessons by stepping into cold waters and trying different things.

Applying product discovery is anything but trivial. During my experiences, I've faced two sides of the same coin:

- **Mindful product discovery.** It helps uncover what you don't know and equips you to create valuable solutions. Teams work in a collaborative flow, helping each other learn and progress.

- **Biased product discovery.** It distracts you by giving expected answers or traps you because you neglect reality and continue investing in flawed ideas. Teams focus on coordinating tasks instead of collaborating.

I want to help you apply the first approach and avoid the latter. That's why we must discuss what blocks you from open-mindedness toward learning: dangerous biases.

Biases: Blocking Learning Opportunities

The more we think we know, the less we can learn. Product discovery aims to help us uncover what we don't know, enabling us to create value while dropping flawed ideas. Yet, how can we benefit from that if we assume we know what's best?

More often than we imagine, we hold our own opinions higher than anything new. That's what biases are. They cloud our judgment, impeding us from evaluating what we learn in an open-minded manner. We search for positive signs to confirm we're right or convince ourselves to continue investing even when the potential result looks undesired. Until we manage to set our biases aside, uncovering the unknown is nearly impossible.

First, we need to step back and recognize our biases. Here are a few questions to reveal bias:

- Am I investing further because of a previous choice or because this is the best option to progress in the desired direction?

- Am I extending my commitment because I'm already invested or because this path is still worth pursuing?

- Am I doing this because our competitors are doing it or because I learned how that will drive value for customers and the business?

- Am I searching for positive signs to prove myself right, or am I open-minded to learning, even if that proves me wrong?

The more your answers relate to the first options in these questions, the more biases will block you from expanding your knowledge. That will inevitably trap you into biased product discovery. When your answers focus on the second options, you've got a higher chance of having a mindful product discovery.

Let's explore different types of biases further so you can figure out how to set them aside.

Confirmation Bias: The Art of Missing Opportunities and Creating Waste

Falling in love with solutions is one of the most common traps I've observed. It doesn't matter where I am; I see the same dangerous pattern. Someone comes up with an idea and quickly falls in love with it, more people connect to it, and suddenly this idea becomes the ultimate goal, even though nobody knows which problem it solves.

It's not wrong to have ideas or to like them. Yet, it's a trap to go all in and continuously stay blind to reality. That's the confirmation bias. It traps us because we search for positive signs and will pursue anything that hints we're right.

With confirmation bias, we will misuse interviews to learn how customers *like* our solutions instead of learning what matters to them. We trap ourselves because customers are polite and *promise* to use our solution once it's done.

Confirmation bias transforms weak evidence into reasons to build full-blown solutions.

Commitment Escalation: Making a Bad Situation Even Worse

As humans, we hate losing or anything related to losing. We may react irrationally and make suboptimal decisions whenever we feel we're losing something.

Let me give you a real example of a relationship.

A close friend of mine was in a relationship for two years. The relationship was fast-paced because they already lived together and had a kid.

One day, my friend came to me upset because they had broken up twice that week. I couldn't believe what he shared.

They first argued on Saturday. He left home, and she asked him to return, which he did on Tuesday. On Wednesday, things heated up again, and he saw no choice but to walk away. On Friday, they made peace, and then they decided to continue.

He concluded they had a kid and had already spent two years together, so he should not throw away those two years.

What do you think happened later? The couple stayed together for another five years, bought a house and car, and got some credit from the bank. They were never happy again. Today, they don't even look at each other and face constant legal disputes. Had they broken up the moment they realized their relationship wasn't good for either one of them, none of the following problems would have happened.

Our mental model is our challenge. *The more investment we make into something, the more we're willing to invest.* That's another type of bias, called commitment escalation.

We don't recover from losses by persisting with something that's not working, but rather make it worse and lose more. The same happens with digital products. That's why it's essential to have mechanisms to help us drop bad ideas fast enough (more on that in Chapter 7).

Sunk-Cost Fallacy: The Fear of Losing Triggering More Losses

When a past decision convinces you to invest more, it's a sign that the sunk-cost fallacy[1] is knocking on your door. When working with digital products, many situations trap you with this fallacy. Let me take prioritization as an example.

Suppose you've got plenty of ideas but don't know which to invest in. To ensure you make the most promising bet, you use a complex scoring system, defining the reach, effort, potential impact, confidence, and frequency of use. You go through all of your ideas with your team and give them a score. It takes you long hours, but now you have the winner. So you go all in.

---

1. The sunk-cost fallacy is the phenomenon in which individuals resist abandoning a strategy or course of action because they have invested heavily in it, even when it is clear that abandonment would be more beneficial.

Robust prioritization methods create a false expectation that we know what will work even when we don't even know what we don't know. A high investment in prioritization will discourage you from changing direction when you learn your idea wasn't that good. Sadly, our cognitive bias will anchor the prioritization investment into future decisions. We will think, "We already invested hours into prioritization. We must be right." And you wouldn't be the only one thinking this: Business stakeholders would feel the same.

Don't let past decisions block you from adopting a new course of action. It's fundamental to make iterative investments. When it comes to prioritization, remember that it's always a bet. The faster you learn, the sooner you can adapt.

Bandwagon Fallacy: Following the Masses Without Knowing Why

Do you know why you do what you do?

As a teenager, I dreamed of becoming a rockstar, so I let my hair grow and started wearing only black clothes. Why did I do that? Simply because rockstars did that, and I wanted to look like them. Yet, I had no clue what the message behind it was. The long hair was a misfit for me because my hair was pretty oily, and my skin was too sensitive. Quickly, my skin reacted to the oiliness of my hair, giving me more pimples than one could imagine. That wasn't fun at all.

Following what others do without knowing why is the effect of the bandwagon fallacy. Returning to digital products, how do companies fall prey to this fallacy?

You may have heard a few stories about teams that copied their competition because everyone else had a particular feature. A company may have started doing something because the market leader had done so with its product.

Let me share a real story from a senior product manager working for a traditional bank. I'll call him Peter for confidentiality reasons.

Blindly Copying Competition and Getting Nowhere

It was the yearly roadmap planning time, so the product manager expected heated discussions. However, what happened was anything but that. The session lasted around an hour, contrary to the planned half a day. How did that happen?

Top management presented the financial results and shared a substantial concern. The growth of a competitor digital bank was too significant to ignore. In an attempt to prevent a customer exodus, top management decided that all teams should invest next year in copying whatever the other bank was doing to ensure they offered the same.

Peter was speechless at the decision. He couldn't believe the strategy of a multi-billion-dollar bank was to blindly copy the competition. So he asked, "How do we know we're successful?" The answer was, "As soon as we have nothing else to copy."

Over the next year, Peter observed the competitor bank growing and innovating while copying features seemed a never-ending game at his own bank. Worse than that, copying features didn't prevent customers from moving to the competition.

While the traditional bank focused solely on copying features, they missed the core part. They didn't know why the feature existed in the first place. So, they created many "nice features" without understanding how they drove customer value.

Untrapping Lesson: Doing something because your competition is doing it cannot guarantee you create value for your customers.

Striving for feature parity with a competitor is a lame strategy. One can never be a better shadow. Here are the lessons a senior product manager shared with me about competition obsession:

1. *You move far away from your customers' needs,* developing an anti-pattern of valuing more competition than customers.

2. *You build features unrelated to your product,* losing consistency and purpose.

3. *You create an unbearable technical debt* because you want to react fast, creating several half-baked features nobody understands how to benefit from.

4. *Employees get demotivated* because they cannot innovate since being copycats becomes the goal, which makes the company vulnerable in the face of disruption.

It's hard to believe the effects of the bandwagon fallacy, but sooner or later you'll undoubtedly face something similar. We must remain alert and challenge ourselves to understand what drives our decisions. If we don't know why we're doing something, we probably should not continue doing it.

As you learn how to avoid dangerous biases, it's time to get closer to value drivers.

Value Drivers: Doing What Matters for Customers and the Business

I imagine you're wondering, what are value drivers? A value driver has the power to create value for customers and the business. I use the term *value driver* to ensure we keep the outcome in mind instead of engaging with problems that yield no value or distracting opportunities.

Don't confuse value drivers with solutions, because they aren't. They represent opportunities you identify that both customers and the business can benefit from. When you find a value driver, you can explore different solutions.

Value drivers have different flavors. They relate to solving a relevant problem, covering a recurrent need, or fulfilling a desire. Let me elaborate on that by referring to a few digital products I use:

- **Problem:** As an expat in Germany, tax declaration scares me. Given its complexity, I feel anxious about making a mistake or missing an opportunity to receive my taxes back. Many other expats suffer the same. Wundertax.de solved my pain by providing an English web solution that deals with all the complexity. All I had to do was fill out a few forms, and it issued my tax declarations.

  Value driver: Expats living in Germany struggle to declare their annual taxes.

- **Need:** When I started my career as a product manager, I quickly realized how unprepared I was. I wanted to advance in my career, so I needed to evolve my skillset. Over the years, I found many ways of meeting my need to sharpen my skills. For example, Udemy provides affordable video-based courses, which create knowledge for students, income for instructors, and revenue for the platform. Products covering user needs can drive and collect value steadily.

  Value driver for students: Professionals need to develop skills to advance their careers.

  Value driver for instructors: Experienced professionals want to monetize their knowledge.

- **Desire:** In 2020, my wife and I wanted to improve our cooking skills. We could cook to survive, but the results were nothing special. Yet, we had a wish to cook more elaborate dishes. Neither of us had an eating behavior problem, nor did we need to change our food choices. However, we desired to become better at cooking. That's when we found HelloFresh, which covered our desire by delivering recipes and ingredients to our homes. We sharpened our cooking skills and enjoyed that experience. Even better, we didn't even need to figure out how to find specific ingredients; they came straight to our home. Meanwhile, we paid a monthly subscription for HelloFresh.

  Value driver: Cooking enthusiasts wish to level up their cooking skills.

  Value driver: Wanna-be chefs long for easy ways of having restaurant-level dishes at home.

In summary, the value driver represents anything worth doing for customers and business.

You will find other terminologies. For example, Teresa Torres uses *opportunities* as a term with the same meaning. I share her view, but I still see many teams derailing. That's why I use the term *value drivers*. It's a reminder to focus on what moves the needle for customers and the business.

To uncover the value drivers, you must learn from end users and understand the business. The closer you are to them, the better. Let me walk you through another story.

> **The Power of Learning from Reality**
>
> Circling back to the car dealer example, I decided to understand how we got where we were: Dealers disliked our app. I didn't want to blindly redesign the app as the CEO wanted. So, I approached many colleagues to understand the status quo. The more people I talked to, the more surprised I got.
>
> Under the assumption that "the world is going mobile," the team conducted several focus groups to understand how the app worked for dealers (biased discovery). I challenged this approach and decided to confront reality. It was time to get out of the office and meet car dealers where they do business (mindful discovery).
>
> I planned to present myself as a start-up member. However, as I opened the door of the first store, I changed my mind. I felt acting as a potential buyer and seeing how the car dealer would react would be better.
>
> Spontaneity can work well when you listen to your gut.
>
> I looked at cars they didn't have and said I was looking for a BMW Series 3. The dealer said, "Nice one, buddy. I don't have it, but I can find one for you. Give me a few minutes." The dealer went to his computer, searched in some car portals, then called some people. After about 20 minutes, he told me, "Would you give me your number? I will call you in a few days to share when I can get the car." I agreed and left the store. The dealer never called me back.
>
> After six visits, I had already identified some patterns. Car dealers struggled to find the cars they didn't have but didn't use their smartphones to search for cars. I realized our mobile app was a misfit because it wasn't natural for our audience.
>
> **Untrapping Lesson:** Build what's natural for your customers instead of what's rational for you.

Do What's Right, Not What's Easy

I'm not a researcher. Going out and interviewing dealers wasn't my turf, but someone had to get this job done. I couldn't accept doing what the CEO wanted without knowing whether that made sense. I used my best skills to observe, interview, and empathize with car dealers. I gathered several insights and shared them with the team.

I got scared when stepping into the unknown, but it was tremendously exciting to learn from real users. The first step was hard, but afterward, I couldn't get enough of it.

Looking back on this story, redesigning the dealers' app would be a biased product discovery as the solution became the focus. Happily, my rebel spirit didn't let me do that. I applied mindful product discovery because my unwillingness to do something I didn't understand was stronger than my fear of being fired by disagreeing with the CEO.

By doing what seemed right, we uncovered the following value drivers:

- **Problem:** Dealers struggled to find cars their customers wanted and sometimes got fooled by a few sellers. Solving this problem enabled us to acquire more dealers.

  Value driver: Car dealers struggle to find the cars they need without being scammed.

- **Need:** Dealers needed to make profits to survive and feared overpaying for cars. We enabled them to compete in multiple auctions while knowing the car market value. Ultimately, we engaged more dealers with auctions, driving our conversion rate up.

  Value driver: Car dealers need to pay affordable car prices to remain profitable.

- **Desire:** Convenience was the key wish of most car dealers I visited. They were busy with their daily activities, so we figured out that delivering cars to their doors instead of asking them to pick up the cars would increase convenience. No one offered such a service, so we started offering it free of cost. That drove satisfaction up and reduced churn while dealers saved their time.

  Value driver: Car dealers lack time to pick up cars outside their districts.

Your job is to find value drivers that can move the business forward while delivering value for customers. That's what product discovery is all about.

Key Takeaways

- We all have biases. The challenge is knowing how to deal with the different biases we carry. Asking questions to trigger reflection helps us avoid falling prey to biases, enabling us to apply mindful product discovery.

- The more we rely on our available knowledge, the less we can benefit from product discovery. We have better chances of creating value when we strive to run product discovery with an open mind.

- Value drivers represent alternatives from which the business and customers can benefit. They are not solutions, but rather possibilities to drive value that you can capitalize on in different ways.

- Focus on finding value drivers because they enable you to work on what creates value for customers and helps the business thrive. When you don't know how something creates value, don't fear dropping the idea; be afraid of investing in it and creating a solution nobody needs.

- Relevant problems, recurrent needs, and desires are different flavors of value drivers. The key is distinguishing how you drive value from what you choose to work on. From there, you can craft solutions worth building.

This chapter covered dangerous biases and clarified what you need to reflect on to step aside from them. We also addressed what value drivers are and why they are critical. In Chapter 7, we'll embark on a discovery journey and clarify how we identify value drivers and drop bad ideas fast enough. Shall we?

7

Embarking on a Journey to Discover What Matters

Discovering what creates value requires an open mind and the courage to quickly drop bad ideas. By now, you should be familiar with the challenges of dangerous biases and their adverse effects on discovery, which can lead to biased product discovery. Now, we'll clarify how to apply mindful product discovery and escape from the threat of biased discovery.

This chapter will explore how a discovery journey enables you to drop bad ideas fast enough and uncover value drivers.

Understanding the Discovery Journey

My first contact with product discovery left me overly optimistic. I thought we could repeat specific steps and consistently achieve success. But then I tried that and had to swallow the bitter taste of failure.

Understanding why a strict discovery process wouldn't work took me a while. My conclusion came out of the blue. A lightbulb popped up in my head while driving from Munich to Vienna with my wife to celebrate our second wedding anniversary.

We planned to get to Vienna by early afternoon, but some unpredictable roadblocks forced us to change our route, and then a heavy rain made us stop in Salzburg by lunchtime. Unexpectedly, we had one of the best Italian lunches of our lives. This unplanned lunch made the journey more romantic, and we didn't care about arriving in Vienna several hours later than we had expected. Then, I concluded what product discovery is: It's about the journey, not the plan.

When you start a discovery journey, you set a goal, which serves as your north star. Then, you learn as much as possible from your customers and strive to uncover the value drivers that can get you closer to your goal. You'll potentially have more options than capacity, so you prioritize, identify assumptions, test the critical ones, run experiments, and reimagine the future. As with a road trip, it's about the journey, and you're the driver. You can decide whether to drive forward or backward or detour if necessary.

I'd love to give you a magic process to ensure you'll create value at the speed of light, but I won't try to fool you. I will share the elements for a valuable discovery journey and help you understand what they enable you to achieve. *As the driver, you will use your judgment to decide what to do, when, and for how long.*

The discovery journey is illustrated in Figure 7.1. You might look at this figure and think: "This is a waterfall approach." The biggest difference with the discovery journey is that you don't get stuck with phases. You can always go back and forth as much as necessary. You continuously search for value drivers and reserve the right to drop bad ideas whenever you identify them.

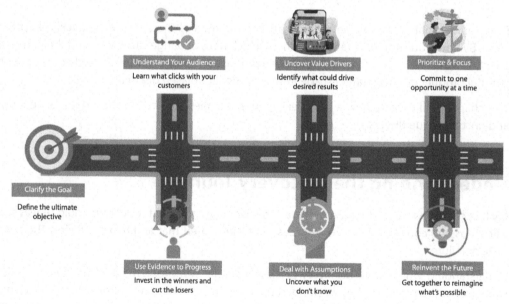

Figure 7.1
Discovery journey

Let's explore each element in depth

Clarify the Goal: Know What Success Looks Like

When you have outcome-oriented roadmaps, applying product discovery is simple: You pick one item from your roadmap and continue with your discovery journey. Of course, real life tends to be more complicated than that. You may end up in a situation where you lack a roadmap, or you have an output-oriented one. That means you've got to step back and clarify the goal you ought to achieve.

Having clarity on the goal is critical. Otherwise, you'll end up discussing every opportunity, ultimately discussing much and getting little done. Yet, a poor definition of goals won't make your life easier, either. Let's look at some typical definitions:

- Increase growth by 30%

- Decrease return rate by 20%

- Increase basket size by 15%

- Decrease churn rate by 20%

> **Note:** If these metrics confuse you, don't worry. In Chapter 9, we will talk about metrics in depth.

How much do these definitions help you accelerate decisions? Sadly, not a lot. They don't give you everything you need to play the game. Increasing growth tells you what to reach for, but not what you could sacrifice and what not to. Without knowing the other side of the coin, endless discussions will drain your energy.

When I worked for the car dealer start-up (see the story in Chapter 6), the CEO wanted me to increase the conversion rate by 30% in three months. I didn't know which trade-offs I could make, so I went to the CEO and asked him some questions.

- *What can I use to increase the conversion rate?* He promptly answered, "You can drive costs up. We don't need to be profitable now; we must prove market fit."

- *What's something we cannot sacrifice?* Another easy question for the CEO: "Too many car dealers are leaving us. We cannot afford to make it worse."

After this exchange, I had a high-level goal: "Without impacting retention, increase the conversion rate by 30%, even if that hurts profitability." The CEO promptly agreed and said the ultimate goal was to enable car dealers to get the vehicles they wanted while helping owners get a fair offer. As I clarified our constraints, we simplified decision making, enabling us to find value drivers.

It's uncommon to talk about potential trade-offs to reach a goal. The typical scenario is to focus on outputs, but even when companies move to outcomes, they often ignore the trade-offs.

You'll face resistance once you try my recommended approach. Business stakeholders will claim they are unwilling to sacrifice anything to achieve the desired outcomes. I'd suggest not approaching them with empty hands but bringing a trade-off that accelerates progress.

For example, when you understand your audience, you'll eventually uncover tremendous opportunities to drive value, but they will have side effects. Share them with business stakeholders. Collaborate and find compromises when necessary.

When you face biased discovery, business stakeholders will push you to commit to features. Producing those features then becomes the goal, because the stakeholders have already fallen in love with them. To move to mindful product discovery, you need to help the business stakeholders step back. Get them to share what they want to achieve with their requests, so you know the goal you need to pursue.

Alignment on what success means is vital. Without it, confusion takes over, and getting stuck is your punishment.

Understand Your Audience: Know How Customers Use Your Product

How do customers interact with your product? You may think you know the answer to this question well, but does everyone in your team and business share the same view? The more you see the world through different lenses, the less value you can create together.

Customers will always surprise us. We imagine they will use our product as we designed it, but they do things differently. Knowing the reality is what matters.

A lack of understanding about your customers' journey will get in the way of creating value for them. Over the years, I've used two approaches, one from Jeff Patton (2014) and another from Teresa Torres (2021). Both will get the job done well. Let me help you understand them.

Jeff Patton created the user story mapping method, which has the narrative flow at its core and focuses on clarifying the activities, steps, and details behind this flow. The narrative flow represents the sequence of customer activities, which I assimilate into the customer journey. This approach is my favorite to build a shared understanding with teams and businesses. It's simple and valuable. You can complete it with the following steps:

1. **Organize a session:** Set up a four-hour session with a multidisciplinary team, including product team members, business representatives, and customers. You may need less time, but four hours will probably be necessary if it's your first time.

2. **Prepare:** If you're meeting in person, reserve a room with a wide wall that you can use to capture the dynamics. If you're meeting remotely, prepare a digital board.

3. **Collaborate:** Start with the narrative flow of your customers' journey, then define each step's tasks. Don't go in depth at this stage. Focus on building a shared understanding with the participants.

4. **Sharpen:** Address conflicting parts and refine the user story mapping until everyone understands it.

The user story mapping evolves based on your learning and is not a means to set scope. I love Jeff Patton's take on it: "Scope doesn't creep; understanding grows."

Figure 7.2 presents the high-level user story mapping for the car dealers start-up.

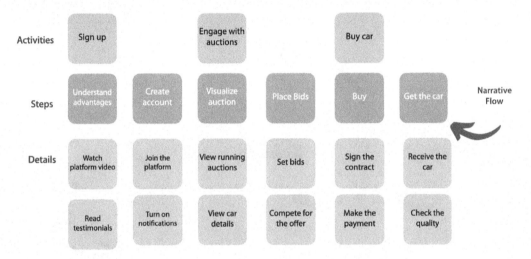

Figure 7.2
User story mapping: car dealers

Alternatively, you can create a customer journey, as Teresa Torres (2021) suggested in her book *Continuous Discovery Habits*. Take the following steps to work on it:

1. **Individual understanding:** Everyone from the product team creates a customer journey based on their perception. They can make it as visual as they want. The key is to evaluate decision points, where customers progress and drop.

2. **Learn from others:** Each team member shares their customer journey and exchanges about it. The result is learning from everyone.

3. **Repeat:** You can repeat steps 1 and 2 to increase the quality of the journey.

4. **Shared customer journey:** After a few exchanges with your team, agree on one customer journey. This step will ensure everyone speaks the same language.

5. **Test:** As you agree on a customer journey, you should test it with your customers and see how much it reflects their reality. You can then adapt it and have a more solid journey, enabling you to uncover value drivers.

Figure 7.3 is an example of the customer journey for the car dealers start-up. You can observe the exit options and progress steps. Dealers would not sign up when our message didn't speak to them. They wouldn't return when our auctions lacked cars they considered. And they missed most auctions, but we didn't know why.

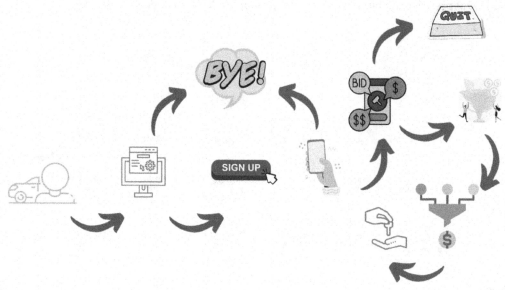

Figure 7.3
Customer journey: car dealers

It's up to you to decide whether you prefer user story mapping or the customer journey. I vary between the two approaches depending on the situation. However, I often opt for user story mapping because I can reuse the results to identify value drivers and assumptions.

Clarity on the customer journey is essential to apply mindful product discovery. Failure to achieve clarity leads to biased discovery because you assume you know best how customers engage with your product.

Uncover Value Drivers: Identify What's Worth Pursuing

Despite learning from multiple failures, companies continue to implement solutions that solve nobody's problems or wishes. I know this pain very well because I contributed to many useless features. But that's behind me, and I hope it will soon be behind most companies.

Our current challenge isn't delivering high-quality solutions, but rather uncovering what users genuinely care about. Those are the value drivers (discussed in Chapter 6): anything that benefits customers while giving something in return to the business. Let's understand how this transaction works in some products:

- **Substack:** It's a platform where content creators host newsletters, and readers can subscribe to newsletters to whose creators they relate. Readers get exclusive access to content when subscribing to paid content. Creators receive 90% of the payment, and Substack gets 10%. Everyone gets value from that. Substack's premium subscriptions represent one of the value drivers.

- **Instagram:** People can interact with one another and consume content they enjoy. The platform is free for users, but they provide value to the platform by giving it their attention because Instagram creates revenue from ads. The more active users, the more revenue Instagram can make. Attention from users is one of the most substantial value drivers for Instagram.

Every product has different value drivers, so it's critical for you to find what drives value for your audience and business.

How to Uncover Value Drivers

You can identify the value drivers in many different ways, but here are six promising methods applicable to B2B and B2C business models:

1. **User interviews:** I encourage you to conduct interviews with your real users at least once a week. The reason is simple: Only they know what matters to them. The more you empathize with your end users, the more quickly you will learn what creates value.

2. **Shadowing:** Great solutions are natural, not rational. To learn what's natural for your target audience, you have to get in touch with them and observe how they do the job in real life.

3. **Data:** You can learn a lot from data— on user behaviors, demographic information, frequency of use, flows, most used features, least used ones, and more. Companies have loads of data nowadays, but I doubt they use it wisely. Gathering actionable insights from your available data is powerful (more about that in Chapter 9).

4. **Expert interviews:** You'll face more complexities in the B2B business model. Talking to experts can boost your knowledge. Such interviews are generally paid but worth the investment.

5. **Search trends:** Knowing what people search for gives you hints about where you can uncover hidden opportunities. This approach tends to reveal demand and interest. Yet, the evidence is weak because you lack context, but it will at least point you in a direction.

6. **Customer service:** When you're running a business, talking to customer service representatives can give you invaluable insights. You'll learn about pains and common complaints. If you want to go a step further, you can become a customer service agent for a few hours and get a natural feeling from your customers.

The key is to get outside your comfort zone and strive to uncover what you don't know. It's easy to stay behind a computer screen and expect magic to happen. Innovation doesn't happen like that. Get out, go after customers, and learn from their reality—not yours.

Structuring Your Value Drivers

Once you identify value drivers, how do you structure them? A common way is to drop them into a backlog and eventually work on them. I'd discourage you from that because your ideas will quickly get lost. I'd recommend two ways:

1. **User story mapping by Jeff Patton:** This approach is similar to that discussed in the context of the customer journey. However, instead of using the details of the tasks as inputs, you name the value drivers you identified for each step.

2. **Opportunity solution tree[1] by Teresa Torres:** This approach is direct and collaborative. You start with the ultimate goal as the root, then add the customer journey steps as leaves. For each step, you then name the value drivers you identified.

I prefer the opportunity solution tree to structure the value drivers. Focus is the reason. When we set the root as the ultimate goal, we consider how the value drivers relate to the goal more carefully. User story mapping is also powerful, but teams may derail and start naming value drivers unrelated to the agreed goal, which can cause distractions.

Returning to the car dealer experience: Sadly, I didn't know about the opportunity solution tree, so I used the user story mapping approach. Ultimately, I got distracted by the many discussions of potential value drivers we could pursue instead of focusing on the ones that mattered most. If I had to tackle the same situation today, I'd use the opportunity solution tree. Figure 7.4 shows how I'd structure it.

---

1. Read this blog post by Teresa Torres to learn more about the opportunity solution tree: www.producttalk .org/opportunity-solution-tree/. In addition, I recommend that you read her book *Continuous Discovery Habits* (2021).

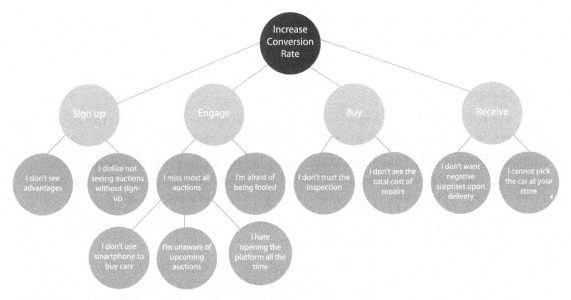

Figure 7.4
Opportunity solution tree: car dealers

Untrapping Tip: Write value drivers from your users' perspective. The opportunity solution tree should reflect their situation rather than what you wish for.

Prioritize and Focus: Take One Value Driver at a Time

What do you focus on after structuring your value drivers? The typical approach is to divide and conquer. Working on many topics in parallel is common, but it stretches the team thin, leading to disappointment and frustration. Failure to prioritize will get in the way of creating value.

The real challenge is picking one value driver per team. I know you believe you're the master of multitasking. We all believe that. But the reality is different. Focus is what enables you to create value sooner.

Now, I have to alert you that falling into analysis paralysis is easy. For example, suppose you adopt a prioritization framework to ensure your bet is the best. Such an approach will create the illusion you know what's best, and then you over-commit to the solution, getting frustrated when the results don't go beyond mediocrity.

Given the endless ideas you have, why shouldn't you invest too much time prioritizing? Unless you want to fall prey to the sunk-cost fallacy, you shouldn't go wild with prioritization exercises.

As we noted in Chapter 6, it's about having the courage to step into the unknown. Focus on learning instead of getting locked in meeting rooms.

Untrapping Tip: The best alternative is to pick one value driver, start small, and grow gradually. Connecting to the car dealer start-up example, let me share another story with you.

Betting on One Value Driver at a Time

We realized that dealers didn't engage in our auctions because the mobile app wasn't a natural fit to them. So, we decided to focus on creating a solution fitting their scenario.

I reasoned with business stakeholders about options and possibilities to make our priority choice. We had more than enough dealers on the platform, but they weren't active. Our bet was engaging them with auctions, which we believed could lead to a higher conversion rate.

The prioritization exercise didn't take an hour. I presented the value drivers we identified. Then, we committed to one and decided to focus on it.

We also reflected on the "I miss most all auctions" and "I don't use smartphones to buy cars" responses (Figure 7.5). We concluded if we could get dealers to find auctions of cars they wanted, they would benefit from our platform, we could make better offers to car owners, and we could close more deals and collect our commission. Solving this puzzle would get us to a better position, and we didn't need to reflect on anything else at that moment.

Untrapping Lesson: Focus on one value driver at a time instead of jumping into many in parallel.

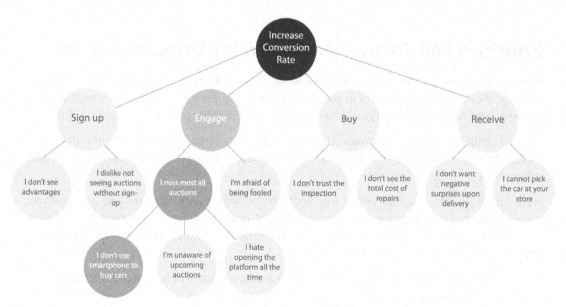

Figure 7.5
Prioritized opportunity solution tree: car dealers

You might wonder what happened to the other potential value drivers. We parked and ignored them for a while. As we evolved with the selected value driver, we eventually returned to the different topics and picked another to pursue.

Reinvent the Future: Diverge and Converge

The next step isn't crafting a high-fidelity solution and getting approval from management. That's not going to help you become empowered. Yet, designers and product managers often get excited about possibilities and go far in the future without involving the whole team. They create a pixel-perfect design without talking to anyone, then expect the team to deliver the solution.

This approach is detrimental to collaboration and will lead to a lack of commitment. Collaboration is vital to reinventing the future. It's the objective of this part of the journey.

As you agree on the value driver, it's time to identify solutions to explore. Herein lies a common trap: committing to a single solution and pouring all your energy into it, which leads to biased discovery. I learned it's worth experimenting with two or three solutions to enable mindful product discovery. The goal isn't to implement them, but rather to learn from different options.

Exploring three solutions in parallel is valuable because it avoids commitment escalation and confirmation bias. Sadly, most teams I worked with were trapped in feature factory mode, making it hard to understand how they could explore three solutions simultaneously. But I'd see some alternatives to it.

The first consideration is to ensure the whole team is involved in reinventing the future. Getting everyone's creative genius to imagine what could be possible is fundamental. Those members working on the future (product trio) share the learnings with the whole team and reflect on different ways of solving the problem.

Multiple ideation techniques can be used at this point. I won't cover all of them in detail, but here are two possible techniques for you:

- **Crazy eights:** Every team member gets an empty page folded into eight parts; they will use each quadrant for an idea. Then, they get a few minutes to draft eight ideas. They share, learn from each other, rerun the session, and develop more ideas. After some iterations, you pick a few ideas to explore in depth. This method works best for offline ideations but can create good results with hybrid formats when well prepared.

- **Ideation session:** Ask team members to ideate alone, share in the group, and learn from each other. Repeat this iteration a few times to get different ideas. The more diverse the group is, the better the results will be. It's fine to think outside the box and suggest unimaginable ideas. The goal is to broaden perspectives and then select up to three ideas.

Returning to the car dealers example, our thoughts went wild as we explored potential solutions. I remember someone suggested building a configurable bot that hunted the cars the dealers wanted. After hours of intense brainstorming, we agreed on testing two solutions (Figure 7.6):

- **Web platform:** Create a web version of our mobile app. The app was a misfit for car dealers, and having a web solution could engage them.

- **Concierge:** Dealers are busy and miss auctions. Trusting someone with a budget to search for specific cars could be a way of engaging with them.

I still pondered the problem and wanted to commit to a single solution as the feature factory hunted me. Yet, I agreed to test both solutions and learn from the results. We committed to investing two weeks into both alternatives. We aimed to identify assumptions and test them with quick and dirty solutions.

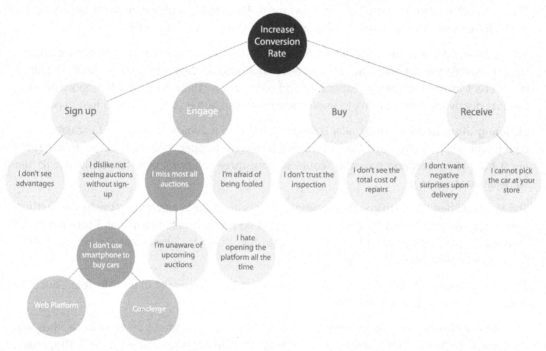

Figure 7.6
Opportunity solution tree with solutions: car dealers

Deal with Assumptions: Drop Bad Ideas Fast Enough

Too often, the solution inspires us, and our imagination wanders far from reality. This scenario is a double-edged sword. Your imagination enables you to create a better future, but at the same time, you may neglect reality and commit to a solution that solves nobody's problems. *Falling in love with the solution will get in the way of solving real problems.*

Identifying and testing assumptions is mandatory to transform your ideas into meaningful solutions. Yet, it's hard to accept how little we know.

Let's clarify the meaning of "assumption." The *Longman Dictionary of Contemporary English* offers the following definition: "something that you think is true although you have no definite proof."

Whenever you hear one of the following sentences, strive to name the underlying assumptions:

- This is a game-changer, and revenue will grow at least 20%.

- I'm sure this is what users need.

- When we have this feature, we will beat our competition.

- I'm convinced they will buy our product.

Such statements represent assumptions because they aren't based on evidence but instead on our impressions or desired results. The more energy you invest without testing assumptions, the bigger the chance of failing becomes.

The challenge is to step back and ask questions when everyone wants to jump into implementation. Before investing in solutions, you need to identify what you know and what you don't know.

> **Note:** You may hear the word *hypothesis* used instead of *assumptions*. In product development, they have the same meaning. A hypothesis is more scientific and based on some minimum level of evidence, but don't get bogged down with that distinction. Both hypotheses and assumptions lack evidence and, therefore, require testing.

Identifying Assumptions

"Assumption is the mother of all [f*ck-ups]."
—Marion Huwatscheck

The preceding quote is from a former colleague. Whenever I heard it, I got reflective—because it was true in most failures I faced. I assumed something, didn't check, and stumbled upon undesired results.

I see two extremes in life: too optimistic or too pessimistic. Both are dangerous. The extreme optimist assumes nothing will go wrong, while the extreme pessimist takes it for granted that everything will go wrong and so avoids taking risks at all costs. One progresses fast and faces substantial setbacks; the other doesn't progress at all.

In Chapter 2, we briefly touched on identifying assumptions. Now, it's time to make this step more concrete. One question might be enough to identify your assumptions: "What needs to happen to make this solution successful?"

Returning to the car dealer example: We wanted to implement a web auction platform. When I asked what needed to happen to make it a success, we made several assumptions:

- Dealers will actively use the platform. (desirability)
- Dealers will understand how to interact with the platform. (usability)
- Dealers will place more bids than they do on the mobile app. (viability)
- Dealers will compete in more auctions, leading to higher conversion rates. (viability)
- Web auctions and mobile auctions will be correctly synchronized. (feasibility)

When I discussed the platform with the team, I asked them how long they needed to get a solution together. They told me it would be around three months. That made me panic, because we simply didn't have that much time. I also didn't want to make such a high bet on a solution without knowing whether it was right. That meant I had to work on prioritizing assumptions and testing them as quickly as possible.

One part of the challenge is identifying assumptions, and the other part is knowing which ones to test and which to ignore. Once you agree on the critical assumptions, you can explore experiments to accelerate learning. Before I clarify these parts of the discovery journey, let me suggest more alternatives that you can use to identify assumptions.

I cannot emphasize enough how important it is to name assumptions. Here are two additional approaches:

- **User story mapping:** Craft a user story mapping for the solution you picked. Here's the trick: Instead of creating the tasks related to the narrative flow, you name the assumptions related to each step. It's a practical approach because you look at the experience.
- **What could go wrong:** Imagine you launched your solution, which went tragically wrong. What happened? Name the potential problems and rephrase them into assumptions.

Both methods work well. You can pick which one suits you best. I like combining both approaches because they tend to reveal different unknowns.

How you formulate assumptions is critical. Write them as the behavior you expect to observe. It's better to write assumptions as affirmative statements to simplify the subsequent experiments. Otherwise, you get confused about how to test them. Let me give you examples:

- **Bad:** Dealers churn as the web platform becomes available.
- **Good:** Dealers remain active as the web platform becomes available.
- **Bad:** Dealers miss auctions of cars they are looking for.
- **Good:** Dealers engage in auctions of cars they are looking for.

I know it's sometimes easier to write in the negative, but that won't help you with the experiments later. The challenge is avoiding confirmation bias, as discussed in Chapter 6. Strive to test assumptions to learn what you don't know, instead of trying to prove yourself right.

Prioritizing Assumptions

Prioritization is fundamental to test assumptions. Devoting your energy to the most critical assumptions for which you lack evidence enables necessary learning. I recommend keeping things simple.

I use the assumption matrix method developed by David J. Bland.[2] With this approach, you create a 2×2 matrix, where one axis represents the evidence strength and the other represents the business importance. This method is a collaborative exercise and not a scientific one. You don't need to have all the data available to work on it, but you need to know the evidence you have or lack and how critical the assumption for the business is. The result is a list of prioritized assumptions you should test immediately.

To evaluate the business importance, take each assumption and ask if it is proven wrong: "Is your idea still viable?" When it's not, that's business critical. For the evidence, reflect on what you know and how trustworthy the evidence is, and be as realistic as possible.

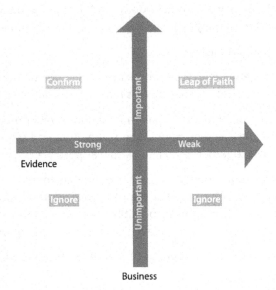

Figure 7.7
Assumption matrix, developed by David J. Bland

---

2. Watch the YouTube video where David Bland explains how to use the assumption matrix: www.youtube.com/watch?v=PyCvsBrKO4w.

As shown in Figure 7.7, when you prioritize your assumptions, you have clusters that define your actions:

- **Ignore:** You can ignore assumptions unimportant to the business, no matter how weak or strong your evidence is. Such assumptions don't deserve your attention.

- **Confirm:** When you identify business-critical assumptions you believe there is solid evidence for, double-check their validity. You don't need to run experiments if your data gives you enough confidence. Otherwise, you move the assumption to the Leap of Faith quadrant.

- **Leap of Faith:** When you identify business-critical assumptions that lack evidence, you better test them immediately. These assumptions will make or break an idea.

Once you've prioritized your assumptions, it's time to run experiments to gather evidence.

Defining Experiments

What are product experiments? They test assumptions and prove them right or wrong, enabling you to decide whether to invest further.

You will have a multitude of experiments to utilize. I don't intend to give you a walk-through of all possible experiments. You can find great books[3] on this topic, and I don't intend to reinvent the wheel. Instead, I want to simplify how you can run product experiments.

Here are five steps to make your life easier:

1. **Definition:** Get together with your product trio and agree on the experiment method to test your assumption. Define what success looks like, its target audience, and its runtime.

2. **Preparation:** Most experiments require a minimum level of preparation—for example, interviews, prototypes, landing pages, and so on. Agree on responsibilities and get the pieces of the puzzle together. Keep it as simple as possible.

3. **Execution:** Ensure your product trio runs experiments together to benefit from all perspectives. The goal is to learn, rather than to prove yourself right. Remain curious and strive to collect as many insights as possible. Even when you prove yourself wrong, it's reason to celebrate—because that prevents you from building something useless.

4. **Debriefing:** After each experiment, get together with the product trio and review the results.

5. **Conclusion:** As you run the planned experiments, review the results. Remain as pragmatic as possible. The ultimate result should be a pass or fail, enabling you to decide what to do.

---

3. Read *Testing Business Ideas* by David J. Bland (2019), the best book about product experiments you can find.

I'm practical, and I hate wasting time. I use a simple template with the required elements for a valuable experiment. The template enables the product trio to align. To illustrate it, I created Figure 7.8, an example for the car dealers web auction platform.

Exp-2024-09 001

Assumption	Date
Car dealers will understand our web auction platform	September 2024

Target Audience	Test Method
Dealers that opened auctions over the last three months but didn't place bids	Interactive Prototype

Reach	Duration
8 Dealers	One week

Expected result	Evidence Strength
5 out of 8 will conclude the assigned tasks without help	Moderate

Figure 7.8
Experiment template example

A common challenge I see with product managers is applying such practices in a B2B environment. It's tough to get access to the end users in this context. You have to explore different alternatives to make it possible. I've worked with a few B2B companies, and I know the level of complexity varies considerably.

No matter which industry I worked in or consulted, I had the same struggle: finding end users to interview. Solving that problem is no easy job, but two alternatives worked for me:

- **User panel:** Form a selective group of people representing the users. To discover them, you can use groups on social networks where such people are or attend events in which they participate. Alternatively, contact recruiters to understand where they find employees for that industry. The group doesn't need to be extensive. A few dozen end users can enable you to run your experiments well.

- **Outsource:** Another alternative is to use platforms like User Testing (www.usertesting.com/) and hire them to put you in contact with end users. You can conduct interviews, unmoderated prototypes, and surveys on such platforms.

Creativity empowers you to run experiments. Don't let the "this doesn't work for us" fallacy block you from doing what's necessary.

Another challenge with the B2B world is connecting customers' needs with end users. You may create a product the end users love, but still get no traction if you fail to address what customers look for. Strive to understand what those who pay the bill need. Then, ensuring your product delivers on that demand while being valuable for end users creates a win-win-win situation. Customers get what they look for, end users love the product, and the business gains revenue.

As Ash Maurya, author of *Running Lean* (2022), said, "Speed of learning is the new unfair advantage." So, keep your experiments as small as possible to boost learning.

Use Evidence to Progress: Experiment, Learn, Decide

Evidence should talk louder than opinions. Don't let noise cloud your judgment.

Product experiments are powerful. They validate or invalidate your assumptions. That's what enables you to adapt continuously.

Evaluate the gathered evidence and decide what to do next. Your experiments don't need to be perfect or high-fidelity prototypes. They should give you enough information to justify increasing the investment or convince you to cut it.

Coming back to the car dealers example: The concierge idea mentioned earlier went sideways. Only a few dealers were interested in using it, which didn't contribute to higher engagement as expected. So, we dropped this idea, but the web auction platform looked promising. Let me tell you what happened.

When we decided to test how dealers would understand our auction platform, I got together with a designer and shared what I had learned. In less than two hours, we crafted a low-fidelity prototype. At that point, the designer asked, "Should I invest now in doing a high-fidelity prototype based on this one? It will take me around a week." I promptly said no, and asked, "How long do you need to make it clickable?" The designer estimated they could finish by the end of the day. That was all I needed. My next step was bringing the clickable prototype to car dealers to experiment with.

I found dealers who were willing to test our clickable prototype. I ran the experiments. During the tests, something became apparent: Dealers didn't get our message, and only a few could complete the assigned jobs. I also noticed they expected to see more information on the car summary. I ran eight experiments in two days. And that gave me enough evidence to decide what to do next. The experiment summary looked like Figure 7.9.

Assumption		Date	Result
Car dealers will understand our web auction platform		September, 2024	Fail

Experiment	Evidence
Exp-2024-09 001	3 out of 8 dealers concluded the tests without help

Learning

Our copy doesn't reflect what dealers are used to. Also, the car summary is missing car damages, market price, customer desired price, number of owners.

Recommendation	Evidence Strength
Address the feedback and test again with different dealers	Moderate

Figure 7.9

Experiment result example

After reviewing the summary, we agreed to refine and test the app with different dealers. The choice of different dealers was intended to avoid the bias effect. The designer and a software engineer refactored the prototype while I contacted dealers to test it. I was convinced we could get this auction right, but didn't want to invest in implementation because the solution wasn't sharp enough.

By the end of that week, I had tested the new prototype with different dealers. This time, seven out of eight got the jobs done without any help. I still received feedback on details, but now the evidence was convincing enough to put a simple solution together and make it available to our users.

Yet, I had a dilemma. Software engineers and designers insisted that we needed at least two months to build a valuable solution. That was too long for me. I told them, "Car dealers don't use our current solution. If we could do something quick and dirty and release it to 10% of our dealers, we'd learn faster and have a higher chance of success." At that moment, the tech lead said, "We can put something together in a Sprint, but that will create tech debt, and eventually we need to pay it off." That's when I saw a light at the end of the tunnel, and it wasn't a truck coming!

When you remain curious and use your creativity to boost learning, you benefit from mindful product discovery. But when you overuse your current knowledge, you give too much attention to solutions and miss hidden opportunities.

Key Takeaways

- Product discovery isn't a silver bullet to guarantee you create value, but rather a method to help you separate good ideas from bad ones as fast as possible.

- Knowing the cards on the table is critical when setting goals. Strive to understand which potential trade-offs the organization is willing to make and which aspects the organization is unwilling to sacrifice.

- Get out of the office and meet your users. You won't find the most promising value drivers by limiting yourself to behind-the-scenes work. You can learn what's natural for users once you meet them in their usual environment, which will potentially reveal hidden opportunities.

- Confirmation bias and commitment escalation are common traps faced by product teams. Dealing with them is mandatory to avoid creating useless solutions. A simple technique is to experiment with different solutions for the same problem. Then, based on the evidence, decide which one to commit to.

- Testing assumptions requires curiosity and humility to accept you might be wrong. When you strive to prove yourself right, you will miss your unknowns. But when you are curious, you learn what you don't know and identify the value drivers.

This chapter covered what mindful product discovery looks like, which bonds with valuable product delivery, resulting in products customers love and unlocking business growth. In Chapter 8, we will address product delivery. I will share my take on it and offer some ways how to minimize time to value while building scalable solutions.

8

Enabling Product Delivery Beyond Outputs

Building features is one thing. Driving value from them is an entirely different challenge. Product delivery is about maximizing customer and business value, not shipping features at lightning speed. In Chapter 7, we discussed how to identify value drivers. Now, it's time to explore how to create value steadily.

In this chapter, I will walk you through the most critical aspects of product delivery, including how to apply these elements to meaningful product delivery in practice. It doesn't matter which framework you use. Whether you work with Scrum, Kanban, Scrumban, LeSS, or something else, you will get applicable insights from this chapter. Figure 8.1 highlights the delivery elements we will discuss in this chapter.

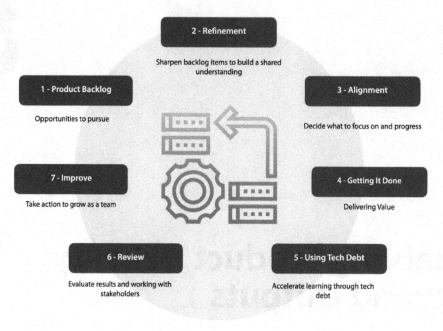

Figure 8.1
Product delivery elements

Before we jump into the delivery elements, let's start by exploring what product delivery isn't.

How the Wrong Approach to Product Delivery Leads to a Feature Factory

When I first landed in a team wearing the Product Owner hat, I thought my role was to optimize delivery. I did my best to keep the team delivering at their maximum speed. What I missed was the connection between outcomes and outputs. I didn't even evaluate results beyond meeting deadlines. That was my faulty perception of product delivery.

Following a plan and delivering all features from your product backlog isn't a meaningful strategy. Unfortunately, that transforms teams into feature factories. Product delivery is fragile, and it's natural to face anti-patterns that get in the way of creating value. Here are some classics:

- Every request you receive becomes a backlog item.
- Teams strive to implement perfect features instead of learning.
- Delivering more features is the definition of success.
- Nobody dares to remove a feature from the product.
- Commitments are made to outputs instead of outcomes.

A common mistake is separating discovery from delivery and having a handover between teams. With this approach, one team uncovers what's relevant, and the other builds it. That's another type of coordinative flow that won't help you create value faster. As we discussed earlier, discovery and delivery are intertwined: One depends on the other. That's why teams should have end-to-end responsibility.

Product delivery isn't about following a plan. It's about creating value at a steady pace.

Making that possible requires a growth mindset (check Chapter 2). Some solutions will go wrong, even though you have strong evidence supporting them. The challenge is finding the courage to drop poor solutions fast enough to double down on the promising ones.

Let's examine each element of product delivery to understand how you can benefit from them.

Product Backlog: Organizing What Drives Value

A meaningful product backlog reflects your ultimate goal. It's an emerging list based on your learning. Outdated items go out, so relevant items come in. You manage the product backlog by looking forward, not backward.

Many people believe the product manager is the only person who maintains the product backlog. That's a misunderstanding. The product manager is accountable for the results but doesn't need to be the only person to work on the backlog. *Good backlog management requires teamwork.*

Using tools like Jira, Asana, or Click-Up is the usual way of maintaining the backlog. Yet, the tool isn't the most important consideration, but rather the clarity the backlog brings. Focus on the collaboration, not on the process.

Be Careful with Excessive Backlog Management

Managing the product backlog represents one of the biggest traps for product teams.

- *Product managers mutate into backlog managers* when most of their time goes into maintaining the product backlog.

- *Software engineers get trapped by implementing requirements* and fighting against product managers when details are missing.

- *Product designers focus on creating high-fidelity prototypes* to enable teams to match expectations.

Whenever you observe any of these behaviors, it's a sign you need to step back and challenge the status quo.

The product backlog isn't a wish list that includes everything everyone wants. It's a means to organize tasks that enable product teams to reach goals. Ideally, the product backlog emerges from a goal. Realistically speaking, that's seldom the case.

Most teams have a running product with tech debt, bugs, improvements, and feature requests. These items tend to be added to the product backlog with the hope the team will work on them once they find the time. When this process continues unchecked, sooner than you imagine, you have an unmaintainable product backlog that leads to distraction instead of alignment.

Basecamp realized how detrimental the product backlog can be and decided against having one. Within its Shape Up framework,[1] Basecamp doesn't have a product backlog at all. Every six weeks, its teams decide what to pursue next. They benefit from having a fresh perspective and not getting stuck with the past.

Coming back to reality, you will probably have to deal with a product backlog. Most companies use frameworks that have a product backlog. So, how do you keep that list balanced?

New products and running ones tend to be different. Let me help you understand that.

Product Backlog for New Products

Getting started with a new product is exciting. Enjoy this opportunity whenever you have it, because it's rare. Unfortunately, it's easy to get excited about everything and dump all your ideas into your product backlog. Don't do that. This approach will block you from focusing on what matters.

Do you remember the user story mapping technique we discussed in Chapter 7? That's a great way of starting to organize your product backlog. You set a goal, craft the user journey, and then align on the customer's tasks you want to address. That allows you to create the first version of your product backlog. Then, you need to sit down with your software engineers and create the tech tasks, such as developing the environment, infrastructure, architecture, and so on.

You'll undoubtedly be tempted to register ideas unrelated to the desired goal, but product management requires mastering the art of saying no. Just remember what Steve Jobs[2] famously said:

> People think focus means saying yes to the thing you've got to focus on. But that's not what it means at all. It means saying no to the hundred other good ideas that there are. You have to pick carefully. I'm actually as proud of the things we haven't done as the things I have done. Innovation is saying "no" to 1000 things.

---

1. https://basecamp.com/shapeup

2. Steve Jobs explained the meaning of focusing during the Apple Worldwide Developers' Conference, 1997.

Three things you have to keep in mind:

1. Focus.

2. Focus.

3. Focus.

I had a few chances to start with a new product and struggled to know where to begin. I thought the focus should be writing backlog items, but I got it wrong. It's about commitment and alignment. You commit to reaching a goal and align on what you need to deliver and what you don't.

Product Backlog for Running Products

With running products, the story is different. You should balance keeping the lights on and working on new items. Whether you like it or not, you will have to do some maintenance (bug fixing and refactoring) along the way. That's normal. You can prioritize what happens when.

A common challenge is keeping the backlog lean. A good practice is to review the content of your backlog continuously and remove items unrelated to your goal. I know teams seldom do that, and that's why I urge you to follow a new path. Eliminating distractions isn't something you ask for permission to do—you just do it.

Once you have a lean product backlog, you can reflect on your goal and add the related items. This approach is a collaborative activity. It's normal for product managers to bring the initial version, but it doesn't mean they're the only ones working on the product backlog.

Backlog Items Format

All backlog items should have a standard format. You can opt for user stories, for example, and create everything that way. To ensure a minimum level of quality, you can establish the Definitions of Ready.[3] Only when items meet all criteria can team members work on them. This way, you avoid confusion.

Wait a minute. Reflect on what you've just read. Do you see how nuts this is?

Forcing backlog items to fit a particular format is nonsense. It doesn't sound like a collaborative flow, but it does sound like a strong coordinative flow—and you know how unhelpful that is. Establishing Definitions of Ready is one of the best ways to kill collaboration.

---

3. The Definition of Ready is a form of working contract. It defines what needs to happen so the team can consider the item in the next development cycle.

You don't need any rules for your product backlog items. I strongly recommend you avoid Definitions of Ready at all costs. They force teams to follow arbitrary rules instead of collaborating.

Keep your backlog items as simple as possible. You don't need a contract to define how teams manage the backlog. Collaboration should be more important than specifying a backlog management process.

It's not about writing backlog items. It's all about building shared understanding with the team. However, you won't be able to develop a shared understanding with a cluttered backlog. Let me help you solve this problem.

Extreme Backlog Cleaning

How often do you clean your home? I imagine you have different levels of cleaning.

- **Daily:** You make the bed, clean the toilet after using it, wash the dishes, and do other small activities.

- **Weekly:** Maybe once a week, you perform a more serious cleaning, removing the dust, cleaning the floors, and washing your clothes.

- **Special occasions:** In certain moments, you take cleaning more seriously. You make your home shine as never before because you will receive special guests and want to impress them.

What would happen if you stopped cleaning daily? It wouldn't take long to have a disgusting home you wouldn't want to visit anymore. And if you stop removing the dust for a week or two, you might struggle to breathe.

Now, let's return to the backlog, your product's home. Once you have a cluttered product backlog, you cannot breathe. It frightens and pressures you, and you have no excitement in your job. To solve this pressure, I encourage applying my extreme backlog-cleaning strategy. Here's what to do:

1. *Every backlog item has a due date.* A good rule of thumb is three months. If you don't touch it in three months, it's good to go—backlog items age like milk, not wine.[4]

2. *Set a routine to remove your backlog clutter.* Once a week, delete everything that has reached its due date or that nobody touched in the last three months. I know you will fear doing that and will find a wealth of excuses to avoid it. Let me tell you one thing: It's not because you have unlimited space in your backlog that you should keep it cluttered. If deleting an item scares you, archive that item so you don't see it.

3. *The backlog focuses on goals.* I recommend doing a more profound cleaning once a month. Go item by item and verify how relevant each item is at the moment. The ones

---

4. This is one of the 12 principles of the Agile Product Manifesto, which I coauthored. Read it here: https://agile-productmanifesto.com/

unrelated to your overarching goal are good to go. Also, placeholders are generally good to go because they rarely add value.

4. *The backlog enables the future.* When you agree on a new goal, it's a moment for radical cleaning. As a lazy person, I delete the backlog and start it over, focusing on the new goal. I understand this step is extreme, but extreme measures are necessary to create value and enable focus.

My extreme backlog cleaning may frighten you, but once you experience it, you'll regain control over your product's future.

Refinement: Building Shared Understanding

Refinement sessions have one goal: build a shared understanding of the opportunity so the team can work on a solution. Pay close attention to this goal. It doesn't say that the team defines a technical implementation plan, nor does the team give precise estimates for the items.

A valuable refinement session will follow this agenda:

1. **Setting the stage:** The product manager shares why the upcoming challenges matter and connects them to an overarching goal, ideally the product goal.

2. **Refining items:** This part is iterative. Timebox the refinement of each item; ten minutes tends to be enough. The product manager shares the context and why that's important. The team members ask clarifying questions, and the product manager refines the product backlog item with the team. After that, the team sizes the item (keep it simple). This cycle repeats for as many items as possible.

3. **Feedback:** Refinement sessions can be exhausting. Leave around ten minutes at the end to collect feedback to improve future sessions.

I suggest timeboxing your refinement sessions and turning them into a routine. At least once per development cycle, take from 90 minutes to 2 hours to refine your backlog items. I've tried different ways, and what worked best for me was conducting a refinement session two days before the end of the development cycle. That gets closer to the next cycle, leading to a smoother transition to starting the new cycle.

It's essential to keep the session as dynamic as possible. You can alter the format according to your needs. For example, if you start a brand-new solution, you can benefit from crafting a user story mapping with the team, and then you create your backlog items.

Remember, the outcome of the refinement session is building a shared understanding. It's not about having a session just for the sake of it. Keep the goal in mind, and work toward it.

Untrapping Tip: Don't over-refine. If you don't intend to work on something in the foreseeable future, don't invest your time in it, because things change. If you refine something but don't work on it for two or more development cycles, I'd recommend refining it again before jumping into execution. This approach ensures you refresh the understanding based on the current situation.

Let me share with you what happens when refinement becomes an obsession.

How the Refinement Slowed Down Progress

At one point in my career, I was coaching a product team. I was shocked when the product manager told me, "We have refinement sessions four times per week, and each session lasts an hour." I was astonished and asked, "How did you come to this approach?" The product manager confidently said, "I read in the Scrum Guide that we should invest 10% into refinement. That means 4 hours a week."

I had to decide between lecturing the team and helping them understand. I chose the latter. So, I started an exchange with the software engineers. I asked them, "What are your challenges now?" I got the answers I expected: "We have too many meetings and no time to code." Then I continued my inquiry: "Which meetings distract you the most?" Then I got what I needed: "Refinement sessions. I'm coding, and then I have to stop and refine items we will implement god knows when. I have a refinement session almost daily that doesn't help me with my current Sprint or the next one. It distracts me, and when I pick something to work on, I need to refine it again because we did it months before."

Then, I asked the product manager, "What will you do about it?" The answer was, "I don't know. We have items refined for six months now, and I have no idea what to keep bringing to the team. I thought we'd deliver more value by following the Scrum Guide. But I guess I need to cut our sessions, which honestly makes sense."

Untrapping Lesson 1: Applying frameworks without knowing why will create unwanted results.

Untrapping Lesson 2: Help the team speak up so they can figure out the solution independently.

Note: The Scrum Guide 2017 states: "Refinement usually consumes no more than 10% of the capacity of the Development Team."[5] That means no more than 10%, not exactly 10%. In 2020, the Scrum Guide removed recommendations on how much teams should invest in refinements.

---

5. The Scrum Guide 2017 can be read here: https://scrumguides.org/docs/scrumguide/v2017/2017-Scrum-Guide-US.pdf.

Alignment: Setting the Next Goal

What's the team going to work on next? That's the necessary alignment to foster collaboration. Yet, this is a thin line between love and hate. Many software engineers despise cycles because they claim cycles get in the way of getting the job done. I don't see the situation as that black and white. I see both the advantages and the disadvantages.

Scrum uses Sprints as development cycles, lasting from one to four weeks. Shape Up sets a cycle of six weeks, but suggests teams find their own, suitable cycle size. Kanban and Scrumban, by contrast, don't have any cycles. Now, let's understand what speaks in favor of cycles and what doesn't.

Advantages:

- Renew the goal every cycle
- Digestible chunks of work
- Celebration when the team reaches the goal
- Reflection and learning from each cycle
- Prioritization

Disadvantages:

- Routine that may hurt creativity
- Danger of cutting corners to fit the cycle
- Plan by capacity instead of goal setting
- Potential of breaking the team into micro teams

For me, the advantages justify having a stable cycle. You can overcome the disadvantages with strong collaboration and leadership.

If having cycles isn't an option for you. I'd still be mindful of aligning on the goal and ensure that team members have this clarity before picking anything from the backlog. Having or not having a cycle doesn't exclude the need for alignment on the direction the team should follow.

Let me elaborate on how you establish alignment when you work with cycles.

How to Set Alignment on Goals

Whenever the team starts a new cycle, the essence is committing to a goal because that empowers individuals to make decisions quickly and adapt the course of action. It's not about creating a detailed plan for the next cycle, but instead about committing to the goal. Maarten Dalmijn's

(2024) book, *Driving Value with Sprint Goals: Humble Plans, Exceptional Results,* addresses this topic. Let me quote him:

> We struggle when we must deal with uncertainty and complexity. We try to apply our usual and familiar approaches of spending more time on planning and analysis to gain control. But those methods are ineffective and often just make things worse.

A common mistake is planning cycles without a goal or a pointless one—for example, "Deliver all features by the end of the Sprint." No goal is a no-go. This trap will force the team to use a divide-and-conquer approach to deliver all features, and they'll commit to outputs instead of outcomes.

Here's how I see the alignment for each cycle:

1. **Setting the stage:** The product manager sets the stage by stating why the cycle is important and what matters most for the business and customers.

2. **Crafting the goal:** The product manager shares a goal draft based on why the cycle matters and sharpens it with the team.

3. **Making it memorable:** The team suggests a name for the cycle. The name can be anything: a superhero, a song, a movie, etc. The point is to make it fun, engaging, and memorable.

4. **Alignment on the focus:** Based on the goal, team members align on how they will reach it. Team members discuss their strategy to collaborate and ultimately achieve the goal. They just need the first few steps, not a plan for the whole cycle.

5. **Wrap-up:** When you have the goal, a strategy to reach it, a cycle name, and commitment, you can start the cycle and communicate it to your stakeholders.

Depending on the cycle and team size, the length of this session varies from 90 minutes to 4 hours. For a two-week cycle, 2 hours tends to be long enough. If you're investing more time than that, it's a sign you're investing a lot of time in discussion instead of progress.

Let me share a story with you about how having a name for the cycle made it memorable for us.

Unbreak My Heart

Product teams have different flavors. You may be part of a company and work closely with your business stakeholders, or you may be part of an agency and work for it, creating products for the agency's customers. For some years, I was part of the agency world. That's a complicated game because of the challenges of getting access to end users.

In one of our development cycles, we felt the burden on our shoulders. Our client wanted to get the product live as soon as possible, so we committed to an unachievable goal. Yes, we committed to it. The name of the cycle was "Under Pressure." We messed up with everything and barely delivered anything we agreed to. As a result, we pissed off our client and had to do something to recover the relationship during the next cycle.

For our next cycle, we aligned on our challenges and why the cycle mattered. Then, we came up with a clear goal. "Editors are empowered to get pages live without talking to anyone." We gave the cycle name "Unbreak My Heart." After two weeks, we over-delivered and regained the trust we had lost in the previous cycle.

Untrapping Lesson: Give your dev cycles a fun name; work doesn't have to be boring.

The magic of cycles is getting a new shot. You craft a goal and may miss it, but then you have another chance to develop a new goal and evolve. It's essential to calibrate the goal. You're setting the bar too low if you consistently achieve the goals. I like moonshots, so a 70% success rate is reasonable from my perspective.

Don't be afraid of aiming high and missing it. Be afraid of aiming low and reaching it.

Getting Things Done

The moments between starting the cycle and closing it are when the magic happens. Teams get together to craft meaningful solutions and ultimately create value for customers and the business. Yet, a common threat lies ahead of you: complexity.

Look at the workflow in Figure 8.2 and reflect on how it contributes to collaboration. Figure 8.2 uses Jira as an example to illustrate an unnecessarily complex workflow because Jira is the most widely used tool for backlogs worldwide. I'm not blaming Jira, but we end up with complex and confusing workflows when we abuse its flexibility, which forces us to coordinate instead of collaborate.

Whenever I'm coaching teams, their workflow is one of the first things I look at. The more steps they have, the less they collaborate. You might disagree, but stick with me, and I will help you understand where I'm coming from.

With coordinative flows, teams work in silos. Everyone has a specific responsibility, and that's what they do—nothing more and nothing less. It's similar to a factory, where employees repeat their tasks daily. The more steps you have inside a workflow, the more handovers the team faces and the less accountable they feel. Here are two workflow steps that hurt collaboration:

- **Ready for QA:** Does that mean software engineers won't guarantee the quality of their work? I understand some teams have quality assurance engineers, and even though that doesn't mean a handover, it means a need for collaboration.

- **PM approval:** This is the first stage I remove from any workflow. The product manager isn't at a higher level than the team and should not approve their work. Having product managers sign off on software engineers' work diminishes their accountability. Instead of approval, I encourage product managers to collaborate closely with team members.

You probably guessed what I do instead. I simplify as much as possible to ensure team members collaborate. Figure 8.3 illustrates a simplified workflow created in Jira.

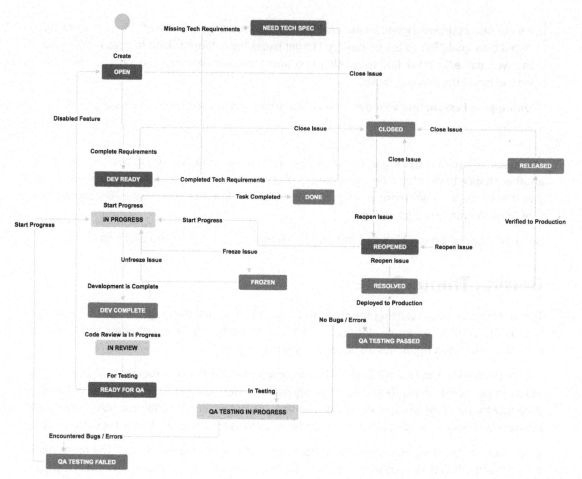

Figure 8.2
Complex Jira workflow

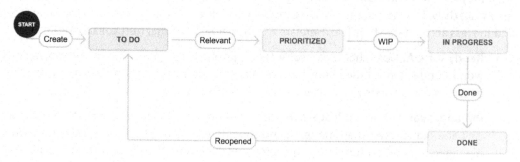

Figure 8.3
Simplified Jira workflow

Unless you work in a place that is intolerant of mistakes, you don't need a rigorous process. I can understand that happening where it's a matter of life and death. But most products aren't like that. So, use simplicity to diffuse complexity.

When the team is working on a cycle, their commitment is to achieve the goal and not to deliver a list of outputs. The team can pivot the strategy during the cycle whenever they see it as relevant.

A critical aspect of getting things done is having the same understanding of what *done* means. A lack of understanding on this front will lead to frustration and frequent conflicts.

Definitions of Done

The Definition of Done (DoD) is what enables teams to progress at a steady pace. They agree on the necessary aspects to define the work as done, and every item they work on must meet these criteria. If you ignore that DoD, you can expect software engineers to be angry with one another, product managers to complain that things lack quality, and designers to be frustrated. No one wins, and everyone loses.

It's common practice for product teams to craft their DoD and revise it as often as necessary— at least once a quarter. The DoD is similar to a contract, which everyone commits to following strictly, and the task is *done* once it meets the agreed conditions.

I discourage teams from establishing strict processes, but I make an exception for the DoD. When teams don't know what *done* means, it negatively impacts how fast they can drive value. Here are some examples of DoD:

- Code reviewed by at least one software engineer
- Minimum 85% of test coverage
- Acceptance criteria are met
- Continuous integration build succeeded
- Browser compatibility tests done on the top three browsers

The criteria for the DoD don't need to be extensive. Between five and ten items tends to be enough. The DoD goes beyond bringing clarity on what *done* means; it sets your quality level bar.

Using Tech Debt: Accelerate Learning to Avoid Poor Investment

Apologies in advance to the software engineers reading this book, but tech debt isn't always evil. It is a handy tool to accelerate value creation when used prudently. Yes, you read it right. It's a tool and not just a problem. The problem is how teams use or misuse this tool.

To explain why prudent tech debt is a handy tool, I want you to imagine a hammer. Is a hammer bad? If you ask a carpenter, the answer is no. But suppose you give a hammer to a five-year-old and let the kid play with it for a while, then ask the parents what they think. They'd probably tell you the hammer is evil because everything at their house became a nail.

Depending on how you use tech debt, you can either destroy your whole application or accelerate learning. You may disagree with me, and that's fine. But if you look at Figure 8.4, how do you convince yourself to start building right when your knowledge is close to zero and the risk is at its maximum?

Despite how much evidence you've gathered during your product discovery journey, users will surprise you. Don't underestimate them. That's why our initial knowledge about the solution isn't enough to justify building right from day one. A better approach is to build to learn first and then to scale. Using tech debt prudently allows you to quickly understand how users benefit from your solutions, which empowers you to adapt them accordingly.

It's unlikely you'll get everything right from the beginning. Also, the first solution should not be intended for your whole audience. Limit the reach to a small percentage (5% is a good number) and then scale gradually. This approach shows when solutions don't work, allowing you to drop the bad ones and focus on the good ones.

When users benefit from a solution, that drives business value. At that moment, it's time to pay the tech debt off instead of jumping to another solution. Failing to pay the tech debt will lead to unmaintainable solutions.

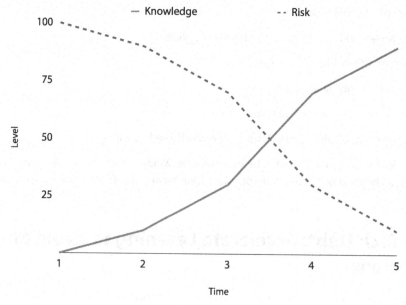

Figure 8.4
Risk and knowledge relationship over time

I understand why software engineers are reluctant to use tech debt. They're afraid of creating a monster they cannot sustain, and they don't trust product managers to give them the space needed to pay the tech debt because many push for output.

It's important to clarify that using tech debt doesn't mean intentionally writing poor code or creating something terrible. Instead, it means prioritizing learning over scalability. It's not about cutting corners or dropping quality, but about searching for the fastest route to accelerate learning. To illustrate what I mean, let me share a story with you.

Using Tech Debt and Avoiding a Pointless Investment

Our growth target market was China, so we found a partner to advertise our products. I was skeptical about the process because everything seemed too easy, and I lacked evidence we'd achieve the results we wanted so quickly. Life isn't that easy.

I was a product manager then and decided to try a simple integration with our new partner. During the first talk with the potential partners, they mentioned they had no API but could read CSV files. We needed to drop the files in a folder, and the partners would automatically process the files. They'd also put the received orders in the same folder. A software engineer was with me and asked some technical questions to ensure understanding.

After that call, we had a refinement session, and I brought the integration proposal to the team. They pushed me to build the solution right from the beginning, saying the whole process would take at least a month. I didn't want to invest that much time and effort, so I asked what we could do in a day to test the collaboration with the potential partner. They laughed in my face and said, "At best, we can create a script and put our products on their servers once a day. But the orders will be something manual." I said, "Okay, let's go for that."

A full-fledged solution would have meant creating a service to exchange files with the partner server. Also, it would have required performance tests and high test coverage. To match our DoD, we needed at least 85% test coverage. I would have had no problem making such an investment if we were certain the partner would reach the minimum orders per day, which we didn't.

We decided to compromise on tech quality, and the software engineers didn't build a service. Instead, they created a simple way of exporting data into a CSV file. We cut the test coverage to 50% and didn't worry about scalability.

We put the products' CSV files on the server. On the next day, our products were available on the partner platform. The next day, no orders. The next week, no orders. The next month, two orders. It turned out that the partner couldn't drive the promised 200 orders a day, so we ended the partnership.

We invested no more than a day of work, dropped the initiative, and pursued another alternative. I wonder, if we had built the solution right at the beginning, how I would have explained to management that we invested a month of work in getting two orders worth no more than 50€ each.

Untrapping Lesson: Wise use of tech debt can prevent you from building worthless solutions.

Review: Getting Business and Product Aligned

Product teams must frequently collaborate with both the business and customers. It's essential to have a routine that ensures continuous exchanges with key stakeholders. A great moment to do that is at the end of the development cycle. This interaction isn't a presentation or a status report, but rather a collaborative session to engage with customers and business stakeholders.

Once again, reality hits us. Most reviews will happen with business stakeholders, and you will struggle to get a customer in the room—which doesn't mean you shouldn't strive to get customers to participate. Even if you cannot, I see value in review sessions with business stakeholders.

One important point here: Reviews aren't the only moment to evaluate what you created. You should create multiple opportunities to test your output to review how it delivers the expected outcomes.

I've been part of hundreds of review sessions and, sadly, misled many of them at the beginning of my career. As a product manager, I often took the stage and led the session. Although the software engineers enjoyed that, they missed the opportunity to interact directly with the business stakeholders. After several attempts to figure out how to run valuable reviews, I found a suitable format. Here's how you can nail it:

1. **Setting the stage:** The product manager reminds everyone of the overarching goal and how the results connect. Then, they share a summary of the cycle, including whether the team reached the goal.

2. **Review outcomes:** Keeping the review related to the last cycle makes it too shallow. It's important to reflect on how the previous outputs drove outcomes. The product manager makes this connection and gets business stakeholders excited about results, not just outputs.

3. **Cycle results:** As the previous outcomes become clear, team members (software engineers, designers, etc.) present their achievements for the current cycle. They start with why and connect with how and what. In other words, they name the problem they are addressing, and explain how the output created solves that.

4. **Hands-on:** Team members (software engineers, designers, etc.) define the missions and assign attendees to get them done. The goal is to observe how stakeholders interact with the product to get the job done. This approach keeps the session interactive and creates more valuable feedback.

5. **Opportunities:** Based on the results from step 4, the stakeholders and the product team interact to identify potential improvements.

6. **Next steps:** The product manager shows a high-level idea of the next goal so the stakeholders know the team's direction.

The more interactive you make this session, the more value you can collect from the participants.

This session doesn't need to be longer than 90 minutes. Depending on your team and cycle size, you might be able to bring it down to 1 hour. It's better to have a shorter session with more attendees than a longer session with fewer participants. Business stakeholders may initially resist attending a 90-minute session. Try getting them used to how the session works. Then, you can probably increase the time if necessary.

Let me share a story of when a brave software engineer changed our reviews.

From Boring Reviews to Engaging Sessions

When we noticed business stakeholders would skip every second review, we knew we had to change something. A senior software engineer took a stand and said, "Our reviews are mechanical, boring, and soulless. We need to spice them up." He got all of us curious, and I asked what he had in mind.

The software engineer wanted the attendees to be active, not passive. He suggested presenting what features are for and letting business stakeholders try them out during the session. We all loved the idea and decided to give it a go.

Our next review was different. Business stakeholders move from spectator to participant after a few minutes. Finally, they found value in the session and could think out loud, helping us connect to their points. The more engaging we made reviews, the less often participants missed them.

Untrapping Lesson: Help participants be active during reviews so the sessions are engaging, not boring.

Improve: Strive to Continuously Become a Better Team

No team is so good that it has nothing to improve. Dedicating time to reflect on the cycle and search for opportunities to grow is essential. Teams don't become high-performing units from one day to the next. Instead, a series of minor improvements tend to lead to unprecedented results.

If you use Scrum, this moment for team improvement is called a Sprint Retrospective. And if you don't use Scrum, I'd encourage you to conduct recurrent retrospectives. Biweekly should do it.

Sadly, many teams face so much pressure that they see no alternative but to cut corners to meet expectations. Often, the retrospective doesn't take place because the team has too much to do. As a result, they always have a lot to do, and no retrospective happens. It becomes a vicious circle: The retrospective would be a way of taking action and avoiding this drastic situation, but it is ignored, and the team remains frustrated.

The retrospective isn't a conversation where the team complains, becomes powerless, and starts the next cycle demotivated. Sure, that happens with flawed retrospectives. But with good ones, the team commits to a maximum of three actions and, step by step, becomes stronger.

You don't need to solve all issues at once. Prioritize the most relevant ones and ignore the others.

There are hundreds, if not thousands, of different ways to run valuable retrospectives. It's in this book's scope to go through all of these methods. To broaden your knowledge, I recommend you check the templates created by Chris Stone.[6]

Allow me to share my way of running retrospectives.

1. **Icebreaker:** Help team members arrive at the session by bringing an icebreaker. For example, define the last cycle with a song, movie, or image. You can find dozens of icebreakers from various sources, so try different ones. You'll be surprised by how five minutes of this fun activity can bring the mood up.

2. **Review actions:** The team reviews the actions they committed to in the last session and then evaluates whether they acted on those commitments and how they helped meet the team's goal.

3. **Learn:** Use a dynamic to help the team inspect the last cycle—for example, Sailboat, 4Ls, Sprint Timeline, or Stop–Continue–Start.

4. **Commit to actions:** Based on the inspection results, the team searches for opportunities to become more effective. They craft a maximum of three actions and commit to work on them during the next cycle.

5. **Tune out:** Wrap up the session by closing the cycle. You can alternate between giving kudos, a weather report for the next cycle, a session evaluation, or something else. The result should be closing the current cycle and opening up for the next one.

If you're using Scrum, the Scrum Master will prepare and moderate the session. But if you don't have a Scrum Master or Agile Coach, anyone from the team can take on this responsibility. It works well when team members alternate the responsibility of preparing and organizing the retrospective over time. It's important to vary the dynamic to avoid a mechanical session.

Key Takeaways

- The focus of product delivery isn't meeting deadlines or creating predefined features, but rather creating solutions for problems worth solving.

- Collaboration and alignment are essential to ensure progress in the right direction.

---

6. www.thevirtualagilecoach.co.uk/retros

- Backlog management presents multiple traps. It's easy to fill the backlog with wishes and promises, but hard to keep it lean and aligned on goals. The former creates confusion, and the latter focuses on what's most relevant.

- Avoiding tech debt at all costs will ensure massive waste because not all solutions work as expected. Using tech debt to accelerate learning will speed up value creation. Yet, you must pay the tech debt off on time for the solutions that remain in your product.

- Don't let a busy routine block the team from stepping back and reviewing how they work. Retrospectives are fundamental to enable teams' growth and help them evolve.

In this chapter, we covered different elements of product delivery and saw how they connect the dots to enable value creation. However, we didn't cover how you measure the results and ensure the work from the team leads to the desired results. That's the topic of Chapter 9.

9

Defining and Measuring Actionable Metrics

Products have so much data today that product teams can quickly get overwhelmed. Analysis paralysis dominates, and teams take no action. They wonder which data matters, what it tells them, where to pay attention, and how to digest and create insights.

Let me be blunt: Having data just for the sake of it is nonsense.

The magic happens when teams can transform data into actionable insights. That's the discussion we'll have during this chapter. I won't give you an extensive list of metrics, because that isn't the point. But I will share how I define which data to use, when, and how.

Up to this point, we haven't addressed how to effectively measure results, but now it's time to do that. Knowing how and what to measure is an essential skill for any product professional because it helps you evaluate the impact caused by your work and act accordingly.

By the end of this chapter, you should have applicable insights on measuring results. Here are the aspects we will discuss:

- **Data traps:** Common pitfalls ahead of you and how to avoid them.
- **Leading versus laggard metrics:** Clarity on actionable and non-actionable metrics.
- **Input versus output metrics:** Understanding where you can influence.

- **Defining metrics:** Crafting questions and identifying fitting metrics.

- **Measuring results:** How to measure results and take action.

- **Sharing results:** Engaging with business stakeholders and getting them onboard.

Data Traps: Avoid Common Traps

Have you ever heard the term *vanity metrics*? If not, you should know it, because these kinds of metrics distract product professionals from what matters.

Many teams still work with velocity, though I see no value in it. Yes, you read that right: I see no value in velocity. I know some people freak out when I say that, but I freak out when I waste my or others' time.

When I got my first product manager assignment, I focused on increasing velocity. Management highly appreciated that. The team has never delivered at that speed. We were flying high, and I even got a salary increase because of my ability to increase velocity. I was proud of myself—until I learned that our features created no business value.

Increasing output speed offers no guarantee that you're creating business value. That was a harsh lesson for me to digest. Velocity is an example of vanity metrics. I strongly encourage you to ditch velocity if you use it. Don't let the noise distract you.

Another common trap is related to top-of-the-funnel metrics. Some examples are page views, impressions, and engagement. Let me use LinkedIn as an example.

Sometimes, I post on LinkedIn to drive readers to my newsletter, aiming to convert them into subscribers. I have posts with hundreds of thousands of impressions that led to no more than a hundred subscribers to my newsletter. In contrast, I have posts with around 10,000 impressions, leading to several hundreds of new subscribers. Subscribers matter because I can engage with them in the future, whereas impressions or interactions don't help me distribute my content.

Vanity metrics don't help you take action to create value, but instead distract you from it. To identify them, reflect on how the metric enables you to get closer to the value you aim to drive.

Data obsession is another issue I commonly stumble upon. Teams claim to be data-driven and become resistant to making decisions when data is lacking. This behavior traps the team into analysis paralysis. To illustrate this scenario, I need to share a story with you.

How a Clearly Better Product Had Its Launch Delayed by Six Months

As I started a new job, I got an assignment to get the new e-commerce site live. The team had worked on the website for six months but couldn't get it live. I compared both website versions with my fresh eyes, and the new one stood out. I couldn't understand why the old one was still in use.

The team aimed for a complete switch once the new website performed at the same level as the old one. To assure it did, the team set up several experiments and ran A/B tests.[1] I was shocked when I noticed 30-plus A/B tests running for different parts of the website. The new website performed better in most aspects but worse in others. The strategy was to optimize the low performers until they reached the same level as the previous website.

The team was frustrated because the A/B testing approach dragged on for months. My gut told me to get the website live gradually and measure the key metrics, average basket size, conversion rate, revenue generated, and so on. However, I got no support because top management wanted a thorough analysis of the whole website, comparing it step by step. I knew that would last forever. I had to act decisively.

I did what I do best: I took risks. I talked to the team and agreed to stop all A/B tests and gradually release the new version to our audience, as the most relevant metrics confirmed we wouldn't be in trouble. The next day, we started at 6 a.m. and got the e-commerce site live to 5% of our audience. By the end of the day, the revenue from the new website beat the revenue from the old version by around 2%. We waited a few days to increase the reach, and revenue remained steadily higher. Then, we increased the reach to 10%, 20%, 50%, and 100% of our audience.

We didn't lose anything. On the contrary, our revenue increased. When top management asked me to show the reports supporting my decision, I said that I didn't have them, but had focused on measuring the most critical metrics. Once I saw a positive increase in those metrics, I increased the reach. They were surprised that I didn't look at everything. But they ultimately agreed it was more important to deliver the business value instead of focusing on keeping session time, bounce rate, and other metrics.

Untrapping Lesson: Use data to enable you to progress, not to block you from it.

Leading versus Laggard Metrics

Leading metrics (e.g., daily active users) are easy and quick to measure. Meanwhile, laggard metrics (e.g., customer satisfaction, revenue growth) take time to measure.

---

1. A/B tests, also known as segmented tests, represent a way of comparing two or more versions of a feature and evaluating which one performs better. They can also be used with slogans, call to action, etc.

Identifying leading metrics is critical to fostering action. Yet, it's common to use laggard metrics as goals, which makes it hard for teams to connect their actions to the desired outcomes. You may realize you have a problem only after it's become too big, forcing you to surrender to the undesired situation.

Leading metrics are empowering because teams can measure them swiftly. For example, after releasing new functionalities, team members can immediately evaluate how those features contribute to the desired outcome.

I don't want to vilify laggard metrics because they also have a helpful role to play. For example, it's better to use a laggard metric as a roadmap goal instead of clearly defined features. Let's take two scenarios and evaluate what teams could do.

Roadmap with Laggard Metric: Identifying Actionable Metrics

Suppose management decides to increase customer lifetime value. This metric is a laggard because you cannot effectively connect small changes to the ultimate result. Yet, the team can explore different solutions to reach this goal. Question what leads to the desired laggard metric that reveals your leading ones.

By asking what leads to higher customer lifetime value, you might identify these potential leading metrics:

- **Recurrence:** How often customers use the product.

- **Customer effort score (CES)[2]:** How much effort customers put into getting a specific job done (e.g., finalizing a purchase, solving issues with customer service, asking for a refund).

- **Average basket size:** The average order volume.

Once you identify leading metrics like recurrence, customer effort score, and average basket size, you can quickly find where customers struggle and improve the experience. People will stick with products that give them a good experience, but if you ignore that, they will switch to your competitors.

With a laggard metric, the team can work on coming up with leading metrics, create assumptions, and then use product discovery techniques (read Chapter 7) to uncover the value drivers. Success depends on you.

---

2. Customer effort score (CES) is a metric to assess the ease of using certain features. The objective is knowing where customers struggle so you can improve that area quickly. For example, how easily can a customer sign up? How straightforward is the process by which a customer can report an issue? CES focuses on specific and actionable tasks so you can immediately learn how your customers perceive those tasks.

Roadmap with Output Defined: You've Got One Shot to Thrive

Suppose management wants to tackle the same problem: customer lifetime value. But instead of empowering the team to address that issue, top management defines what the team should do. They establish a roadmap with features like a loyalty program, product recommendations, and a redesign of the product detail page. Success means delivering everything on time.

With an output roadmap, the team has low outcome accountability. They follow orders instead of uncovering what matters to customers.

Laggard metrics enable you to ask questions. That gives you choices, so it's up to you to find the ones that enable you to drive value. In contrast, an output orientation limits your options to what's predefined. (Read the section on prescriptive roadmaps over embracing the unknown in Chapter 2 to find ways to overcome this trap.)

Input versus Output Metrics: Understanding Control and Influence

Leading metrics enable you to act when you select what's within your control. But when you select metrics, you cannot control them. You can influence them but cannot guarantee any desired change. Progress accelerates when you use input metrics within your control.

Let me use a real example.

Moving from Output to Input Metrics

In one of the e-commerce companies I worked for, we realized that our search feature had a poor conversion rate. Initially, we measured the number of products added to the cart after users searched. I thought that was the right way of looking at it because we wanted to convert the search into products added to the cart. But no matter what we did, the results didn't change. It was frustrating.

Although we could promptly measure the search conversion and connect our actions to it, we struggled to improve the results. For a few weeks, we ran in circles, and I realized we had asked the wrong questions.

Search conversion is a leading metric that we can influence but cannot control. Collin Bryar and Bill Carr, authors of *Working Backwards* (2022), would define search conversion as an output metric because your actions cannot guarantee the desired results. So, frustration becomes unavoidable. The alternative is to identify input metrics because you can control their outcome and quickly see the impact of your work.

After running around in circles, I started asking different questions. I wondered what we could do to improve the search results. One opportunity was the ranking strategy. We presented the products matching the search alphabetically (yeah, you can laugh about it). We changed the ranking to show the high-runners first. This simple change increased the conversion by 0.5%, which was quite representative.

Later, we addressed the issue of searches that did not produce any results (input metric). We initially showed "no results found" with a tile of our best-selling products, which annoyed users and led them to bounce. Then, we tried something more advanced and presented products similar to the one the customer searched for. We ensured that we offered the most similar high-runners and stopped showing the message "no results found." Curiously, this change drove the conversion rate (output metric) up again.

Untrapping Lesson: Focus on what you can control instead of what you can influence.

Knowing which metric you're working on helps you decide on the best action. No, I'm not suggesting you ignore output metrics. Instead, I'm urging you to understand which metric you're using and ask better questions that enable you to take immediate action. Otherwise, you will run around in circles like I did.

For example, suppose you're looking at your net promoter score (NPS; a satisfaction metric representing how willing your customers are to recommend your product). NPS is an output metric. You need to take immediate action when you realize the score is too low, but that might be too late to recover the customers you lost. A helpful question would be, "What can I do now to improve satisfaction?" You can measure the CES for different tasks related to your product and then evaluate how to reduce the effort for specific customer experiences.

The strategy is to focus on the input metrics because you own them and can define what happens when. Consequently, the desired output metric will probably improve as a side effect.

Defining Metrics: Focus on Signs While Ignoring Noise

Track everything and decide later what to use. If that's your strategy, your future is analysis paralysis. I know the drill. I have faced this trap several times. Defining the proper metrics, though, can be pretty exhausting.

When I started my career, I was proud I could give answers to any question as fast as possible. Today, I don't value this skill as much as I did. Questions are often more powerful because they force you to consider different answers. Knowing the questions will point you in a more appropriate direction, enabling you to uncover the relevant metrics.

Start with a simple question: What does success look like? As obvious as this question may be, finding a meaningful answer enables you to define your metrics properly. Before you come up with an answer, let me warn you about some pointless metrics:

- **Deadline:** Delivering a solution nobody needs on time won't help you thrive.

- **Features:** Building all the features stakeholders wish for won't guarantee success.

- **Quality:** Creating a high-quality, bug-free product is nice, but it doesn't mean you've created value.

When you're trapped in the feature factory, the preceding metrics will define success. Although teams following that path may perceive themselves as successful, the value created will be minimal. You might disagree with me, because such metrics may be what you're familiar with. In project organizations, they do define success, yet they won't lead to it.

Let me share a real story with you to elaborate on this scenario.

Accelerate Sellers' Onboarding

When I started my new position as the marketplace product manager, I had to define the team's focus for the upcoming quarter. I analyzed our business plan and noticed an ambitious goal of onboarding 300 sellers on our platform. So, I tried to understand how we onboarded them.

I was surprised that partner managers couldn't onboard sellers because software engineers had to do it manually. In short, the team could onboard a maximum of eight sellers per month, and we had a target of 300 for that year. That math didn't work.

The goal was to onboard 25 sellers per month. Success for us came from empowering partner managers to run onboardings without any software engineer help, and eventually enabling self-onboarding. When we asked ourselves what success was, we came up with the following metrics:

- Onboarding time: Knowing the onboarding speed allowed us to review whether we'd get to our objective.

- Sellers activated: Onboarding was the first step, but we had to ensure we acquired relevant sellers. An active seller would have sold at least one item.

- Products per seller: That metric helped us assess sellers' engagement.

- Sales per seller: It was key to understand how our sales spread across sellers.

Such metrics empowered us to act and correct our direction whenever we derailed.

Untrapping Lesson: Define metrics that enable you to act fast enough.

You will have tons of metrics you can look at. Don't let that confuse you. Focus on what success looks like and work backward. Define a few metrics and focus on measuring them frequently enough.

Measuring Results: Be Careful, You're Not a Stockbroker

How often should you measure your results? You may think you should be like a stockbroker and have several screens with dashboards and pivot whenever something goes off. But how sustainable would that be?

Let's explore several different options for measurement frequency:

- **When you release a new feature:** Measuring results only when you create a new feature will be too late, and you won't be able to assess the overall state of your product. This approach isn't sustainable and will ensure you miss valuable insights.

- **Once a month:** Looking at your results only once a month will show you problems only after it's too late to act. With this approach, you'll become powerless. I've observed some teams barely looking at their data despite having many data points. That's unhelpful.

- **Once a day:** My favorite pick is looking at your results once a day. I recommend doing that because you can measure what happened on the previous days and compare that metric with other data points. I see value in having actionable dashboards showing how sustainable your product is. Then, you can quickly look at the dashboard and act whenever something is off.

- **Multiple times a day:** I compare this approach to the stock market. You will freak out if you continuously look at the data several times daily. You may see something you dislike, start creating hypotheses about why that is happening, and drown in endless possibilities. The day ends, and you've done nothing but get lost in the data.

I recommend you simplify your life with dashboards[3] that show high-level information, so you can act whenever you see key metrics are off. You don't need to panic and look at your results multiple times daily; that will just make you anxious. I speak from experience because that's what I used to do, and it isn't mindful.

Another aspect of measuring results is the depth of data. For example, you may realize that your revenue is declining. You can look at this same metric in different scenarios to determine how that happened. For instance:

- Conversion rate per device

- Conversion rate per region

- Conversion rate per traffic source

---

3. You can use multiple tools to create dashboards. My favorite one is MixPanel because of its flexibility. You could also use Tableau, PowerBI, Looker, and similar tools.

Looking at the data in-depth will show you where the problem lies and enable you to react. Let me share a brief story with you.

The Importance of Looking at Data from Different Angles

At one time, I was part of a team charged with creating a referral program to reduce our customer acquisition costs and increase loyalty. One morning, I looked at our numbers and noticed a decrease in our activated referrals. I started exploring the data from different angles and quickly noticed that the conversion per device had changed compared to the previous week.

Desktop devices had performed similarly, but the mobile app had a significant drop in the conversion rate. I tried to understand whether something had changed in the user experience. After testing, I noticed no difference. So, I dug deeper, and the issue became apparent: Devices with smaller screens had a conversion rate close to 1% instead of the 7% we previously had.

When testing the app with a smaller device, I noticed the call to action (CTA) wasn't visible in the first view, which forced users to scroll before activating the referral program. That problem happened because the marketing team changed our program's explanatory text. A simple change impacted our overall conversion rate by around 15%.

Untrapping Lesson: Look at data from different angles so you reveal hidden opportunities.

To measure the results, you need to start at a high level and then search for different perspectives to understand where you can optimize the overall results.

Sharing Results: Spread the News about Outcomes

Who's responsible for measuring results? You may think it's the product manager, but I'd say everyone is ultimately responsible for the result. That includes software engineers, product designers, business stakeholders, and others involved in building the product. But the product manager is accountable for the final result—which doesn't mean they're the only person measuring it.

Product managers need to take full accountability for failures. This role holds decision-making power for the product direction, but the product manager acting alone will never be enough to guarantee success. That's why involving others is critical to acquiring relevant perspectives and identifying promising opportunities.

The question is, how should you share the results? You can drop a message to everyone involved saying, "Hey, please have a look at our cool product dashboard." The moment you do that, people will get confused because they lack the context you have.

Results alone aren't enough. They need context. That's where storytelling comes in handy.

In Chapter 7, I shared the story of my first experience with product discovery. When we reached the desired results, I didn't come to the business stakeholders and share the rough numbers we had. Instead, I invited them for a presentation to walk them through what we had uncovered.

You can follow a simple framework called PAS (problem, agitate, solution) to share results. You start by laying out the problem you're addressing, spice it up, and finally lay the solution down. Let me share what I did back then with the challenge I faced with that start-up.

- **Problem:** The car dealers didn't engage with our auctions, which led to low conversion rates and unsatisfied car owners.

- **Agitate:** We were burning money and struggling to find market fit. If we didn't make a change, we'd fail to prove market fit and struggle in a second investment round.

- **Solution:** After our late discoveries, we became hopeful. Car dealers connected to our value proposition but not to our previous product. Luckily, after pivoting from a mobile app to a web platform, engagement increased by 30% and our conversion rate skyrocketed. Continuing this growth enabled us to prove our product's market fit in a few months.

With this simple structure, I got everyone's attention. Then, I shared the results in a digestible way. After that, I gave them access to our dashboards as they understood why the metrics were progressing that way.

Bringing people to the same page as you is crucial for their support. You don't need to make things complicated. Ensure the context is clear and the message will speak to your audience.

Sharing results isn't something dry. It's about the product's story and how that matters to your audience. Don't assume people know what you know. That's why crafting the message is critical to getting your audience to listen to you. Otherwise, it's just about numbers, and nobody connects to that.

Pro Hints: Saving You Hours per Week

You're lucky because technology is highly advanced and unstoppable. You can benefit from modern tools and optimize your time. No, I won't recommend you use tools like ChatGPT to make decisions because I'm not convinced that AI tools can replace human expertise. I may change my mind as I acquire more experience with such tools, but for now here are three tricks to save you valuable time:

- **Scheduled reports:** I recommend you look at your dashboards once a day. To optimize your time, you can have the most critical reports scheduled for you and the other relevant people once a day. This approach will ensure you don't forget to look at them.

- **Alerts:** You don't want to realize something went off track only after the problem becomes unbearable. To avoid that, you can set up notifications when certain deviations happen. The metrics will depend on your business, and you should decide on them. For example, if your conversion rate plunges from one day to another, that's a bad sign, and you could receive alerts for this situation.

- **Insights from AI:** Although I don't see AI entirely replacing human expertise, AI can considerably supercharge our knowledge. You can use AI to generate insights from your datasets to identify patterns, value drivers, and more. The more creative you are with your prompts, the more value your insights can collect.

Usual Metrics: The Bread and Butter of Analytics

I told you I wouldn't give you a list of metrics to use mindlessly. But I want to help you understand the critical ones for different aspects. This list is by no means a definition of metrics you must follow but a clarification of the usual metrics for various purposes.

You can use the information in this section as a high-level overview of potential metrics to help you measure the results that matter. If you'd like to go further and learn more about metrics, I'd recommend the book *Lean Analytics* by Alistair Croll and Benjamin Yoskovitz (2013).

Engagement: How Users Interact with Your Product

The following metrics will help you understand how your audience engages with your product:

1. **Unique visitors:** The number of unique users visiting your product. This metric is highly relevant for landing pages.

2. **Bounce rate:** Percentage of users abruptly leaving your website after visiting a single page.

3. **Conversion rate:** Percentage of users who go through a preestablished funnel and conclude a desired action (e.g., order a product).

4. **Customer retention rate:** Percentage of customers who continuously do business with you.

5. **Click-through rate (CTR):** Helps you understand the percentage of users clicking on a link, the CTA, or something else you wish to measure.

6. **Average session duration:** The average time users spend on your product per session.

7. **Return visits:** How many users return to your product.

Monetary: How You Play the Numbers Game

To understand the financial state of your product, the following metrics will help you:

1. **Monthly recurrent revenue (MRR):** Helps you understand how your revenue develops over the months.

2. **Customer acquisition cost (CAC):** Helps you understand how much it costs to acquire new customers.

3. **Churn rate:** The percentage of customers who stop doing business with you over time.

4. **Gross margin:** The revenue percentage left after deducting the direct costs of getting your product into your customers' hands.

5. **Customer lifetime value (CLV):** How much revenue a customer brings you. You will have different ways to calculate this metric. The formats depend on your business model. For example:

   a. Subscription model: CLV = subscription price $\times$ subscription length.

   b. General model: CLV = (average revenue per customer $\times$ gross margin) / churn rate.

6. **Customer lifetime value ratio:** Shows the relationship between CLV and CAC. For example, a ratio of 3:1 is sustainable in most businesses. A ratio of 5:1 means you could invest in marketing and acquire more customers, but a 2:1 or 1:1 ratio shows your CLV and CAC are unbalanced and suggests you need to work on them immediately.

Activation: How You Convert Leads into Customers

Understanding how well you activate your users will help you grow your product value. The following metrics can help you with that:

1. **Sign-up rate:** The percentage of visitors you convert into users. This metric helps you understand if you're getting the right audience or if your message is convincing enough to potential users.

2. **Onboarding completion rate:** Percentage of users who complete your onboarding process.

3. **Activation rate:** Percentage of customers who reach a desired milestone.

4. **Feature adoption:** Helps you decide whether the feature should remain in your product. You can understand the percentage of users who benefit from it.

5. **Referral rate:** Percentage of customers acting as promoters by bringing their contacts to the platform.

These metrics are just some examples. My recommendation when you're considering which ones are right for your company is the same: Define what success looks like and work backward.

To conclude the tips for metrics: Start on a high level and then explore different angles—for example, regions, devices, genders, or age groups. A deep dive into your data will help you identify opportunities to improve the experience for particular audiences and uncover winners and losers.

Key Takeaways

- Use data whenever you can, but don't let a lack of data block you from making decisions. Even a bad decision is better than no decision. No decision gets you stuck, whereas a bad one creates learning.

- Differentiate laggard and leading metrics. Laggard metrics take a long time to measure, whereas leading metrics indicate whether the direction is right.

- Focus as much as possible on the metrics you can control instead of the ones you can only influence. That enables you to see a direct impact on your results faster.

- Understand the frequency with which you need to measure results. Looking at dashboards every hour will be more distracting than helpful.

- Share stories instead of raw data with your business stakeholders. Help them connect the dots instead of bombarding them with numbers.

This chapter addressed evaluating progress and identifying turning points to take action. We also approached the shared responsibility of measuring value, which may have intrigued you about who does what in high-performing product teams and what common misconceptions of different roles are. That's the topic of the next chapter.

10

Getting the Teams Right

> *"If you give a mediocre idea to a brilliant team, they will either fix*
> *it or throw it away and come up with something better."*
> —Ed Catmull

Getting the team right is paramount. In his book *Creativity, Inc.* (2014), Ed Catmull, former Pixar CEO, noted that a good team can improve mediocre ideas. Conversely, when your team setup is dysfunctional, collaboration suffers, and creating value becomes more complex than it should be. You maximize the odds of thriving once you have a team structure that fosters collaboration.

If you're a leader, this chapter will equip you to set up your teams to succeed. But if you can't change the team structure, you'll get the information you need to help leaders see what good and bad look like.

In this chapter, I will share what makes or breaks most teams and how each role can function well or poorly. Please don't expect an extensive guide to team management, but rather pointers on simplifying structure and roles within product teams.

Understanding what constitutes a sustainable dynamic with teams and meaningful deployment of each typical role is essential. Topics covered in this chapter include the following:

- Common product teams setup
- Roles and responsibilities
- Product managers versus backlog managers

- Software engineers versus coders
- Product designers versus pixel-perfect designers
- Agile Coaches versus Agile Rulers

Common Product Teams Setup

The team's skillset is a pillar of its success. When something is missing, dependencies grow, and delivering value gets more complex.

In the ideal world, teams would have all the skills required to uncover value drivers, experiment with solutions, and drive outcomes. That would enable them to progress without dependencies.

In the real world, it's common for teams to be responsible for specific tasks. For example, external teams perform quality assurance, user interface design, and other tasks. The more this happens, the less accountability teams have for their ultimate result. I imagine you may be in this situation. I know it's exhausting and tiring. After reading this chapter, you might want to invite your company leadership to reflect on different working methods.

The real world isn't always bad. Sometimes, you may encounter outstanding team setups, enabling steady value creation.

Have you ever worked in an empowered team? Such teams have all they need to transform ideas into valuable solutions. Leadership trusts them with problems to solve and lets them do the work. Collaboration and independence are the key aspects to enable empowered teams.

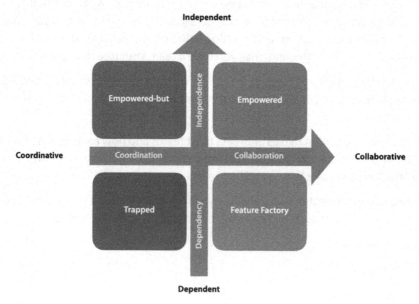

Figure 10.1
Different types of teams

Figure 10.1 shows several possible types of teams. First, let me clarify what each axis in this figure means.

- **Collaboration versus coordination:** As discussed in Chapter 1, teams face two usual working approaches: collaborative and coordinative. The first focuses on collaboration over processes and empowers teams to adapt to reality faster. In contrast, the second is tight to the process, and teams must coordinate to progress, leaving them with little space to adjust their approach.

- **Independence versus dependence:** How autonomously can teams create value? The more independent, the better. Sometimes, however, teams lack the skills to transform ideas into value, creating strong dependencies with other teams. The more dependent teams are, the more slowly they will deliver value.

Now that we have clarified what I meant by collaboration and independence, let's look more in-depth at each quadrant in Figure 10.1:

- **Trapped:** Teams working with a coordinative flow and strong dependencies are trapped. They can barely create output because they must coordinate their activities with stakeholders while lacking the skills required to deliver features. Being trapped is demotivating because teams talk a lot about how to get the work done but progress occurs very slowly.

- **Feature factory:** These teams have all the skills required to finish their work. However, they struggle to align with stakeholders as their development flow prioritizes coordination over collaboration. At best, they can ship features at lightning speed but will face a rigid process combined with output focus.

- **Empowered-but:** The development flow for these teams focuses on collaboration, enabling smooth decision making. However, the team topology creates dependencies between teams, diminishing their ability to deliver value. It doesn't take long for such teams to get frustrated.

- **Empowered:** Independent teams with a collaborative flow create value steadily. They have all it takes to work autonomously. These are the game changers. That's when the work gets exciting and outstanding products are born.

In Chapter 1, we explored the differences between coordinative and collaborative flows, which relates significantly to the collaboration axis in Figure 10.1. Teams' setup is critical to their independence, which leads to two types of teams:

- **Dependent:** Lack the skills required to transform an idea into value.

- **Independent:** Have all the skills required to transform an idea into value.

Dependent Teams: Disguised Waterfall

When teams depend on other teams to transform ideas into meaningful results, they become dependent teams. The more dependent teams are, the slower they become and the more problems they will face.

To demonstrate the disadvantages of dependent teams, let's consider an online shop with six teams. Four of these teams are focused on specific components of the product, and two are focused on disciplines—UX and QA. Each team has a clear responsibility and set of skills. Figure 10.2 shows how the teams are structured.

In this scenario, all product teams depend on UX and QA teams. This situation creates the following problems:

- **Miscommunication:** The dependencies require constant handovers, leading to broken messages.

- **Lack of responsibility:** Given their dependencies on UX and QA, no team feels accountable from end to end.

- **Decisions based on limitations:** Each team decides what to work on based on what their skills allow them to do instead of focusing on solving meaningful problems together.

- **Superficial domain knowledge:** Each team focuses exclusively on their responsibilities, and the dev team implements what is defined by UX and QA tests whatever they receive.

The more dependent teams are, the slower the business can grow.

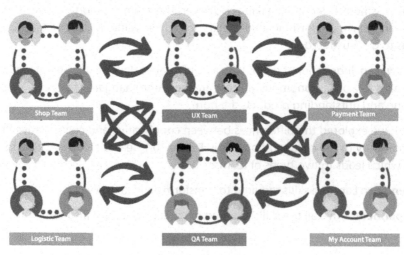

Figure 10.2
Dependent teams

Note: I used UX and QA for dependencies to illustrate the problem, but there are other disciplines to consider—for example, analytics and DevOps.

Independent Teams: Born to Thrive

When teams can create value independently, the results are often remarkable. Yet, it's hard to remove all dependencies and transform teams into independent ones. This change doesn't happen from day to night.

Continuing the previous team example, we would have four teams without dependencies when we convert the teams into independent units (Figure 10.3).

What does it imply to be an independent team? It means the teams have all the skills required to transform ideas into results. They are autonomous and do not need to sync their work with other teams or hand over tasks. Independent teams can create value at a steady pace when working with collaborative flows. That empowers them to focus on goals instead of coordination.

The core advantages of independent teams can be summarized as follows:

- **Accountability:** There is no room for a blame game because teams have all the skills needed to get things done and are accountable for end-to-end results.

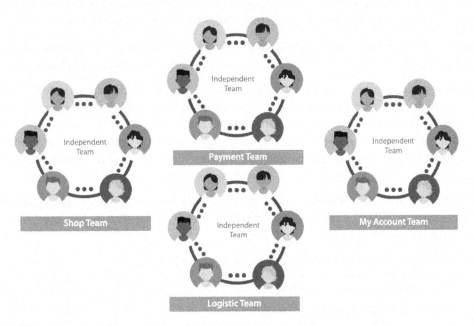

Figure 10.3
Independent teams

- **Speed:** Communication becomes straightforward, and there's no need for handovers.

- **Domain knowledge:** As all team members work toward the same goal, they continuously enrich their domain knowledge. The longer they work together, the faster they can discover valuable insights.

- **Focus on what matters:** Teams don't waste their energy begging other teams to prioritize their requests. They focus on creating value.

Obstacles to Become Empowered Teams

An empowered team benefits from independence and strong collaboration, enabling fast value creation. Empowered teams seem an obvious choice, but many companies still have dependent teams. Why does that happen? *One of the biggest obstacles is moving from an output orientation to an outcome orientation.*

Feature factory teams receive requests to fulfill, whereas empowered teams receive goals to achieve. The difference between these two scenarios is gigantic. Requests mainly require execution, whereas goals require a different strategy because the team must discover what works and doesn't.

As discussed in Chapter 1, the product development flow plays a critical role. Even when teams are independent, they will struggle to create value if they're working with a coordinative flow. That will transform them into a feature factory, rather than an empowered team.

A natural path from a highly dependent team is first to become independent and then to apply a collaborative flow. This approach paves the way to becoming an empowered team.

When teams move from dependent to independent, they will find it complicated to handle various activities simultaneously. For example, a UX designer might look at something far from what the team is implementing. How can that be combined with the other activities? When UX designers define everything alone, software engineers create resistance because they feel ignored and execute tasks instead of solving problems. That's when applying mindful product discovery, as discussed in Chapter 7, will solve this challenge.

Empowered teams face a dual-track agile approach during their development cycles. Some members may be working on the present, and others on the future. That enables them to quickly drop bad ideas and focus on the promising ones.

The following points are essential to creating empowered teams:

- Remove dependencies between teams as much as possible.

- Get the teams used to a collaborative flow.

- A dual-track agile approach is a part of empowered teams.

- Readiness to embrace the unknown is required. As discussed in Chapter 2, a growth mindset will accelerate learning, whereas a fixed mindset will limit the team.

The Importance of Team Size: Strive to Foster Collaboration

Smaller teams are more productive because collaboration flows naturally. The more team members there are, the more challenging communication becomes. The complexity scales exponentially. Figure 10.4 illustrates how the communication lines change as the team grows.

It's better to have smaller teams with a reduced set of responsibilities than bigger teams with more than they can handle. Two teams with five people will outperform one team with ten people.

Small teams can align faster than bigger teams. The bigger the team gets, the more complex alignment becomes, which inevitably leads to confusion, rework, waste, and slowness.

A mindful way of setting teams is as follows:

- Four to seven individuals
- All required skills available to progress
- Follow a collaborative development flow

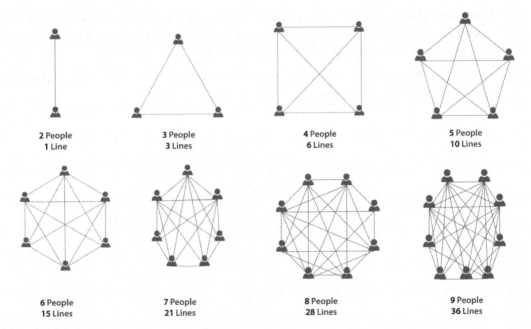

2 People	**3 People**	**4 People**	**5 People**
1 Line	**3 Lines**	**6 Lines**	**10 Lines**
6 People	**7 People**	**8 People**	**9 People**
15 Lines	**21 Lines**	**28 Lines**	**36 Lines**

Figure 10.4
Interaction complexity as the team grows

Roles and Responsibilities: Who Takes Care of What

Have you ever heard about the product Venn diagram? You may have stumbled upon one of the multiple versions already. Let me share my version with you and explain why it's critical for product teams.

The Venn diagram in Figure 10.5 has four main aspects: customers, business, tech, and integrity. What matters most is their intersections:

- **Waste:** It's easy to get distracted when exploring ideas. For example, if you find something desirable and viable, but it's neither ethical nor feasible, investing time in that idea will cause waste. The same would happen with other combinations that lack all aspects.

- **Promising but unfeasible:** Ideas that are desirable, viable, and ethical are promising, but you cannot deliver because you lack the capabilities. These ideas are good to revisit as your expertise develops.

- **Attractive but inviable:** When you identify desirable, feasible, and ethical ideas, you may consider investing in them, but you should be aware they won't create business value, at least in the short term.

- **Doable but undesirable:** These ideas can easily distract you. They are viable, feasible, and ethical but lack desirability. Investing in them will cause frustration and waste. Such ideas relate to business stakeholders' wishes without customers' desirability evidence.

- **Valuable but unethical:** This intersection is tempting because you can create value for customers and the business, but it would be unethical. I strongly recommend dropping such ideas unless you can make them ethically correct.

- **Sweet spot:** The intersection of customer, business, integrity, and technology yields ideas worth pursuing, and that's where you should invest your energy.

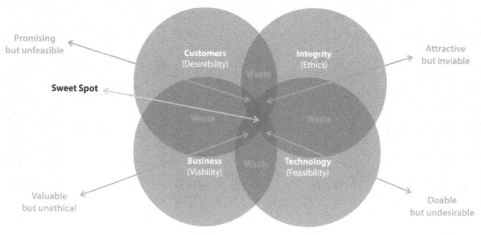

Figure 10.5

Product Venn diagram to find solutions worth pursuing

You may wonder why I'm discussing this Venn diagram in the context of roles and responsibilities. Let me shed some light. You need to have clear responsibilities for each aspect of this Venn diagram. You may believe it's clear, but nobody will take full ownership of the responsibilities as long as they remain unspoken. In most teams I worked, the responsibilities worked well when assigned as shown in Figure 10.6.

Let me give you more details about these roles and responsibilities:

- **Product designer:** Engage with customers to understand their scenarios and uncover value drivers. Strive to empathize with customers, learning their jobs, pains, and gains.

- **Software engineer:** Responsible for bringing ideas to life given the constraints presented. Ultimate accountability for the solution's quality and reliability.

- **Product manager:** Understand the business and collaborate with stakeholders to identify viable ideas. Product managers have the daunting mission of connecting the dots between all parts.

- **Product team:** Together, product managers, product designers, and software engineers create valuable and ethical products for customers and the business.

Accountability should not be an excuse to work in silos. Collaboration is fundamental to uncovering value drivers and creating the desired outcomes. Teams will have little to no chance to succeed when they're working in silos.

The accountability needs to be clear because teams will have conflicts on the way, and the responsibility for each aspect should have a higher stake in the decision. Here are some everyday situations that involve such conflicts:

- Software engineers disagree with product designers on the interface prototype.

- Product designers disagree with product managers on business prioritization.

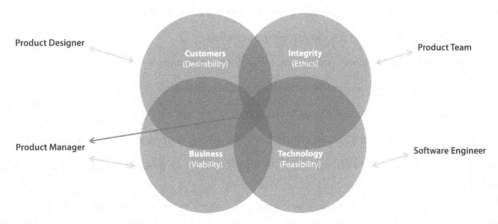

Figure 10.6
Venn diagram: responsibilities and roles

- Product managers push software engineers to cut corners and fit the implementation to the budget to make the solution viable.

Such situations are all too common, and trust is the solution for all of them. Once each role respects and trusts the other, collaboration gets simpler. I'm not saying that software engineers should never challenge designers, or vice versa, but rather that expertise needs to rank higher than opinions.

Another trap with team dynamics is the pursuit of consensus. When you're trying to please everyone, you end up pleasing no one. Consensus ensures the worst product option is selected and leads to slow decision making. High-performing teams trust each other and know when to disagree and commit.

Let's investigate each role, comparing what good and bad looks like in each case.

Product Managers versus Backlog Managers

A product manager is accountable for maximizing the value created for both the business and the customer. This definition is a common understanding of the job, but the biggest challenge is its complexity. Product managers don't code, design, ensure software quality, or set IT infrastructure, yet they massively impact how fast teams can create value. This is not to say the other roles are unimportant, but teams have little chance of creating value when the product manager role is misrepresented or misimplemented.

The corporate firewall is strong, and it's easy for the person filling this role to revert to a backlog manager and fail to live up to the responsibilities of a genuine product manager. That happens because of many factors, as discussed in Chapters 2 and 3. Here are the most common mutations of the product manager's responsibilities:

- Writing detailed backlog items versus uncovering value drivers
- Accelerating output versus maximizing outcomes
- Opinion-driven decisions versus evidence-driven decisions
- Planning by capacity versus empowering to pursue goals
- Trying to please everyone versus building partnerships
- Making compromises to avoid conflicts versus avoiding compromises by solving conflicts

The more you observe the behaviors on the left, the more of a backlog manager the product manager has become.

Product managers are authentic leaders, enabling teams to create value steadily. In contrast, backlog managers are uninspiring managers, guiding teams to create multiple useless features.

It's hard to be a product manager. Almost everyone around you will misunderstand your job, but your job is exciting and purposeful when you strive to meet its full set of responsibilities. It's also stressful and frustrating to be a backlog manager. No matter what you do, it's never enough. You see no value created despite doing all you can, and everyone seems disappointed with the results. The product world needs more product managers and no backlog managers.

Let me share my story about how I started transitioning from a backlog manager to a product manager.

Becoming a Product Manager

We reached all goals we had. Our founder was excited that we had proved our product's market fit and fought for another investment round. It took just a few months to get tens of millions of dollars invested in our start-up. But then we faced a mission we didn't know how to handle: It was time to scale up. That was a different game.

The founder informed me that my team would grow from 8 people to 25. I got scared because I was the only product manager and would remain that way for the following months, and I'd have to deal with three teams instead of one. I had no idea how to do that.

It was the end of the year, and we were all enjoying our achievements during our offsite meeting in the Dominican Republic. As I admired the inexplicable ocean's beauty, Michael, the most experienced software engineer, joined me and started chatting. "Hey David, how are you coping with the upcoming challenges?" That question got me, and I promptly answered, "I'm scared. I don't know how to handle three teams. I think it's more than I can take."

Michael looked at me and said, "I feel that. But let me share what's on my mind. You didn't ask, but I will share it. You've done a great job feeding the beast. With your user stories, anyone could work without talking to you, and we've progressed a lot. You nailed it. But this style isn't scalable. It's time to trust us more. Instead of feeding the beast, I want you to point us to a monster to slay and let us get the job done."

He got me. I reflected on his words for a few minutes before answering. The word *trust* made me realize I was doing the job that way because I didn't trust the team. I wasn't empowering them. I had to change to enable our next phase to be successful.

I will never forget that five-minute chat. It changed my life forever because I understood that my job wasn't to feed the beast, but rather to set the mission. That transformed me. I prioritized, decided on goals, and collaborated with the team. The backlog got smaller, but the results got bigger.

That's how I moved from a backlog manager to a product manager.

Untrapping Lesson: Empower your team to solve challenges instead of feeding them with tasks.

Returning to the complexities of being a product manager, we haven't talked about the elephant in the room—the product owner. Is it a different job than a product manager? Let me simplify that for you.

What Is a Product Owner?

Unfortunately, much noise surrounds the term *product owner*, which may confuse you. Some companies have a product manager working with a product owner, and others have a product manager being a product owner.

Let's start by clarifying the difference between product owners and product managers.

> *"Scrum defines three specific accountabilities within the Scrum Team: the Developers, the Product Owner, and the Scrum Master."*
> —*The Scrum Guide*, 2020[1]

Product owner is an accountability in Scrum, whereas product manager is a job. An experienced product manager is often the best person to take on the product owner accountability. Put simply, you cannot succeed as a product owner without solid product management expertise. That's the theory, anyway, although reality adapts in multiple ways.

Depending on your framework, you will find different types of product owners. For example, in Scrum, the product owner is responsible for the end-to-end product development process. However, in other scaling frameworks, the product owner is responsible solely for execution.

No matter which framework you use, the confusion between product owners and product managers still exists. I've seen many companies working with Scrum that have both roles. The question is, does it make sense to have both parts in the same context? From my perspective, it makes no sense at all.

A product owner or product manager, whatever name you want to call it, should carry full responsibility from end to end. How can you lead a team without being accountable for the whole picture? Take football as an example. Have you ever seen a successful team with two managers? Imagine one person is responsible for the team's strategy and another for the tactics. How would that work? It wouldn't. A blame game would potentially take over because leadership requires full accountability.

When product owners and product managers coexist, it adds unnecessary complexity, and the results are disappointing. Here are some examples:

- **Lack of responsibility:** When the team doesn't reach the expected result, who is held accountable for that? The product manager could say the implementation was faulty, while the product owner could say the direction was wrong.

---

1. *Scrum Guide*, 2020, https://scrumguides.org/docs/scrumguide/v2020/2020-Scrum-Guide-US.pdf.

- **Poor communication:** When product owners and managers coexist, the message tends to be distorted along the way. Product managers talk to customers, and product owners speak to software engineers. It's like building broken bridges instead of working as a single team.

- **Customer distance:** Within the coexistence of product owners and product managers, teams tend to behave as feature factories, putting them further from real customers than they should be.

Both names, product owner and product manager, suck. They don't provide orientation but instead create confusion. As a product owner, you're not the owner of anything; as a product manager, you don't manage anyone. I wish these names could be removed once and for all.

The name *product lead* better reflects the responsibilities the job entails. It's all about leading and empowering teams, and not managing anyone. You lead teams to create value as soon as possible.

Enough discussion about this topic. Let's explore software engineering.

Software Engineers versus Coders

One of the hardest parts of software engineering is its breadth. Creating a guide to determine what each team needs is impossible. Your context matters a lot. Sometimes, you need specialized expertise in machine learning, artificial intelligence, quality assurance, front-ends, back-ends, and architecture, among dozens of other names.

You won't find a software engineer who can do everything alone. Instead, teams have professionals with different types of expertise. Some focus on coding, and others on quality assurance, or infrastructure, or architecture, or security. The title varies across companies, but all of these software engineers must collaborate to thrive.

It's not within this book's scope to define all possible software engineering roles or to judge how companies set them. However, I will elaborate on characteristics contributing to a team's success or failure. Let me share the key traits of software engineering to help you understand what's beneficial versus detrimental:

- Implementing solutions versus solving problems

- Blindly following requirements versus mindfully understanding the context

- Avoiding responsibilities versus taking full ownership

- Accepting requests without understanding versus challenging what's unclear

- Limiting knowledge to the ticket description versus striving to learn from end users

- Resistance to stepping into the unknown versus curiosity and willingness to step into the unknown

- Writing code that causes problems versus crafting code that solves problems

The behaviors on the left side trap software engineers and limit their skills to coding, whereas the ones on the right side empower them to use their full potential.

It's challenging to be a software engineer. It requires understanding users and their problems and developing solutions for them. It's a lot of work, and many things won't click at first. Yet, being a coder is boring and unpurposeful.

Sadly, many talented people mutate into coders for different reasons. Some companies strongly emphasize features, plans, timelines, and other aspects, dramatically limiting software engineers' empowerment. From a product manager's perspective, I always encourage software engineers to reflect on how to solve problems because their potential to create valuable solutions is unprecedented.

You may ask yourself, "How might I empower software engineers?" I asked the same question several times and tried different approaches to solve this problem. One strategy worked well with me, and I'd like to share that with you.

Empowering Software Engineers

After I understood the difference between product managers and backlog managers, I started having conflicts with some of the software engineers. They'd challenge how I kept the product backlog because it wasn't detailed enough for their taste, and I refused to have the famous Definitions of Ready. Yet, I had to improve my relationship with those software engineers to enable us all to succeed.

Lecturing people on how to maintain the product backlog doesn't work. That was my first attempt, and it got me nowhere. But what did help me was understanding why software engineers needed that level of detail.

I was already in Germany, and one person annoyed me during every Sprint. "Hey, David. I cannot work on this story. I don't have the wireframes, and it's missing details." Once, I asked, "What do you need that for?" The answer was straightforward: "Because I'm not paid to design solutions. I code what's written in the story. If it's not there, I don't code."

This situation was frustrating to both sides. I said what came to my mind: "I believe you are better than me at defining the solutions for the problems I bring. You understand the product in depth and know how to connect the dots. When I define how you do your work, I limit your potential and don't want to do that. It would be unfair from my side."

I got the software engineer thinking. The real reason finally came to the table when he said, "What if I make a bad decision? I will get the blame, and I don't want that." I calmed him down: "There's no blame game. If something goes wrong, it's my fault because I set the context. When you make a bad call, it means I didn't give you the right context."

The software engineer was skeptical but willing to try. He asked if I could bring one user story, as suggested, and work closely with him to define the solution. I did that during the next three Sprints. After that, the software engineer got excited about crafting solutions, and we never had this trouble again.

Untrapping Lesson: Empowerment and trust are vital to collaborate with software engineers.

Product Designers versus Pixel-Perfect Designers

Over the years, I have worked with many professionals related to product design. Some were UX designers, others were UI designers, and still others were product designers. Some teams had one person with full responsibility, and others had separate interface designer and user experience roles. In my view, having full responsibility from end to end works better, because it removes the need for handovers.

A trend I've observed is having someone called a product designer who is responsible for crafting a meaningful user experience and interface design. Unlike when designers created high-fidelity designs and software engineers implemented them, now they create low-fidelity designs and improve them with the rest of the team.

Sadly, even today, I observe many anti-patterns with the product designer job. All too often, it becomes a pixel-perfect obsession, missing a relevant part of the job. Let me clarify the key differences in this critical role.

- Designing for business stakeholders versus designing for end users
- Creating experiences business supports versus uncovering what's natural for end users
- Pixel-perfect interfaces pleasing stakeholders versus intuitive interfaces end users love
- Lack of customer understanding versus empathizing with customers
- Fear of testing imperfect solutions versus testing multiple solutions to learn quickly
- Defending high-fidelity prototypes versus representing the user experience

The behaviors on the left side block product designers from doing their actual job, whereas the behaviors on the right side enable them to thrive. Product designers create what users love and business stakeholders accept, whereas pixel-perfect designers craft designs business stakeholders love and users don't understand.

The organization may be unprepared to support product designers, but taking that status as unchangeable will weaken the teams' ability to create value. True product designers craft intuitive designs that are natural for users. They strive for pleasant experiences instead of perfect designs.

Agile Coaches versus Agile Rulers

Do you need an Agile Coach? I can imagine you asking this question. The answer depends on what you want to achieve as a team and which expertise you have available. Let me ask you some questions:

- Do your stakeholders push you to deliver features or trust you to solve problems?

- Do your software engineers focus on receiving requirements or learning the context?

- Are the teams' results questionable or highly satisfactory?

- Are there open conflicts with the team, or can the team solve them without help?

The more of your answers that appear on the left, the more a savvy Agile Coach can help you. Unfortunately, it's hard to find a qualified Agile Coach who can get the job done, but it's all too easy to find someone who can misimplement an agile framework.

I've seen many mutations of Agile Coaches over my life, ranging from the team's secretary or assistant, to its gatekeeper, therapist, or delivery manager. But the worst results happen when the Agile Coach evolves into an Agile Ruler. Here are the extremes you need to be aware of:

- Obsession for frameworks versus focus on finding better ways of working

- Forcing abrupt changes versus fostering a step-by-step journey

- Blocking external parties from interacting with teams versus guiding external parties to enhance collaboration

- Disputing with product managers versus mentoring product managers to empowering teams

- Giving more answers than questions versus providing more questions than answers

- Defining how the team works versus coaching them to grow

When teams observe the behaviors on the left side, they will assimilate to the Agile Ruler, whereas the behaviors on the right side reflect the influence of an Agile Coach. One is unwelcome to teams; the other is highly accepted.

Agile Coaches help teams reach their highest level of performance, whereas Agile Rulers force teams to implement frameworks they don't understand. An Agile Coach will face endless challenges with the organization and team but will ultimately make them better.

Wrapping up this chapter, it's about improving collaboration and not about deploying an agile framework. Use frameworks when they help you and ditch them when they distract you.

Key Takeaways

- Empowered teams are born from independence and a collaborative development flow. They have all the necessary skills to transform ideas into value and work fluidly, focusing on collaboration over coordination.

- No matter what your role in a product team, you may potentially fall into anti-patterns. That's fine. The transformation happens when you are curious about different working methods and strive to learn from how others fill their roles.

- Product teams don't need to have several roles. The fewer roles you have in your team, the easier the collaboration becomes. What matters most is clear responsibilities and transparency with everyone.

- Product managers, software engineers, product designers, and Agile Coaches will struggle to do what they should. It's incredibly easy to fall into anti-patterns and derail into faulty roles. Understanding the difference between the good and bad sides of each role is crucial; with that knowledge, you can foster change.

- Be careful with silos. Roles set clear responsibilities but shouldn't get in the way of collaborating. The team should be greater than the sum of its parts.

We've reached the end of this chapter. We explored different team setups, roles, and responsibilities, and common anti-patterns. You're unlikely to find an organization that is totally free from anti-patterns, but now you know what to look for and what good looks like. That should empower you to foster changes.

At this point, you may be thinking about how you can encourage people to change teams or how they collaborate. That's easier said than done. Let me tell you the secret: It's about building relationships, and that's the topic of our conversation in Chapter 11.

11

Building Solid Relationships

Product professionals cannot thrive without meaningful relationships. That's the foundation of collaboration. Up to now, we have explored different aspects of working with product teams. In certain ways, we touched on the importance of building relationships, but not deeply enough.

I used to think that building the product was the biggest challenge of product management. It takes a lot of energy to understand what to focus on, and then you realize it doesn't work and you need to change it. On top of that, technology evolves at a fast pace, so your product quickly becomes outdated. Building a product is exhausting but not the most daunting aspect.

People and their collaboration is the most complex part of bringing an idea to life.

It's all about people. It's not about the framework you use, your tech stack, or your product strategy. It's about how people collaborate.

Building relationships is what makes or breaks product teams. Without sustainable relationships, you get no customers, business support, team commitment, or meaningful product. You may think your business is about building products, but I daresay it's more about building relationships.

In this chapter, I'll share my takes on building relationships and the critical aspects of dealing with different stakeholders. We'll also explore how to reach alignment internally and externally. Here are the topics we'll cover:

- Who the stakeholders are
- Power and interest

- Sharpening communication

- Setting alignment

- Where the magic happens

Who the Stakeholders Are

I've got a confession. I hate the term *stakeholder* because it's one of the most misleading words I've ever encountered. It's an umbrella term that relates to anyone or anything with any interest in or relation to the product. For example, the customer, a third-party system, an accountant, a software engineer, or an investor are all stakeholders. I don't think it's mindful to put everyone in the same bucket and call them stakeholders.

Clarity matters. I prefer categorizing stakeholders instead of getting trapped by this terminology. For example:

- **Business:** Anyone from the company with an interest in the product.

- **Customers:** Those who acquire the service.

- **Users:** Anyone or anything (yes, systems can use your product) using your product.

- **Externals:** Any external entity that has an interest or influence in your product.

Over the years, I've learned the importance of differentiating business stakeholders from customers. Typically, business stakeholders define what gets built without testing it with customers. Yet, that's a trap, because the wants of business stakeholders often misalign with customers' needs.

Business stakeholders aren't your customers unless you care for internal products. But they aren't your enemies, either. They're your partners. It's naïve to believe product teams have all they need to create valuable products. Teams need support from business stakeholders to thrive. That's why building partnerships is mandatory.

Every product will have different people involved and interested in it. And that's the complex part because everyone wants something, and their wants will often conflict. Most of the time, the product team finds itself in the middle of the crossfire, and it's got to figure out how to create a great product.

You won't find a precise recipe that solves the daunting challenge of managing expectations from business, customers, and everyone else. But working collaboratively (see Chapter 1) and having a sound product strategy (see Chapter 5) will pave the way for success. It's about fostering collaboration and progress in the same direction.

Power and Interest: How to Improve Collaboration with Business Stakeholders

Understanding business stakeholders is fundamental to collaboration. When you're equipped with such an understanding, you can avoid ending up in dreadful situations. The bigger the organization, the bigger this challenge will be.

It's natural to be in a situation where business stakeholders have many wishes, and you cannot deliver on all expectations. That's why prioritization becomes a nightmare. Pleasing everyone is impossible. You've got to align on what makes more sense now and say no to all the other initiatives.

Some business stakeholders will swallow the bitter taste of prioritization easily, but most won't. Keeping the relationship sustainable with all of them is almost mission impossible. The first step is to map the business stakeholders and understand their power and interest in your product.

In 1991, Aubrey L. Mendelow created the stakeholder matrix[1] to enable teams to define how they would behave with the different stakeholder categories. Even though he conceived this matrix three decades ago, I still see its relevance today. My adapted version of the stakeholder matrix appears in Figure 11.1.

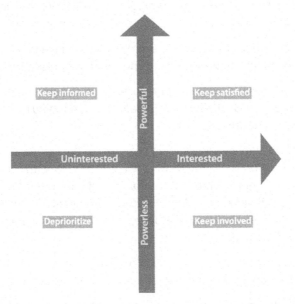

Figure 11.1
Stakeholder matrix adapted by David Pereira

---

1. Read more about Mendelow's stakeholder matrix: https://fourweekmba.com/mendelow-stakeholder-matrix/.

Filling out this matrix can help you clarify your situation and define how you act with business stakeholders. But before we examine each cluster, let me shed light on power and interest—the two axes in Figure 11.1.

Powerful business stakeholders can stop your initiative at any time or influence someone who could do it. For example, the CEO of your company is a powerful stakeholder. In contrast, a business analyst is often powerless.

When it comes to interest, it's more complicated. Some business stakeholders may be interested in your product or initiative for financial reasons. Maybe their bonus depends on your product's performance, or your product directly impacts their work. For example, the marketing team will be highly interested in your product's new features because that enables them to connect with the audience, advertise what's new, and drive traction. In contrast, the chief marketing officer (CMO) might be uninterested because they're thinking more strategically than tactically.

Let's explore each of the clusters shown in Figure 11.1:

- **Keep satisfied:** The people who are powerful and interested in your product are the ones to collaborate with closely. Alignment with them is fundamental for your success.

- **Keep involved:** The people who are lacking in power but highly interested in your initiative can help you progress because they value what you do. Keep them informed. Ensure they know what you're doing and how you're progressing. But make no mistake, you should rank their influence and interests lower than those of the people you've got to keep satisfied.

- **Keep informed:** Powerful but uninterested business stakeholders should be aware of what's going on. You need to ensure they know your progress and results.

- **Ignore:** You don't need to engage very closely with the people who are powerless and uninterested in your product. Identifying them is crucial so you don't spend your time and energy on these relationships.

These clusters are helpful and will give you an overview of the business stakeholders and ways to collaborate with them. I used this matrix for a while, but I missed the stakeholders' attitude— because that would hint where I had work to do. Attitude matters a lot. Some people will be supportive, and others will work against your efforts. You need to know who those people are and how to engage with them in a way that benefits from the positive ones and gets the negative ones to a neutral state, at least.

To visualize the attitude of each business stakeholder, I use colors. Figure 11.2 shows an example of a stakeholder matrix highlighting the various stakeholders' attitudes.

Once you see a matrix like this, you can reflect on the immediate actions you could take. For this example, I'd do the following:

- Talk to Josef to understand his concerns and act to get him on your side.

- Peter is skeptical while he's interested and powerful. Strive to understand his skepticism.

- Talk to Harold to understand his position and get him to a neutral state.

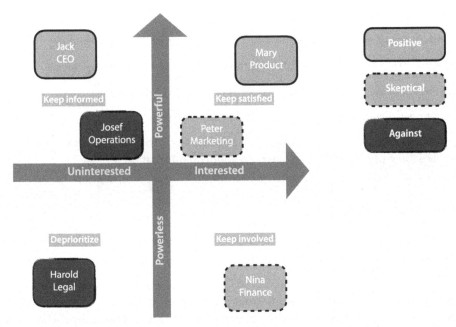

Figure 11.2
Stakeholder matrix including attitudes

The stakeholder matrix should enable you to define actions to improve the relationships. But the matrix isn't an excuse to treat people differently. Collaboration requires treating everyone at eye level and striving to build partnerships.

Sharpening Communication: How to Ensure Shared Understanding

How do you ensure the relevant messages get to the right people and they understand what you mean? This question has no simple answer. Conveying a message is complex while confusing others is easy.

Consistency is fundamental. You must consistently transmit your message to your audience in all mediums, whether speaking, writing, or sharing a presentation. Do you see how complex that is?

Over the years, I learned the importance of creating a system to communicate and distribute information on demand. For example, you shouldn't overload top management with details they don't care about, but you should have those details ready if they ask you to share.

Here are examples of how to fail to communicate:

- Send a colossal email to everyone who you aim to communicate something
- Invite as many people as possible to a meeting and share everything verbally
- Create a slide deck with dozens of slides and send it to everyone

These actions will guarantee your message doesn't come across.

It's key to adapt the communication methods depending on the message you want to convey. Let me share three useful practices to sharpen your communication.

1. Transparent Information

Make the overview of your work transparent. Imagine a world where nobody needs to ask you what teams are working on because they can get answers by themselves and understand where teams stand.

For example, having your product roadmap available to everyone is great. The roadmap can be accessible as a high-level overview, and if someone wants to know more, they should be able to see it. Many tools enable you to do that, such as airfocus and Jira. For B2B companies, you can create a visualization for business stakeholders and a different one for customers if you don't want to share everything with them.

If you don't have enough transparency, people will keep dropping emails or constantly ask you where the team is and how it is progressing. Of course, interaction is necessary, but you need to optimize your time and reduce dependency on team members.

Transparency helps with relationship building, whereas lack of it creates mistrust.

2. Sharing Progress

The more interested business stakeholders are in your product, the more they want to see progress. You can solve that by having frequent product demos where you show what you've created so that interested stakeholders can glimpse the upcoming focus. But what about the other business stakeholders, who are not so interested in your product but have a lot of power? You want your progress message to come across. Different solutions will be appropriate depending on the company's size and culture.

In start-ups and pragmatic companies, you can have product updates in your company's communication tool (e.g., Slack, MS Teams). Don't limit yourself to that medium, though, because such messages get lost. You can go classic with a brief email sharing the progress, results, and next steps. You may elaborate on details but ensure the first two lines of the message offer the most value because not everyone will read the rest.

It's your job to build a shared understanding. Without it, you will struggle to gain support.

3. Structured Meetings

The word *meetings* is becoming increasingly negative. Many people are locked into meetings for most of their working time and are frustrated by achieving little.

Meetings aren't evil. Unstructured meetings are evil.

I'm dogmatic with meeting preparations. I reject any invitation that comes without a goal. If I don't know what the meeting is for, I reserve the right to reject it. Meeting preparation is necessary to improve collaboration, and that's not hard. Here's what I do:

- **Goal:** Set the objective you want to reach by the end of the session.
- **Motivation:** Describe the reason for having the session.
- **Agenda:** Define the meeting structure and what you will cover.
- **Time:** Reserve adequate time for the goal you want to solve. Also, respect other people's calendars by not booking a meeting about a critical topic during their lunchtime. You don't want hangry participants.
- **Preparation:** If participants should prepare, inform them in advance.
- **Participants:** Mindfully select the participants who can contribute to the goal.

If you care to prepare, you will save yourself and others valuable time. As a result, you will create more value.

Another aspect is to ensure understanding. Don't be shy about taking notes and sharing them with the participants. That contributes to reaching a shared understanding. After the meeting, share the notes and ask if any participant thinks anything is missing or sees it differently. A simple notes review can avoid confusion and save you plenty of time.

The last aspect is about taking action. The result of the meeting shouldn't be scheduling another session. This outcome is a sign of a poorly prepared meeting. You may fail to reach the goal during the exchange but should have identified actions. Ensure to set them precisely. My format is "Who does what by when," where *who* is a person.

Establishing Alignment: No More Confusion

It's not about winning an argument. It's about collaborating and progressing. The best option for the product wins, and it doesn't matter how that came to the table. It's not about who's right and who's wrong. The goal is to serve customers and collect value for the business in exchange.

When I started my career as a product manager, I didn't know how to explain my job. Eventually, I found an honest answer. I talk to people. That's what I do—day in, day out. I speak to many people about different topics. Success materializes from aligning with all these people and ensuring we progress together in the same direction.

Never underestimate the challenges behind establishing alignment. That means you must understand others, uncover conflicts, and address and solve those disagreements. It's complex but motivating.

To establish alignment, you need to do your homework. We discussed the right ingredients, which are essential for alignment, in Chapter 4. More often than you might imagine, you will encounter opportunities to derail from your goals, and business stakeholders will come up with conflicting requests. You can avoid conflict by doing a little bit of everything for everyone, but that won't help you create a valuable product. Or you can make your problem their problem. To illustrate that, I will share a story with you.

The Monthly Business Stakeholders Fight

I was new to product management and dealt with demanding and powerful people. Everyone pushed me in different directions, and many of their wants contradicted our goals.

After several setbacks, I found my way of solving this challenge. In the usual scenario, I talked to business stakeholders separately. I noticed that wasn't helpful, so I decided to get all of them in one room once a month and discuss prioritization.

During our first session, I said, "We're here today to agree on what to do next and what not to do. Our current biggest challenge is keeping our customers. They come and go too fast. And we have no profit. I've compiled your requests, and I want you to help me understand which will get us closer to solving our current challenge."

After setting the stage, I stayed quiet and waited until someone broke the silence—the longest 30 seconds of my life. But finally, someone spoke up: "Ignore my requests. They aren't helpful to what you mentioned." Then the head of customer service said, "Our customers are complaining a lot about our delivery time. We should do something about it." That was the moment the meeting heated up. The head of operations shared, "Of course. Someone changed the delivery time from five to three days without talking to us. Now we have more orders than we can handle and don't deliver anything on time."

The marketing director who made that decision was in the room and stayed quiet but seemed annoyed. After a few minutes of discussion, she said, "How are we supposed to drive revenue up? We had to give customers a reason to buy. So, we promised faster deliveries." Then, the problem became apparent.

Departments had conflicting goals, and they put me in the crossfire. Yet, we had to prioritize what mattered most at that moment. After some rounds of discussion, I got what I needed. The operations director said, "Okay. That's what we do. And the rest is for later." And the others shook their heads in agreement. At that moment, we reached the alignment I strived for.

This type of meeting occurred once a month for a year, giving me space to do better work. In the beginning, the decisions were output oriented. We defined features to pursue, which eventually trapped us, but my lack of knowledge didn't help back then. Over time, we prioritized direction and outcomes, letting us discover what would create value. The point is to get key business stakeholders together, and to help them collaborate and support you in pursuing a single direction. That's alignment.

Untrapping Lesson: Don't try bridging communication between multiple business stakeholders; strive to build alignment among them.

Breakthroughs Occur with Real Interactions Instead of Shallow Ones

"Humans are social animals. We seek belonging."
—Simon Sinek[2]

Did you know humans are social animals? Sometimes, I forget that.

Interacting with each other is vital for us, but since the COVID-19 pandemic, our reality has changed. Many professionals work entirely remotely without ever interacting with their colleagues in person. Others have a hybrid mode with only a few touchpoints. This scenario makes it daunting for us to build relationships.

Remote work isn't the same as collaborating in person. Humans are more open to collaborating when we know each other better. I understand some people prefer separating their private lives from their work, but even then, exchanging ideas in person is powerful.

When I worked in the office, I'd have an idea, and then I'd get a few colleagues together and talk about it over a cup of coffee. Most of the time, I dropped the idea, but sometimes I improved and pursued it. The result was impressive. We'd have open exchanges without a strict agenda. We had no rules apart from enjoying coffee and listening to each other.

But now something has changed. Today, when product managers have an idea, they probably search for a slot and then schedule a meeting to discuss it and use it to share their thoughts.

---

2. Sinek, Simon. "Why We Form Tribes." YouTube Channel, 2020. www.youtube.com/watch?v=z8EVzdCBvoA.

That kills excitement, and it becomes mechanical. Breakthroughs happen when we act spontaneously.

Even in the digital era, it's important to remember that we're social animals. We value appreciation, and we can barely collaborate without trusting each other. The following practices are valuable for building relationships in remote or hybrid work modes. They create opportunities to help each other and develop bonds:

- **Random one-on-one:** Have random virtual coffee dates. Once a week, assign random chats with people and have a 15- to 25-minute conversation. This chat helps build bonds and strengthen collaboration. To make it better, avoid work-related topics. Knowing each person as a human being will help to build a bond.

- **In-person exchange:** Create opportunities to have exchanges in real life. They can be quarterly events or monthly get-togethers in the office. Ignoring that need for in-person contact tends to create distance between people and gets in the way of meaningful collaboration.

- **Spontaneity:** Try acting as spontaneously as you can. For example, do what you do in the office when you have an idea. Maybe you just start a call and share what's on your mind with someone. Make it simple. Prioritize collaboration over coordination.

Communication and collaboration don't need to be structured all the time. You don't have an agenda when you have dinner with your family or hang out with your friends. You don't plan everything upfront. You just interact with people and naturally strengthen the connections. A mechanical collaboration won't help you create meaningful products. But a valuable relationship will pave the way to thrive.

Don't be afraid of calling people out of the blue. Be afraid of losing authenticity.

When meaningful relationships are combined with the right ingredients explored in the previous chapters, you're ready to deal with the challenges you face. This chapter concludes Part II of this book, but we're still not finished simplifying what gets unintentionally complicated.

Key Takeaways

- Don't put everyone in the same bucket, because that will complicate collaboration. Separate business stakeholders from customers, and categorize them into clusters according to their power and interests.

- Business stakeholders are neither enemies nor customers. They are your partners.

- Communication is vital to your success. Ensure you adapt your style to your audience and strive to build alignment and shared understanding.

- Face-to-face engagement is a powerful way of building relationships. It's possible to collaborate remotely, but developing a meaningful relationship is better achieved through in-person exchanges. Adapt your practices according to your situation, but don't forget that we are social animals.

Once you've started steadily creating value, the traps won't disappear. On the contrary, they will come back you once you relax. To help you remain untrapped, I'd like to share some beneficial practices like setting product principles and running health checks. These are the topics we will explore in Part III.

PART III
REMAINING UNTRAPPED

"Growth has not only rewards and pleasures but also many intrinsic pains and always will have. Each step forward is a step into the unfamiliar and is possibly dangerous. It also means giving up something familiar and good and satisfying."
—Abraham H. Maslow, *Toward a Psychology of Being*

The last part of this book gives you the tools you need to remain untrapped. This part opens with a discussion of the importance of product principles and ways to craft your own. Then, we move to a sequence of health checks to help you understand where to act. We also consider how you can examine the efficacy of product management in your organization. We close Part III by exploring how you can assess product discovery and delivery to understand their effectiveness. By the end of this part, you should have a well-equipped toolbox to keep your teams untrapped while steadily delivering value.

PART III

REMAINING UNTRAPPED

12

Establishing Product Principles

Should you sit back and rest once you reach a stable level with your product teams? I'm afraid the moment you lie back, the traps we discussed earlier in this book will return in full force. It's one thing to defeat dangerous traps; it's another thing to remain untrapped. That's where product principles can help you.

Have you ever had the feeling that you're discussing the same topic over and over again? No matter where I worked, I frequently faced endless discussions about the same issues. Here are some questions I often stumbled upon:

- Who should we prioritize, the business or customer side?
- Should we build it right from the beginning or focus on accelerating learning?
- What matters most, quality or quantity?

Over time, I realized that such questions are important but tend to distract teams from progressing. Instead of evaluating what they have to do, teams often return to some basic questions. That's a sign that grounding principles are lacking.

The challenge of principles is that context matters, so you'll need to set the relevant principles for your situation. You may use principles from other teams or companies as inspiration, but you will yield more commitment once you bring your own organization's traits into the mix.

I left the discussion of this topic to Part III because I see product principles as one of the key ingredients to ensure teams remain untrapped. Once you have established your guiding principles, you can use them to untrap your teams and keep progressing in the right direction.

Let's discuss how you can craft product principles that fit your particular situation.

Why Product Principles?

Getting stuck is annoying. You want to progress, but face roadblocks and sometimes don't know how to overcome them. Lack of guidance on decision making is a significant factor that slows teams down.

When teams don't know what makes a good decision, they discuss it until they reach a consensus. Such discussions can be lengthy and tiring.

Product principles accelerate decision making by making it clear what's more important. They enable multiple teams to follow the same guidance on decision making.

You may think having an inspiring vision, solid strategy, and compelling goal is enough to accelerate decisions. Those are certainly important factors and fundamental to ensure teams move in the same direction, but teams usually get stuck with making the daily decisions.

If you want your teams to avoid repeatedly talking about the same things, you better define guiding product principles.

How to Craft Product Principles

Teamwork is fundamental when establishing product principles. When top management sets the principles and forces teams to use them, such principles are unlikely to remain alive for long. But, when management and teams collaborate to develop principles, that will create buy-in and commitment from everyone involved.

Before crafting product principles, you need to take some time to reflect on your current situation. Understanding where you struggle with decision making is a good start. From there, you can reflect on principles that could help you accelerate that process.

A common mistake I observe is letting each team define its principles. That quickly backfires because when teams value different aspects, overall collaboration suffers. Product principles should be the same for every product team across the organization.

To understand your situation, reflect on the following questions:

- What's your ideal customer profile?
- What kind of experience do you aim to deliver?
- What's your ultimate success metric?

- What defines your quality standards?

- What's your unfair advantage?

- How do you ensure progress?

The answers to these questions depend on your context, and there are no right or wrong answers. What's crucial is to align them. Do this exercise in collaboration with your teams and leadership, and then you'll be ready to set principles.

To help you put this into practice, let me use an example from the start-up that aimed to help car owners sell their cars without bureaucracy. When I worked there, we struggled to make decisions because we lacked guidance. Coming back to the questions I suggested, the following would be our answers:

- **Ideal customer profile:** Car owners who want to sell their cars in less than a month.

- **User experience:** Ensure customers feel respected and valued even when we don't make a deal.

- **Success metric:** Deals closed per day.

- **Quality standards:** Mistakes are expected, but don't break customers' experience.

- **Unfair advantage:** Pioneering this business model in Brazil.

- **Ensure progress:** Use available knowledge to accelerate progress.

Product teams got together with the top management to produce these answers. The exercise clarified what was most important but didn't reflect reality in prioritization. The product teams agreed on crafting and presenting the product principles to management in a week.

In close collaboration with software engineers, product designers, and Agile Coaches, we came up with the following principles:

- Car owners even over car dealers

- Delightful customer experience in all stages

- Closing deals is what makes us successful

- Set one goal at a time and say no to distractions

- Progress today enables building the future

- Learn from mistakes, don't hide them

- Focus on customers over competition

It took us a few hours to come up with these principles. First, everyone participated in a silent exercise to develop their own set of principles. Then, we shared our suggestions and built on top of one another's ideas. We were confident that these principles would help us progress and avoid getting stuck in the same discussions. When we presented them to top management, they shared some concerns about flexibility but decided to green-light the principles.

Our agreement was simple: We'd step back and check which principle could help us when we got stuck. And whenever someone would break a principle, we'd name it and have a chat.

Before using the product principles, we constantly discussed which audience to prioritize. Some aspects would be suitable for car dealers and not so good for car owners, and we struggled to commit to one option. It was also hard for us to align on our most important success metric, which led to more discussions.

Setting principles means simplifying how you make decisions. Here are some tips:

- **A over B:** You want to see more of A than B, though B isn't irrelevant. For example, with the principle "Progress over analysis," you value progress more than analysis, but you're not discouraging analysis entirely.

- **A even over B:** Both A and B are highly important to you, and you'd need them well aligned to succeed, but when they conflict, you choose A. For example, the principle "Car owners even over car dealers" means you will do your best for both but prioritize the car owner when you face a dilemma.

- **A instead of B:** Only one side is accepted. For example, the principle "Establish alignment instead of pleasing everyone" rejects the attitude of pleasing everyone. Only establishing alignment is accepted.

- **Statements:** Each statement should reflect a desired behavior you want to see across teams. Be objective and use adjectives to reflect the quality you seek. For example, the principle "Delightful customer experience in all stages" clarifies that the customer experience is paramount and should be delightful.

The crucial aspect is understanding the principles and bringing that knowledge into your daily business.

How to Ensure Principles Are Kept Alive

Writing your principles on the wall won't get the job done, but using them will. The question is, how do you put the principles into practice? I'd say you have many possibilities for that. Let's explore three options.

1. Keep the Principles Alive in Your Interactions

No matter how you work, bringing the principles into your interactions is a good start. Connecting to my previous example, we struggled immensely with our assumptions. Our refinement sessions were an energy drainer because we talked and talked, but achieved little. So, we decided to start being mindful of our principles.

I remember our first refinement after introducing the principles. A software engineer began asking "what if" questions and suggested doing research instead of delivering anything. Then, our Agile Coach interrupted and said, "Progress today enables building the future." That caused silence in the room. After a seemingly endless 30 seconds, another software engineer said, "What about committing to create something simple and learn from it?" I was glad she spoke up. From there, we could progress.

Here's another example. The chief operations officer (COO) approached me and dumped several requests, which I would generally put in the backlog. Luckily, I had the product principles this time, so I said, "We agreed to work on one goal at a time. How do your requests support getting car dealers engaged with our auctions?" The COO showed resistance initially, but then stepped back and said, "You're right. That's the most important now. Please ensure the team doesn't derail from this goal."

2. Make It Interactive

You can use your product principles creatively. People are more willing to use them when you add some fun to it. The simpler it is to speak up, the more often people will do it.

In one organization where I worked, we crafted principles, but the teams ignored them because they felt it would cause a conflict. Making it fun was our solution. We designed cards for each principle. Participants could raise the related card whenever a principle could help us, or when someone broke a principle. This simple solution helped the group step back and reflect, which enabled us to simplify decisions.

3. Assess How Often You Use the Principles

Another aspect of keeping the principles alive is to measure how frequently you use them. When the team looks at the principles and evaluates how often they followed them or observed someone following them, it helps the team understand the status quo. After evaluating, you can discuss how the principles helped or let you down. Such learnings enable teams to strengthen the benefits of principles and encourage others to use them.

I recommend doing this review as often as necessary. From four to six weeks tends to be a good rhythm.

Whenever you get stuck, return to your principles and reflect on how they could help you. Use them, learn, and over time, make your principles sharper.

Evolving the Product Principles

It's natural that some principles will become less relevant with time and will need to be adapted. Yet, it's critical to understand that product principles evolve slowly. Changing your principles every four weeks signifies a major problem (e.g., lack of vision, poor strategy).

How do you know it's time to adapt your product principles? When one of the following events has happened:

- A change in the ideal customer profile
- Business model pivot
- New ultimate success metric
- Changes in the quality standards
- Introduction of a new audience

When you face one of these situations, you'll need to adapt your product principles. That's normal because the principles should help you simplify decision making in your context. You don't need to throw everything away; you just need to review your product principles and ensure they reflect your current situation.

You may benefit from tweaking some of your principles even when no change like the ones just mentioned happened. For example, if you've been working with your principles for three months and realize that following one of them always gets you in trouble, that's a sign the principle needs adaptation. Paying attention to the signs will help your team grow.

One mistake I see is continuously adapting product principles without actually using them. Some teams want to get to a state where the principles are perfect, but that will get in the way of benefiting from them faster. And the worst part is that shooting for perfection won't help you learn from practice.

It's not about memorizing the wording, but rather about fostering the desired behavior.

Principles That Helped My Teams

Throughout my career, I've worked with dozens of teams but ran around in circles more often than I'd like. One of the main reasons was the lack of principles to ease our decision making, but that changed once I learned the power principles bring to teams.

My current approach is practical. Whenever I join a team, I observe the dynamics. I pay particular attention to unspoken agreements and frequent confusion. Then, I observe what top management cares about. After learning, I can suggest crafting principles and making them live.

What I'm about to share relates to my experience, which has mainly focused on start-ups and scale-ups. These principles may be a starting point from which you can craft your own. However, I must emphasize that context matters—and it matters a lot.

Some challenges are very particular and require different guidance. For example, scaling up an online shop is entirely different from launching a new digital product for the healthcare industry. That said, let me share 12 principles that have worked in multiple teams I've encountered. I organized them into categories to simplify understanding:

- **Strategy**
    - Focus on the goal and say no to distractions.
    - Stop starting, start finishing.
    - Dare to take risks.
- **Discovery**
    - Start with what you know to step into the unknown.
    - First build to learn, then to scale.
    - Evidence talks louder than opinions.
- **Delivery**
    - Continuously measure the impact of your work.
    - Good enough is better than perfect.
    - Simplify whenever you can.
- **Collaboration**
    - Meet your audience where they are, not where you want them to be.
    - Establish alignment instead of pleasing everyone.
    - Focus on solving current problems over future problems.

1. Focus on the goal and say no to distractions (strategy)

Until you have a goal to rely on, everything requires your attention. It's essential to agree on one goal at a time because teams have no chance but to divide intro micro teams if you have multiple directions to follow. When you craft a goal and get everyone behind it, you can only say yes to what relates to the goal while saying no to distractions.

2. Meet your audience where they are, not where you want them to be (collaboration)

It's easy to complain that your audience doesn't understand you. In B2B, complexity increases quickly, and teams get frustrated because they face change aversion. Experience has taught me that meeting companies or individuals a mile away from them won't work because they won't listen. It's wiser to meet them where they are.

For example, if your company has worked with output roadmaps for a decade, teams won't understand how an outcome roadmap works. Shouting "That's the only way!" won't help you get their support, but leading them on a step-by-step journey will help them understand why moving to outcomes is better for everyone.

It requires patience to meet your audience where they are, enabling you to bring them on a journey with you.

3. Start with what you know to step into the unknown (discovery)

I dislike plans, not because they are bad, but because they are too abstract. I've been part of extensive planning discussions, and none led anywhere except to frustration. The more you plan, the more you speculate, which separates you from reality.

A mindful way to approach the unknown is to use your current knowledge to progress. As you advance, you step into the unknown and uncover opportunities, which enables you to adapt your actions based on learning while keeping your ultimate goal in mind.

As Maarten Dalmijn (2024) said in his book *Driving Value with Sprint Goals: Humble Plans, Exceptional Results*:

> The best way of dealing with friction is to work with what you do know to discover what you don't know—to start with humble plans that acknowledge how little you know and how much you expect to discover and learn. Those humble plans can then be adjusted as you gain confidence and discover and learn what's necessary to achieve your objectives.

4. Stop starting, start finishing (strategy)

The more activities teams have in parallel, the more inefficient they become. Unfortunately, this problem goes beyond efficiency. Creativity takes a massive hit when teams have to juggle multiple topics. Their minds become exhausted, and they can no longer maintain a deep focus.

Many people think addressing multiple topics in parallel is better than focusing on one at a time. But that's not the case. Suppose a small team starts working on three features at once. They will continuously switch contexts. Ultimately, they will finish all three features later. But, if they start with one feature and get it done, users can benefit from it, and the business collects its value faster.

It's vital to serialize the work instead of parallelizing it. Focus on one item at a time. That enables you to realize value earlier. It's a win for all sides.

5. Continuously measure the impact of your work (delivery)

I used to think that my job as product manager finished the moment we rolled out a feature live. I was wrong. The job is finished only when you reach the desired outcomes. It's a different game, as we explored in previous chapters.

Teams deliver outputs (features), but that isn't enough. What matters is the results those features create (outcomes). That's why teams need to continuously measure the impact of their work and adapt from there.

Your product becomes valuable when it makes users better at their craft. Here are some examples of products I use and why:

- **Grammarly:** It makes me a better writer.
- **Mentimeter:** It transforms me into a better facilitator.
- **Canva:** It makes me a better communicator.

I don't use these products because of their features, but rather because of how they upgrade my skills.

Focus on leveling up your customers, not just enhancing your offerings.

6. Dare to take risks (strategy)

Play it safe, and everything will be fine. That can be a choice, and the result isn't beyond mediocrity.

In primary school, we learned to color inside the lines, listen, and follow people with more authority than we had. That kept us out of trouble. But as adults, that kind of behavior won't unleash our full potential in creating digital products.

If teams are not facing any failures, they are not trying anything new. Avoiding failure will ensure you block your chances of innovation. If you want that end result, play it safe, and you'll get it right. Otherwise, dare to go against the masses. The people who dare to take risks are the ones who shape the future.

7. Establish alignment instead of pleasing everyone (collaboration)

It's wrong to believe your job is to please everyone. No matter what you do in a product team, your job is to create value from what you decide to work on. The challenge lies in establishing alignment with the parts involved.

Alignment means business stakeholders know why you do what you do and support that. They may be annoyed that you aren't working on their desired requests, but they follow your reasoning and understand it, which enables them to support you.

This principle is one of the hardest to live. Many business stakeholders will still perceive product teams as a support to the business and won't accept teams deciding what to do. Yet, mindlessly following business wants will quickly backfire when you realize that's not what users need.

8. First build to learn, then to scale (discovery)

The first version of your product will be wrong. Your first attempts to produce a feature that creates value will fail.

Creating value requires multiple interactions, which are a normal part of the journey. Failing to recognize that reality will lead to many perfect features that deliver no value.

It's necessary to accelerate learning time and reduce the costs behind it. That's why, with an attitude of first building to learn, once you have uncovered the unknowns and learned what drives value, you can make your product scalable.

This principle entails making sure your first product version or new features are technically over-simplistic. The team reduces test coverage to the bare minimum or even neglects it, knowing the feature would probably break when multiple users engage with it. Yet, you're able to create something in a few hours or days, reducing the learning cycle and accelerating your speed to adapt.

Following this principle enables you to drop bad ideas fast and minimize waste.

9. Simplify whenever you can (delivery)

> *"Problems are usually pretty simple. We just imagine that they require hard solutions."*
> —Jason Fried and David Heinemeier,
> *ReWork: Change the Way You Work Forever*

When I stumbled upon this quote, I got thoughtful. I had often made things more complicated than they should be. I remember having complex workflows in Jira. Whenever I had a chance, I would add new steps in Jira. I did that so often that I was the only one who could explain our workflow in depth. I made collaboration more complex than it should be.

One of the most underrated skills is the power of simplicity. To unlock the team's potential, you need to identify and simplify what is unnecessarily complicated. Such skills will make you stand out and unlock your team's potential. Most of the time, a great question to ask is "What could we simplify?" You'll quickly find many opportunities.

10. Focus on solving current problems over future problems (collaboration)

Some teams take risk aversion to an extreme. For example, when they find a solution for a problem standing in front of them, they engage in lengthy discussions about all potential issues the solution may cause. Yet, they don't have any future problems, and chances are good they won't face them.

It's essential to understand the consequence of solutions, but not to a point that blocks you from progressing. *What matters most is solving the problems staring at you over the ones you can only imagine.*

11. Evidence talks louder than opinions (discovery)

Opinions are good to hear and reveal assumptions, enabling learning. Sometimes, however, opinions drive the future, which is unwise.

Letting opinions guide you will inevitably get you into trouble. It's better to extract questions from opinions and then run experiments to gather evidence, because that enables you to progress in a meaningful direction.

Following this principle doesn't forbid anyone from having opinions. Instead, it encourages teams to gather evidence to follow or drop opinions. It's about learning and avoiding unpleasant surprises.

12. Good enough is better than perfect (delivery)

What's good enough? Sometimes, teams aim for a bug-free policy, which initially sounds nice but ends in nothing getting done. Of course, you don't want your product to include low-quality features, but when perfection becomes the goal, you can barely progress. Agreeing on what defines "done" is critical, but that should reflect your objective.

When you follow a collaborative approach aiming to create value incrementally, it's natural that the first versions won't be state-of-the-art solutions. Even so, they enable you to discover the gaps and improve the product quality.

These 12 principles have been game changers for me. I hope they inspire you to craft your own principles and pave the way for smoother decision making.

Key Takeaways

- Product principles set the foundations to accelerate decision making, by aligning multiple teams and identifying what characterizes a good decision.

- Craft the product principles in collaboration with leadership and product teams. It's a collaborative exercise to get buy-in from all layers.

- Use your product principles to untangle discussions and ensure progress during daily exchanges. Keep them alive and learn from experience.

- Slowly evolve your product principles as your situation develops, but don't switch principles every two to four weeks because that will cause confusion instead of guidance.

- Develop your principles based on your context. Using another set of principles is possible, but you will need to adapt it to your reality.

Continuing our mission of remaining untrapped: Sometimes, companies' dynamics may impact product teams and diminish their potential. In Chapter 13, I share a company health check and clarify how you can use that information to remain untrapped.

13

Assessing Your Company's Dynamics

Companies are dynamic and constantly changing because people come and go. It's important to understand what makes or breaks teams. For that reason, I encourage you to run a company health check every six months or whenever you join a new place.

I've been searching for the essence of companies that would enable product teams to thrive. After more than 15 years in this game, I recognize the following as the key aspects:

- **Leadership:** How leadership empowers teams and establishes alignment.

- **Product perception:** How the product organization is perceived and treated.

- **Product leadership:** How product leaders can influence the companies' direction.

- **Team topology:** How team topology contributes to empowerment and independence.

- **Risk tolerance:** How companies perceive and take risks.

Use the health check shown in Figure 13.1 to assess your company dynamics. The goal of the company health check is to create a shared understanding of the status quo and then to take action to transform it for the better. I recommend doing this check twice a year with different layers of the organization: product teams, middle management, and top management. In these sessions, ask yourself and the other participants, "How does our current situation help us reach our goals?" An honest answer to this question enables you to devise actions to improve your situation.

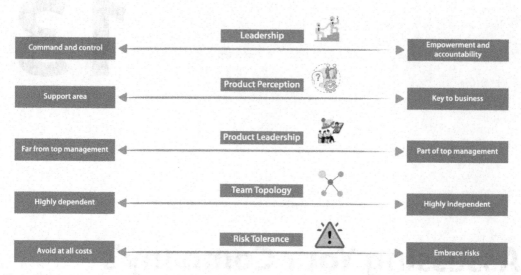

Figure 13.1
Company health check

Let's go into the details of each health check item in Figure 13.1

Leadership: Creating a Space Where Great Ideas Can Happen

Understanding and assessing leadership can be complex, and exploring the depths of this concept is beyond the scope of this book. Let me briefly evaluate leadership in creating digital products and suggest what good and bad look like.

Bad leaders will unintentionally lower the chances of success and increase the odds of unbearable failures. Good leaders will intentionally pave the way for success and diminish the odds of poor results. Bad leaders strive to make all decisions so they remain in control. They tell people what to do by when and how they should get it done. They often use this leadership style because they believe they know best how everyone should perform their job. Although that may be true, the role of a leader isn't commanding but guiding.

It's easy to be a bad leader and challenging to become a great one. And *it's nearly impossible to be a good leader from day one.* It's a journey from bad to good. The turning point will happen once you're open to feedback and willing to adapt your leadership style gradually. The higher you go in the organization, the less you should worry about how tasks get done, and the more you should care about setting the direction and the proper context all over the organization.

I'm genuinely passionate about product management. I love being a product manager, but that's not my job anymore. It's tremendously hard for me to accept I'm no longer the person getting things done, but rather the person charged with creating the space where things get done well.

When I first became a leader, I thought my job was to give answers and help product managers get their job done. But then I realized I was failing—because I wasn't helping them grow but diminishing them. When you tell people how to do their jobs, you're not helping them evolve, and nobody likes being told how to work. It hurts me to say that, but I was a bad leader before I could become a good one.

Good leaders don't worry about defining what gets done; they care about what the organization should achieve. They are humble enough to accept they aren't the people who know best how to do the job and trust their teams to do their best. Teams create outstanding results when they are empowered to bring their best selves to work.

Bad leaders set goals like this: "Deliver features A, B, and C by the end of Q1." This leader would continuously micromanage the team to understand their task-level progress. Bad leaders want to approve the look and feel of features to ensure they match their own understanding of quality. Teams become annoyed in this scenario because everything needs to be run by their majesty, the owner of quality standards.

In contrast, good leaders set goals like this: "Increase growth by 20% by the end of the year, even if that leads to a 10% increase in customer acquisition costs." Such leaders don't care which features the team is creating, nor do they require approval over the look and feel. Instead, they care about progress and the results teams have achieved.

On top of that, good leaders craft a guiding strategy that enables multiple teams to reach their goals cohesively and collaboratively. Bad leaders change direction every other day or give conflicting goals to each team, forcing them to compete against each other.

Good leaders take responsibility for their failures and learn from them. Bad leaders blame others and continuously repeat the same mistakes.

Good leaders hold teams accountable for their results while empowering them to get there. Yet, they remain available to help the teams overcome challenges and make trade-offs. They extend a hand whenever necessary and ask questions more than giving answers. They make tough decisions when required but won't tell teams how they should do their work. Instead, they ensure teams know the context and constraints.

The more command-and-control behaviors you observe, the less value that is created. The more empowerment and accountability teams receive, the more value they create.

Product Perception: Are You Ready to Thrive?

Are the following items present in your situation?

- Feature requirements

- Feature specifications

- Business approval to get features live

These items represent the old-fashioned way of crafting digital products. Software engineers, designers, testers, and similar roles worked to serve business stakeholders, who were the people calling the shots. Teams had to deliver what the business wanted, no more and no less. Teams lacked the power to decide what was worth creating and what was not.

Although that approach should be considered outdated, it's still present in many organizations. Unfortunately, this scenario isn't as fruitful as expected. When product teams serve the business instead of the customers directly, their results are watered down.

I've encountered awkward situations where product teams needed permission to talk to customers. In some organizations, the sales department or another area possessed the customer contacts, and only after their approval could product team members speak to end users. Yet, product teams were accountable for creating features for those customers.

This scenario sounds nuts to me. How can you create something for someone without the ability to talk to them directly?

The equation is simple: The farther product teams are from customers, the more waste they create. Let me be blunt: *Hiring highly qualified professionals and locking them in a cage is nonsense.*

I understand that all companies are different, and situations aren't the same everywhere. But I also understand that product teams don't have a crystal ball to uncover what works for customers without interacting with them.

A better approach is to treat product teams as key members of the business instead of a support area. In this situation, product teams are placed in the center of the business and are empowered to interact directly with customers. They can also determine which problems are worth solving and experiment with different solutions until they uncover what works for customers and drives value for the business.

Business stakeholders also play a critical role in this scenario. They may not set requirements and approve specifications, but they work closely with product teams to develop the conditions in which all of them can thrive. Product teams won't have all the answers for everything related to the business, such as legal restrictions, finance, operations, sales, and so on. But joining forces with business stakeholders enables everyone to thrive. It's not a competition; it's a collaboration geared toward achieving the same results.

When product teams serve customers, the business thrives and customers are satisfied. When product teams please business stakeholders, customers suffer and the business struggles.

Product Leadership: Coordination or Collaboration?

Is a product leader present in your organization's top management? The absence of a product leader in the management team will create many traps. Let me share a little story with you.

Product and Tech: A Necessary Tension to Create Valuable Products

When I arrived in the office on a cold winter day, the company leadership called everyone together for an unexpected all-hands meeting. The CEO shared the bad news: The company had missed all of its goals and had to lay off a third of its personnel. That entailed merging the product and tech teams, meaning the chief product officer (CPO) was removed from the management team and would no longer be part of the company. The chief technology officer (CTO) became responsible for product and tech. I couldn't swallow that change and felt I had to quit.

After the change, I started reporting to the CTO. I was skeptical about it but decided to try it—a decision I regret to this day.

Our roadmaps moved from outcomes to outputs. Suddenly, the CTO instilled a bug-free policy, and we had to focus on preventing any kind of technical debt. Yet, nobody was talking about the elephant in the room: Our churn rate was skyrocketing. When I told the CTO about this issue, she said she would take that message to the C-level alignment. Two weeks later, I heard that we had to focus on what was previously agreed. I was furious.

The CTO wasn't an evil person but lacked product management expertise. Tech and product are different. One depends on the other, which means that having one person wearing both hats will push too much on one side and fail the other. That's a sure recipe for disaster. That's why having a counterpart to balance the tech and product concerns is vital.

For a few months, I tried my best to help the CTO see what was necessary for the product and business, but she ignored me. I saw no choice but to quit. I couldn't accept reporting to tech and missed the product support from management.

Untrapping Lesson: Product and tech are complementary to each other. One should not report to the other.

I'm sad that this situation isn't unique. Even today, I see many companies with a chief product and technology officer (CPTO), or with the CPO reporting to the CTO, or even worse, with no CPO, and many product managers reporting to different business directors.

Until the product unit has a seat on the management team, product teams will waste their energy doing things unhelpful to create value. A product executive must be part of the management team. Without that, you should get used to mediocrity as the ultimate result.

Since my frustrating experience reporting to the CTO, I've no longer supported organizations not having an exclusive person representing product management in the C-suite. The reality is that the farther the product is from top management, the more trapped the product becomes.

Team Topology: Setting Teams Ready to Rock

Some teams are set up to thrive, while others fail. The first is the result of an intentional and well-thought-out structure, and the second is often an accident resulting from poor decisions.

To understand the impacts of team topology, you can explore two questions:

- How independently can your teams create value?
- How fast can you turn an idea into value?

Let me elaborate on each question by injecting an additional perspective from Chapter 10.

The first question relates to the skills the team has available to them. When teams lack skills, they face hard dependencies with other teams, which slows them down considerably. A classic example is having a team of product designers serving multiple teams. Its downsides include a lack of contextual knowledge, numerous handovers, and a web of dependencies.

In contrast, teams with all the required skills can create value without depending on any other team. It's a far better situation because each team acts autonomously. Even so, that's not enough to accelerate value creation. The team's focus strongly impacts their ability to create value, which leads us to the second question.

Transforming an idea into a feature is simple, but creating value for the business and customers is complex. Common ways of working focus on coordinating tech activities with multiple teams. For example, the team is responsible for components instead of a domain. Whenever teams work on an initiative, they must coordinate activities with other component teams to create value. This scenario is a bad situation to be in. Despite having all the necessary skills, such teams have dependencies on the application level.

The desired way of working empowers teams to focus on progressing instead of coordinating technical dependencies. The focus is clear, and each team member can create value without depending on other teams.

A mindful topology will include independent teams focused on collaboration over coordination. Team members will be engaged, motivated, and committed, creating more value for the business and customers.

Risk Tolerance: From Fear to Courage

How often do you stumble upon the following situations?

- Risk avoidance is more important than exploring opportunities.

- Risk analysis consumes more time than understanding customers' problems.

- Knowing the risks is mandatory for most initiatives.

- Teams do all they can to avoid risks.

The more intolerant to risk an organization is, the less innovative it becomes.

Innovation doesn't emerge from a genius who comes up with a breakthrough out of the blue. It takes a lot of small failures until someone comes up with an outstanding idea. That means taking risks and embracing failures with wide-open arms.

When I hear the question "What are the risks?," my standard reply is "What are the opportunities?" We need to look at both sides of the coin. Obsession with risks will, without a doubt, kill innovation chances.

You will stumble over two types of teams:

- **Optimistic:** Such teams say yes to challenges and then do their best to transform an opportunity into reality. They are excited to progress and make a difference.

- **Pessimistic:** These teams default to "no." When asked about an opportunity, they say no and seek reasons to defend it. Such teams slow down progress, complicating innovation.

Now, let me ask you a few questions:

Do you want to thrive?

Do you want to innovate?

Do you want to differentiate?

Do you want to stand out?

If you answered yes to any of these questions, you've got to take risks. Without that, you cannot thrive, innovate, be different, or stand out.

Taking risks means leaving your comfort zone and trying out new things, knowing that some will fail and you will get hurt. Nevertheless, along the way you will learn what enables you to achieve what you didn't even know to be possible.

I'm not claiming that organizations should be reckless and ignore risks at all costs. But I dare to say that risk management is overrated and can be simplified. Teams can focus on product discovery (read Chapter 7) and separate good ideas from bad ones.

Risk-taking means using what you know to uncover what you don't. The more willing an organization is to take risks, the more innovative it can be.

Key Takeaways

- It's unlikely any company will always be in the perfect state to thrive with digital products. Understanding which aspects contribute to success and which don't enables you to devise actions to change the game.

- Product teams will struggle to create value when they're perceived as a support area but will help the business thrive when they're viewed as a key part of the organization.

- Independent teams will outperform dependent teams—but that's not enough. Having a focus on something that enables value creation is fundamental. A mindful topology allows teams to create value without having tech dependencies on other teams.

- The more you avoid risks, the less you can innovate. However, ignoring risks will put you in undesirable situations. The balance between risks and opportunities is vital to success.

When we opened our conversation in this chapter, we noted that companies are dynamic. That's why stepping back and evaluating the key aspects of your organization is essential to understand where to act. But it's not the only part. In Chapter 14, we will continue our discussion by evaluating how effective the product strategy is.

14

Evaluating How Your Product Strategy Implementation Simplifies Decision Making

Product management is complex and easily misinterpreted. By now, you know the most common challenges across companies. You've also learned how to combine the key ingredients (discussed in Chapter 4) to overcome dangerous traps. Yet, even when you have all the right elements, you may end up in undesired situations.

One key issue is bringing the key ingredients to your situation. Another is getting the most out of them. It takes time to get things right. Even when you nail everything down, unexpected problems can arise. The moment you sit down and relax, the traps discussed in the first part of the book may slowly take over.

It's critical to continuously evaluate the status quo. Throughout this and the next two chapters, we discuss how to assess product management's key ingredients. This chapter focuses on product strategy.

Product strategy tends to evolve slowly, but you would benefit from quarterly health checks to uncover opportunities to sharpen it. Compounding the minor tweaks made across multiple quarters will strengthen your strategy.

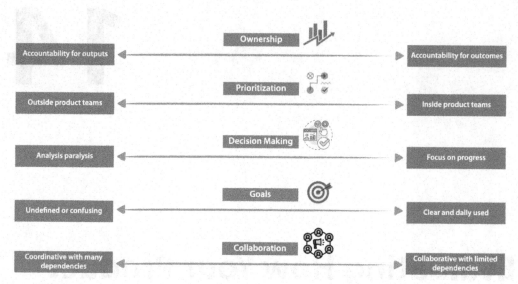

Figure 14.1
Product strategy health check

A sound product strategy simplifies decision making. Yet, that's easier said than done. Here are the fundamental implementation aspects to pave the way for success:

- **Ownership:** Are teams responsible for outputs or outcomes?

- **Prioritization:** Does prioritization happen outside or inside the teams?

- **Decision making:** Do teams focus on analysis or progress when making decisions?

- **Goals:** Are goals unclear or clearly set and used daily?

- **Collaboration:** Do teams have to coordinate tasks or collaborate to reach goals?

When answering these questions, the more of your answers that are found on the left side, the harder it is to create digital products. That means you should first address these aspects before considering frameworks. Use the health check shown in Figure 14.1 to uncover what your product strategy leads to.

Ownership: Clear Accountability, Better Results

Often, teams are accountable for delivering features on time and within scope. Meeting deadlines and roadmaps pleases management and business stakeholders. Yet, sooner or later, they may realize that business results aren't growing and customers aren't satisfied.

Features are worthless until end users can benefit from them.

When teams focus on outputs, the goal becomes delivering the desired features rather than reaching results. When that happens, teams will be busy figuring out how to technically create features while meeting deadline expectations. Sadly, they won't find time to run experiments to learn from actual end users and drop bad ideas soon enough.

Holding teams accountable for outputs will dramatically decrease their chances of success. It's a simple equation, but the solution is challenging. The more accountable teams are for outcomes, the better results they create. The more outputs matter, the more waste teams create.

Prioritization: Moving from Serving to Partnering

When teams don't have a say in the prioritization, their commitment will be lower, and the pressure from the business side will be higher. Such a combination is likely to lead to ugly results. To illustrate that, let me tell you a story about my software engineer journey.

The Pain of Being Left Out of Prioritization

Long ago, I worked as a software engineer for an automaker, and my team was responsible for an internal solution. We worked to automate processes and boost productivity. To define what I'd work on next, I had to wait for a business committee to decide. Sometimes I had no work to do, so I walked and talked to operators.

In one of my conversations, I learned that our automatic order sequence was damaging productivity because it forced frequent machine reconfigurations, which was time-consuming. The operator told me a different way would reduce setup time and increase productivity. Skeptical about it, I talked to other operators and quickly confirmed how detrimental our automatic order sequence was.

I had the solution in my mind and wanted to test it, but I couldn't: I needed to wait for the prioritization done by the external committee, whom I called the prioritization lords.

I decided to share my learning with the business manager who was accountable for prioritization. He told me it was not my responsibility to suggest roadmap items. I was mad because the problem was shouting in my face, and everyone else ignored it.

When we received the roadmap, nothing related to the automatic order sequence was there, despite our operators complaining about it to everyone they could. Instead, we had a prescriptive list of requirements we couldn't challenge. Some items related to features layout, which, in my eyes, couldn't rank higher than a productivity issue.

Untrapping Lesson: Prioritization without involving product teams leads to frustration and lack of commitment.

Decision Making: Progress over Analysis

How long do teams need to analyze something before getting hands-on? The tricky thing about analysis is that the more you analyze, the more you want to analyze. You will always find something you don't know and consider figuring it out before getting hands-on.

Let me share a story where excessive analysis created considerable waste.

Throwing a Month of Work Straight to the Trash

I worked for a marketing agency with thousands of employees across Brazil. An annoying challenge was to plan promoters' routes, defining which stores they'd visit each day. It was an exhaustive task performed by multiple analysts. We couldn't bear that any longer, so we decided to build a solution.

My first action was to analyze the current scenario. After I understood the situation, I invested roughly a month analyzing potential alternatives. Eventually, I finalized the specification of this functionality (around 70 pages) and handed it to a software engineer.

Surprisingly, the software engineer asked me a few questions, for which I had no answers. I felt embarrassed. What happened was simple: As the software engineer got hands-on, he learned different aspects of what I was only speculating about, and my lengthy specification quickly became obsolete.

Untrapping Lesson: Collaboration beats documentation.

A better alternative would be to share the challenge with the team and start experimenting with quick-and-dirty solutions. In the situation I just described, that would have enabled us to learn faster and correct our course.

Analysis obsession leads to illusion and low progress. Don't fall prey to the illusion of being in control. Prioritize progress over analysis; you will benefit from outstanding results.

Goals: Clarity on Where You Want to Land

When goals are absent, teams run in circles and see no purpose in their actions while struggling to prioritize what's relevant. But setting goals is complex. Let's simplify it with different flight levels:

- **Product vision:** Where you want to be in a few years.

- **Product goal:** What you want to achieve in a few months, getting you closer to your product vision.

- **Development cycle goal:** What you want to reach in one cycle that gets you closer to your product goal.

Now let me bring this down to earth by connecting it to the car dealers company I worked some time ago:

- **Product vision:** The fastest way to sell and buy cars for fair prices.

- **Product goal:** Enable car dealers to quickly find cars they want.

- **Sprint goal:** *Don't let dealers down! Let them know when their desired cars are in auction.*

This structure is simple because it breaks the goal down into workable chunks. The product vision would be too broad to work directly on, and the product goal is probably more extensive than a development cycle. Three levels of goals are probably enough to unlock progress.

The challenge is the longing for parallel goals. It's common to be pressured to commit to everything, which will mutilate teams and reduce value creation. I once got tired of dealing with this pressure and decided to ask the CEO to a coffee meeting because she was the main driver of parallel work.

I told the CEO I wanted her to do a foolish exercise to make a relevant point. I also said the activity wouldn't be longer than a coffee meeting as I valued the CEO's time. I took a piece of paper and a pen and asked the CEO to write from 1 to 10 on the first line and then from 10 to 1 on the second.

The CEO was in a good mood and said, "Okay! Let me see where you're going." I timed that with my phone. When the CEO finished, I asked her to alternate the order and write the lines again, and timed the exercise a second time. I saw the CEO slowing down during this round, but not that much. Then, I said, "Now let's add a third sequence, from A to J. Do the same—first time, line by line; second time, alternating between lines" (Figure 14.2). I timed both exercises.

Without context switching

Finish each sequence before starting a new one

1, 2, 3, 4, 5, 6, 7, 8, 9, 10

10, 9, 8, 7, 6, 5, 4, 3, 2, 1

A, B, C, …

With context switching

Start all sequences at once, alternate until you finish them all

Figure 14.2
Context switching exercise: in progress

When I looked at the CEO, I said, "You were 50% faster when you focused on one line at a time. And I noticed that you made some mistakes during the last exercise and had to scratch some letters and numbers" (Figure 14.3).

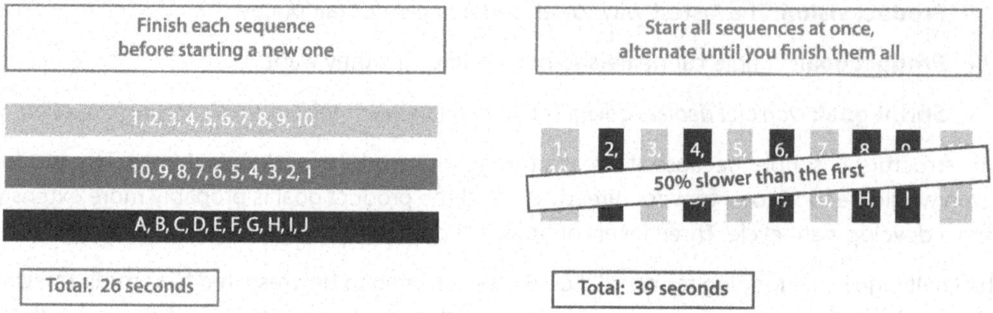

Finish each sequence before starting a new one	Start all sequences at once, alternate until you finish them all
1, 2, 3, 4, 5, 6, 7, 8, 9, 10	1, 2, 3, 4, 5, 6, 7, 8, 9
10, 9, 8, 7, 6, 5, 4, 3, 2, 1	50% slower than the first
A, B, C, D, E, F, G, H, I, J	
Total: 26 seconds	Total: 39 seconds

Figure 14.3
Context switching exercise: comparison

The CEO said, "My brain couldn't deal with this as fast as I imagined with all the sequences together." Then, I came to my point: "How do you think software engineers handle 17 complex roadmap items per quarter?" With this question, I got the CEO thinking, and she looked into my eyes and asked, "Am I killing efficiency?" I asked back what she thought about it, and she suggested running an experiment with one team focusing on one goal at a time while the others continued working as they were used to. A few months later, all teams were working on a goal at a time.

Untrapping Lesson: Help others see what you see.

Collaboration: Getting Together to Create What Matters

A sound product strategy will help teams create value independently from each other. Conversely, a confusing one will force teams to coordinate their activities and fight for prioritization.

Sometimes, each team receives a separate quarterly goal. At first glance, it looks good, as teams have a mission, but you shouldn't celebrate so fast. Reflect on the following:

- Do teams need to coordinate activities with other teams to reach goals?
- Are team goals unrelated to each other?
- Do teams need external approval to reach desired outcomes?

The more times you answer yes to these question, the more you have to coordinate, and the more slowly you can create value.

Chapter 1 discussed the differences between a coordinative flow and a collaborative one. Often, teams have no other choice but to coordinate to progress. This is an outcome of a weak product strategy. In contrast, a sound strategy will enable teams to benefit from a collaborative flow and empower them to make progress independently.

Key Takeaways

- A sound product strategy simplifies decision making, while a lack of one or a confusing product strategy will slow teams down considerably.

- The more accountable for outcomes teams are, the more value they can create; the more output matters, the less value the team can deliver.

- Analysis paralysis is a symptom of fear of failure. Teams will analyze the problem over and over again when failure leads to punishment.

- Without clear goals, teams will lack purpose and waste too much time defining what to work on next.

- The more teams collaborate, the faster they drive value. The more teams coordinate tasks, the less value they can create together.

Understanding how your product strategy simplifies decision making will help you uncover improvement points. The next step is to evaluate how product discovery enables you to drop bad ideas fast enough and what you could do to benefiting from good ones. Let's have this discussion in the next chapter.

15

Understanding How Quickly You Can Drop Bad Ideas

Discovery isn't a process you follow for guaranteed results. Applying practices is one thing; maximizing customer and business value is entirely different.

A busy routine may set you and such key elements apart. I strongly recommend stepping back once a quarter to reflect on reality and commit to improving one aspect at a time. Gradual changes will help you sharpen your discovery practices.

Use the questions to help you reveal what product discovery looks like in reality:

- **Value proposition:** How helpful is your value proposition for accelerating decisions?

- **Customer interviews:** How often do you collect insights from real customers?

- **Identifying assumptions:** How do you identify assumptions behind your value drivers?

- **Testing assumptions:** How fast can you test critical assumptions?

- **Ideation:** How do you identify solutions worth building?

The health check in Figure 15.1 can help you understand how your discovery practices enable uncovering value drivers. We discussed the elements in this health check in Chapters 6 and 7, but now I'll bring in another angle to broaden your perspectives.

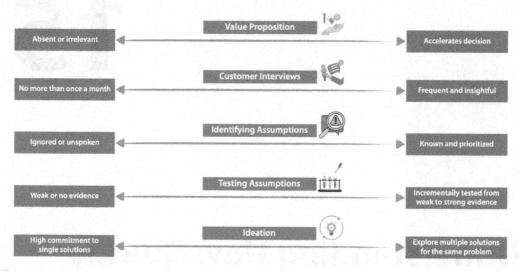

Figure 15.1
Product discovery health check

Value Proposition: Clarity on What's Most Important

Knowing how your product creates value for your target audience is vital to decision making. A busy routine combined with delivery pressure can lead to ignoring the value proposition during daily work, which then complicates decision making.

Let me share a story on the impacts of neglecting the value proposition for the Brazilian car dealers start-up.

Clarifying the Value Proposition to Enable Focus

Once, the product team cornered me and said, "David, you've got to tell us what really matters because now we're juggling lots of issues, and things are falling apart."

We had too many challenges at the same time. Car dealers didn't engage with our auction platform, car owners didn't show up to the inspections, and when they did, many customers were annoyed when they entered the negotiation room. These were problems we had to solve, but something was missing. We hadn't agreed on what our value proposition was. It was my job to nail it down.

I approached the founders and asked them what made our product valuable. They answered in one word: convenience. I asked them to elaborate. The CEO said, "Car owners come here, drop off their car key, and in 60 minutes, they get a fair offer. After they accept it, we make an instant payment and call a cab. They go home happy. All of that happens without any bureaucracy."

I decided the best way to learn about our problems was by using our service. I wanted to sell my car, so I booked an appointment and went through the flow.

As I scheduled the inspection, I got three emails reminding me about it, plus two calls. When I went to an inspection point, I handed over my car key and heard nothing for the next 63 minutes. I was clueless about the progress. Then, I entered the negotiation room and heard how bad my car was, its damages, and why the offer was fair.

I knew the car issues and how much that devalued the car, but I felt the company negotiator tried to fool me. I'd never come back. That gave me more than I needed to address experience points to provide the convenience promised in our value proposition.

Untrapping Lesson: Becoming your customer can reveal unforeseen value drivers.

Customer Interviews: Creating Insights to Unlock Learning

Nothing can replace contact with real customers. Here are two questions for your reflection:

- How often do you talk to your customers?
- How insightful are those conversations?

The closer you are to your customers, the more unknowns you can uncover.

Falling into execution mode is a common trap with product teams. There's always more to do than available capacity, and many business stakeholders believe they know what's best for the product and customers. Neglecting direct contact with customers will ensure you create too much waste before you can create value.

A healthy balance is having each product team talk to at least one customer per week. In the ideal world, each team would talk to three or more customers per week and learn from them, but that's not as simple as it sounds. Businesses are different.

For B2C scenarios, you can create a user panel and offer a small reward to get closer to your target audience. B2C is simpler because your end user is your customer. In short, the one paying for the service is also using it.

In contrast, B2B scenarios are more complex because the users of your product are rarely the people making the buying decisions. You need to understand what the actual decision makers care about and how you can align that with users' expectations.

For B2B, I recommend setting up a customer advisory board (CAB) and aligning on frequent exchanges with them. Restrict your CAB to your ideal customer profile (ICP). Putting any random five customers on the CAB won't help you get the feedback you need.

Real contact with customers empowers you to understand what drives actions, motivations, and wishes, revealing opportunities.

Identifying Assumptions: Knowing What We Don't Know

Confidence is important, but an excess of confidence can lead to unbearable results. Once we identify our assumptions, we can test them. But without that kind of testing, we're left to discover we're wrong the hard way—maybe when it's too late and the loss becomes too big to digest.

To illustrate the importance of identifying assumptions, I will share another story with you.

The Pain of Ignoring Real Users

When I worked for a digital agency, one of our clients wanted us to digitalize a complex process. In short, this process involved four audiences: research institutions, private companies, the public sector, and investors. Our client (the one hiring the digital agency) claimed to know best what to do and needed our expertise in building digital products.

When I was assigned to this project as the product owner, I quickly realized how complex the scenario was and the high risk of getting it all wrong. After talking to our clients about the potential threats ahead of us, I hit the wall. They insisted we did as they said because they knew what to do and everything would be fine.

I had gotten myself into a tricky situation. I lacked the empowerment to challenge the client, and our agency would quickly fire me if we lost the account. The outcome seemed obvious to me: We'd fail by doing as the client wanted, and that would make them lose trust in us.

I decided to be open with our clients: "We can do as you say, but I am afraid the results may be undesired because users generally react differently than expected. If we build everything upfront, changing the application later will be costly. But if you allow us to follow another approach, we can experiment with some solutions and identify what works best. That would prevent painful setbacks."

The clients carefully listened to everything. Yet they opted for going their way.

I'm persistent, so I made a second attempt. Before implementing anything, I named the assumptions with the team and presented them to our client. For some assumptions, the client had evidence validating it; for others, they were unsure how that would play out. That planted the seed I needed to run experiments.

Sadly, after a day, I got an email from the sponsor saying they'd like to follow their way. I realized they needed to digest the bitter taste of failure, but I had to minimize the damage. We decided on a Sprint Goal, and I agreed with the client that we'd present the results to the target audience and gather their feedback.

When we showed the result to the audience, they were confused and didn't know how to benefit from what we created. We had failed, but the failure was small enough to convince our clients to test assumptions.

Untrapping Lesson: Overconfidence will inevitably lead to tragic results.

Testing Assumptions: Confronting Reality

Identifying assumptions is a critical piece of the puzzle, but it won't create enough knowledge to help you drop bad ideas quickly. As I illustrated in the previous story, even when you identify the assumptions, you will fail if you don't test the critical ones.

In Chapter 7, we discussed how you can identify and test assumptions. I don't want to be redundant here, but I want to ensure you reflect on how you test assumptions in your situation because the equation is pretty simple: The more you neglect critical assumptions, the more failures you'll have to swallow.

Coming back to the previous example:

How a Painful Experience Enabled Important Changes

When the client saw the result of two weeks of work going straight to the trash bin, they panicked. They feared the project would be a disaster.

The sponsor wanted to have a conversation with me. She said, "David, we cannot afford for this project to fail, but we don't have more funds to extend our runway. How can we best move from now on?" With that, I got all I needed to start running experiments.

Our next step was to prioritize the critical assumptions. After that, we defined experiments. Time was critical, so we started with simple experiments.

We had many assumptions about challenges related to the current process. I wanted to interview users but quickly realized the complexity of organizing the interviews. Instead, I created a survey with our UX designer and sent it to our target audience. The results were eye-opening: Our clients' perceptions differed from those of real users. With that, we insisted on interviewing six users who were involved in the current process.

Through these interviews, we learned users' real pains and identified patterns. It was time to test high-level wireframes to understand how they would resonate with those users. Once again, we learned a lot.

At that point, we felt we could experiment with some solutions before committing to one. But then we hit the wall: Our client wanted only one solution and was reluctant to try different options. It was time to have an ideation session and get them more involved.

Untrapping Lesson: Strive to uncover unknowns instead of confirming your biases.

Ideation: Creating a Better Future

I used to be happy when teams knew the why behind the solutions they faced pressure to deliver. But I missed one crucial aspect: Knowing the why behind the solution enables the team to improve it. Yet, it doesn't empower them to create a better solution.

In Chapter 7, we discussed the importance of experimenting with at least two solutions in parallel to avoid falling prey to confirmation bias and commitment escalation. Here's a refresher on how we can make this possible, based on the story from the previous section.

Slowing Down to Avoid Betting Too High in a Single Option

After running a few experiments, we learned that one of the main struggles of our audience was remaining updated on the projects in which they were involved. After recognizing that, our clients immediately wanted a notification center solution.

I had to slow our clients down, so I offered an ideation session with our team. In preparation for the session, I asked all participants to reflect on the following question and come up with potential solutions: "How might we ensure that project participants remain informed about relevant updates?"

Despite the skepticism, the clients accepted my offer. They thought having an ideation session would waste time, and I was all in to prove otherwise.

During the session, everyone presented their ideas. We clustered them and dropped the ones unrelated to the challenge. After that, we selected the most compelling ideas. None of the solutions related to a notification center, and each had barely anything to do with the others.

Our clients wanted to pick one solution and go full in, but I warned them about the dangers of that approach, as they already had tasted the bitterness of failure. I was ultimately able to convince them to try out three solutions in parallel.

Instead of just building all three in parallel, the team hacked a quick-and-dirty prototype for each solution and tried them out. That allowed us to learn what made more sense for our target audience, not us.

Untrapping Lesson: Experimenting with multiple solutions for the same value driver lets you learn what's most valuable to your customers.

Key Takeaways

- Lacking or ignoring a value proposition will make simple decisions complex. Teams will struggle to agree on what deserves their attention and what doesn't.

- Identifying and testing critical assumptions can help you avoid building a solution that misses the mark. The faster you test critical assumptions, the faster you can adapt your solution to something meaningful.

- Overconfidence will blind teams to reality and lead to tragic results; solutions nobody cares about will become typical outcomes. To avoid this fate, ensure evidence ranks higher than opinions in the decision-making process.

- Nothing can replace contact with your actual users. Having data can allow you to generate insights, but relying solely on such data is foolish.

- Committing to a single solution might potentially lead to an "output over outcome" attitude, meaning delivering the solution becomes the goal instead of creating value.

By reflecting on the five elements discussed in this chapter, you can identify ways to improve how you play the discovery game. Our next and last step in remaining untrapped is to examine how product delivery takes place.

16

Examining How Fast You Can Drive Business and Customer Value

The speed of delivery tends to get more attention than it should. Sadly, focusing on speed often happens to a point where it obfuscates what's most important: creating value for end users and the business.

It's much easier to accelerate output than to maximize outcome. Even when teams have been through a transformational journey from being output-driven to becoming outcome-focused, it's natural to fall back to what's more convenient.

Perform a health check once a quarter to examine the health of your product delivery. Then, choose one aspect at a time to improve throughout the quarter.

Here are five characteristics to help you understand how sustainable your product delivery is:

- **Implementation:** Do you build it right from the beginning, or do you focus on building to learn first and making it right after?

- **Measuring results:** Is it more important to maximize features or results?

- **Feature removal:** Do you keep features forever in your product, or do you dare to remove the ones that do not contribute to value creation?

- **Facing failures:** Do you perceive failures as evil or a necessary step towards success?

- **Product backlog:** Do you let everything get into your product backlog, or do you fill it based on the current goal?

Reflect on these traits for a few minutes. Let it all sink in. The more of your answers that are found on the left side, the more chances you have to improve.

Use the health check in Figure 16.1 to understand your product delivery reality. Only when you know the status quo you can change it.

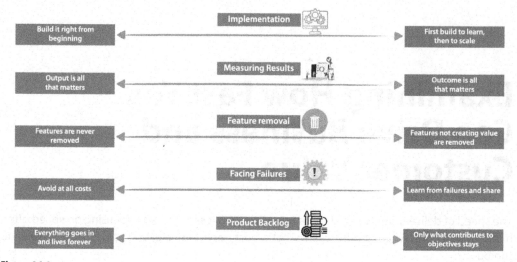

Figure 16.1
Product delivery health check

In Chapter 8, we discussed how to create value through product delivery. This chapter aims to help you ensure you're on track to drive value steadily.

Implementation: Prioritizing Learning over Scalability

Some guidance I got over my career confused me:

- Tech debt is evil. Don't let your team ever create it.

- Our solutions must be scalable and work for hundreds of thousands of customers.

Had I followed these pieces of advice, I'd have transformed teams into feature factories. The hard truth is that I did follow them until I painfully learned how misleading they were. Let's evaluate them.

Avoiding tech debt is desired by most teams. The danger lies in trying to build everything perfectly when you lack substantial evidence. When you uncover a solution worth building, you're unlikely to get everything right from the beginning. That's why avoiding tech debt is unwise when you don't know whether the solution is right for your audience.

When teams strive to build everything right from the beginning, solutions will take too long to get into the hands of users. Software engineers will spend most of the time discussing software architecture and making decisions to find the most scalable one. The problem with this approach is the assumption that the solution itself is what end users need. I wish life were so simple.

A better approach is to accept that you don't know everything upfront and start as small as possible. Your first solution doesn't need to be scalable or free of tech debt, but it must help uncover your unknowns. That's what enables you to create value faster and adapt your solution on the way.

The more problems with scalability and tech debt you try to avoid at the early stages, the more slowly you can learn.

Measure Results: Focusing on What Moves the Needle

What do you do once you've added a new feature to your product? If you had asked me this question a decade ago, my answer would be straightforward: I take the next priority and start working on it immediately. Success meant delivering more.

The magic isn't how fast you can deliver output. As technology advances, developing software gets easier. Nowadays, artificial intelligence can accelerate delivery considerably.

The magic happens when you learn which features drive desired outcomes and which don't. That lets you understand why that happens and create better solutions for your audience.

Measuring outcomes is mandatory. But it's not the only thing you should care about. Another trap lies in who measures the result. Naturally, product managers will be accountable for outcomes, which shouldn't limit software engineers, product designers, and other team members to measuring results. Outstanding product teams have a culture where everyone is responsible for results, which means everyone understands how their outputs drive outcomes.

Feature Removal: Getting Rid of Distractions

When I work with customer-facing products, I frequently talk with customer service agents because it gives me direct insights into what's painful for customers. Let me tell a brief story about what I learned from customer service at an e-commerce company.

Adding Value by Subtracting the Clutter

I asked the customer service coordinator if I could talk with the team to learn about common customer challenges. The coordinator was surprised and asked me if any of their requests were on the roadmap. When I said that I was there to learn and not to evaluate roadmap items, she told me no one would visit her team to learn. I was astounded.

Nonetheless, the coordinator introduced me to a customer service agent. I asked some questions about common requests from customers and complaints. Most of the requests were related to the following areas:

- How to process a return

- Return and refund status

- How to cancel an order

- Order status

Such issues related to information customers could get without talking to anyone. That confused me. I decided to look at our product's heatmap, particularly the "My Account" functionalities. It was a tough lesson: Customers interacted with no more than 20% of our features.

I wanted to hide ignored features, meaning features that no more than 5% of our customers interacted with. Luckily, we had all tracking in place and quickly identified those features. I couldn't believe what I uncovered. Customers had ignored 60% of the "My Account" features over the last half-year. Yet, almost nobody supported me in hiding the forgotten features. Anyway, I decided to run with my plan because I felt I had to listen to the signs instead of opinions.

We quickly adapted the "My Account" functionalities and ran an A/B test for two weeks. Then, I cross-checked the customer service requests. Curiously, the group with access to fewer functionalities reached out to customer service 50% less often.

We kept the experiment running for another week and concluded it was worth removing features. We added value by subtracting distractions.

Untrapping Lesson: Ensure you assess the value of your current features for your users. Naturally, some features become obsolete, and it's wise to remove them.

Facing Failures: Learning versus Blaming

The more risk-averse the team is, the less innovation they can create. Teams seek to avoid failure for multiple reasons—but especially out of fear. It's common to perceive failure as bad, and few people are likely to welcome something bad with open arms.

Here's a story I love about shifting perspectives:

Creating Space to Learn from Painful Experiences

At one scale-up I worked for, failures became a dilemma, and no one wanted to discuss them. The founders perceived this attitude as detrimental because failures would continue to happen. Hiding failures and neglecting lessons from them wasn't what they wanted.

The founders wanted people to learn from failures. To encourage this behavior, they sponsored a monthly event called "F*ck-up Night!" The idea was simple: Set up a stage where employees could share learnings from a recent failure.

The first event was quite engaging. One of the founders took the stage and said, "I'm here today because I led three start-ups into bankruptcy. My lessons are:

- Don't overcommit to solutions because that's not the goal.

- Focus on identifying problems your target audience has and go from there.

- The first solution will suck, but it will help you learn. Speed matters. But it's more about learning than delivery."

The employees looked excited by the honesty of one of the founders. After that speech, a product manager said, "I have something to share." They then took over the mic and shared a story on how doing what customers ask you to do leads to what customers don't need.

The "F*ck-up Night!" event encouraged teams to talk about failures to each other. After several events, I noticed teams were more open to exploring the unknown instead of creating plans to prevent setbacks.

Untrapping Lesson: Create room to treat failures as learning opportunities.

You may be able to prevent failures by playing it safe, but that will extinguish your chances to innovate. Facing failures is an intermediary step toward success.

I know failures taste bitter, and you're unlikely to enjoy the experience. But it's unrealistic to think that you can deliver the most outstanding solution from the beginning.

Here are two examples of successful pivots:

- Kevin Systrom and Mike Krieger developed a check-in app with gaming elements and photos. The app was called Burbn. Given the number of features, the creators noticed it was hard to gain traction. They cut everything they could, leaving only the photo features. That was the birth of Instagram.[1]

---

1. "Instagram: What It Is, Its History, and How the Popular App Works": www.investopedia.com/articles/investing/102615/story-instagram-rise-1-photo0sharing-app.asp.

- Odeo was a network that enabled users to find and subscribe to podcasts, but then iTunes came and took over this niche. The company decided to take a massive detour by following the idea of status-updating micro-blogging conceived by Jack Dorsey and Biz Stone. That's how Twitter came to exist.[2]

Product Backlog: Past Promises versus Future Opportunities

When you look at your product backlog, do you get trapped in the past, or does it enable you to explore the future? The more the product backlog relates to the past, the more detrimental to learning it becomes. In Chapters 3 and 8, we discussed in depth the impacts of a cluttered backlog and the benefits of an uncluttered one. We also explored how to overcome this trap.

I won't bore you by repeating those points here, but I will bring in another perspective. Let's talk about trips.

What Would Make a Better Vacation, a Detailed Plan or a Flexible One?

In 2017, I went to Boston to attend an MBA extension program at Babson College. That was my first time in the United States, and I wanted to get the most out of it, so I combined my studies with vacations. Around six months before landing in the United States, I planned a seven-day trip from Boston to multiple cities, including New York City, Philadelphia, and Washington, D.C. I booked everything upfront. I had tickets to all the attractions I wanted to visit. All of this happened before I ever stepped into the country, and I was proud of my planning because I knew what I'd do for seven straight days, from 7 a.m. to 10 p.m.

Six months passed, and I concluded my MBA extension in Boston. Then, I headed to the meeting point of my seven-day tour, but one thing shocked me: I was the only non-Chinese there. When I asked around about the tour, barely anyone could speak English. Eventually, I found the tour guide, and she told me the trip would be in Chinese and not in English because I was the only non-Chinese person in the whole group. I felt stupid and didn't know what to do, but my backlog was full, and one thing depended on the other. So, I followed the plan.

The trip was stressful. I had headaches all the time due to the excessive guidance in Chinese. I couldn't understand a word. Eventually, we got to New York and stopped at Central Park, so I sat and peacefully relaxed. I enjoyed the atmosphere and wanted to explore more but couldn't because I had tickets to other attractions. So, I moved to another place and didn't enjoy it. My head was never in the present, and it was a stressful situation. I connected my plan to the next step and never enjoyed the moment.

---

2. "The Origins of Twitter": https://penningtoncreative.com/the-origins-of-twitter.

Now, let's look at a different trip.

> For my second wedding anniversary, I went to Vienna with my wife. Our goal was to have a romantic escape. We didn't have tickets to any particular place, nor had we planned what to do. We checked tour guides but decided to walk around the city and choose what to do spontaneously. We walked around 15 kilometers on the first day, and one thing got our attention: the Vienna Opera House. We decided to go there. We were lucky because the venues were just reopening after a COVID-19 lockdown, so we got tickets.
>
> We stayed in Vienna for a week. We'd wake up every day and decide what we were up to. It was a magical trip. We enjoyed it so much that we decided that every trip would have a goal, and we'd focus on that and not on the plan anymore.

Returning to the product backlog: The more cluttered it gets, the more opportunities you miss. When I was in New York, I had to rush from place to place. I'd take a selfie and move on, but I didn't enjoy anything because I was trapped by my plan. Yet, when you start with the goal, you enable yourself to remain open, and you can have outstanding experiences.

Whenever you notice your product backlog relates to a plan or promise, remember how horrible my seven-day trip in the United States was. I failed to adapt my backlog to what I discovered (which I could have), but following the plan was more comfortable. Don't let that happen with your product backlog.

Key Takeaways

- Focus first on learning, then on scaling. Your first version of the solution should enable you to learn, and then you can decide between investing further or dropping this solution altogether if it fails to create the desired results.

- Delivering more features doesn't mean more customer value and business value. It's vital to continuously measure results and adapt according to what you learn.

- Features will have a limited lifespan. Eventually, they stop creating value and start distracting users. That's the moment you need to remove them from your product.

- Failures may hurt, but they can enable you to create better solutions if you're open to learning from them instead of creating plans to avoid mistakes.

- The product backlog should enable you to explore the future without getting trapped in the past. Keep your backlog uncluttered by focusing on your goals.

With the product delivery health check, we conclude the last part of this book. Remember, it's a journey, and there will be ups and downs. Remaining curious and eager to improve will help you keep untrapped.

Wrap-Up

I doubt you will ever work in a company where the situation is totally favorable for creating digital products.

I doubt outstanding teams won't face the traps most teams face.

I doubt teams will reach high performance by settling into their comfort zone.

I believe teams will always have opportunities to improve their work by identifying dangerous traps, adding a pinch of simplicity, and removing complexity.

I believe the best teams are humble enough to understand they always have something to learn, and curiosity drives them to reinvent how they work continuously. They are open to the new and afraid of becoming obsolete. They despise the status quo, and their optimism for a better tomorrow inspires everyone around them.

Throughout this book, we've explored what complicates creating value and how simplifying your work can drive you to steadily deliver value. We evaluated the key elements of product management and considered the best ways to combine product strategy, delivery, discovery, and measurement of results. That discussion revealed the Herculean challenge entailed in creating truly valuable digital products, but I hope it gave you insights that you can apply from now on.

You've learned the importance of stepping back and assessing how you work, because dynamics change, potentially impacting how you play the game. It's about inspecting and adapting, not about complaining and becoming a victim.

No matter where you work and how successful you are, you can benefit from frequent assessments of your product strategy, delivery, and discovery. Once a quarter, get together with your key stakeholders and team members and run the health checks shared in this book. That will enable you to talk about reality. If you don't like what you see, you can change it.

My mission with this book is audacious: I aim to empower product professionals to overcome the most dangerous traps. That's daunting because it's a rollercoaster. One moment, you're on top; the next second, you're on the bottom.

The hardest part isn't overcoming dangerous traps but getting comfortable with the uncomfortable. It would be all too easy to sit back and relax once you reach the top, but that's unwise. You've got to remain alert, pay attention to the signs, and act accordingly.

Returning to the example of El Bulli, what brought this pioneering restaurant to the top couldn't keep it there—five times the best restaurant in the world, then permanently closed a few years later. Ferran Adrià pioneered experimental culinary skills and got to the top, but he failed to adapt the strategy fast enough and faced recurrent losses year after year, forcing him to close El Bulli.

Don't expect to always see the same outcome from a continuous process. The complexity requires constant adaption. Whatever got you to the top cannot guarantee you will remain there. Remaining flexible is fundamental to progress.

Flexibility reminds me of my second wedding anniversary trip. I had a goal and a plan. But Mother Nature decided to disrupt my plan several times. I got annoyed but enjoyed the trip once I focused on the journey. Ultimately, the journey is what matters, not the plan. Start with the goal and have the courage to adapt as you uncover the unknown.

Remain open to the new, and don't get stuck with the old. That's what empowers you to remain untrapped.

Uncertainty is your only certainty in the digital product world. How do you cope with such a stressful situation? Simple. By knowing the cards you hold and making the best move. You will probably lack some cards you'd like, but using what you have enables you to get what you don't. Meanwhile, complaining about the cards you're missing will frustrate you and block progress.

Remember, you're not the victim of your circumstances. You're the hero of your story.

I'd be more than happy if this book motivated you to challenge the status quo and encourages you to implement changes of whatever magnitude are needed in your scenario. I know it's hard. That's why only a few people stand out among the crowds.

Untrapping Product Teams is for the brave ones, those willing to face more resistance than you can imagine. Sometimes, you will wish you had never started because the journey isn't always pleasant, but the results will speak for themselves. If you've gotten this far, you can do it!

Enjoy the journey and remain bold to simplify the uninvited complexity:

1. Face your reality as it is.

2. Take one step at a time.

3. Learn from results.

4. Improve and repeat.

Thanks for reading this book. If you have questions or comments, drop me a message at contact@d-pereira.com. You can join my newsletter, *Untrapping Product Teams* (d-pereira.com/newsletter), to keep updated with my insights. You can also get updated resources for *Untrapping Product Teams* at https://d-pereira.com/resources:

- Get my recommended reading list.

- Learn the necessary skills to rock as a product manager.

- Product leaders to follow.

- All untrapping templates and health checks.

- Product courses to level up your game.

- Broaden your strategy with 50 business model examples.

If you'd like to help me, the best way is by writing an Amazon review, sending me feedback, or recommending this book to a friend or colleague.

I wish you all the best in your journey. Let's rock the product world together!

Untrapping Lessons

1. Ask questions leading to a "no" answer because it relates to loss aversion and triggers reflection. [Chapter 2]

2. Understand the problem before you implement the solution. [Chapter 2]

3. Do what's necessary to focus on progress, even if that frightens you. [Chapter 3]

4. Help others say no to themselves instead of bluntly rejecting their requests. [Chapter 3]

5. Don't make prioritization complex. Simplicity is the key to adapting fast. [Chapter 5]

6. Be brave to do what's necessary, even when you lack support. [Chapter 6]

7. Doing something because your competition is doing it cannot guarantee you create value for your customers. [Chapter 6]

8. Build what's natural for your customers instead of what's rational for you. [Chapter 6]

9. Focus on one value driver at a time instead of jumping into many in parallel. [Chapter 7]

10. Applying frameworks without knowing why will create unwanted results. [Chapter 8]

11. Help the team speak up so they can figure out the solution independently. [Chapter 8]

12. Give your dev cycles a fun name; work doesn't have to be boring. [Chapter 8]

13. Wise use of tech debt can prevent you from building worthless solutions. [Chapter 8]

14. Help participants be active during reviews so the sessions are engaging, not boring. [Chapter 8]

15. Use data to enable you to progress, not to block you from it. [Chapter 9]

16. Focus on what you can control instead of what you can influence. [Chapter 9]

17. Define metrics that enable you to act fast enough. [Chapter 9]

18. Look at data from different angles so you reveal hidden opportunities. [Chapter 9]

19. Empower your team to solve challenges instead of feeding them with tasks. [Chapter 10]

20. Empowerment and trust are vital to collaborate with software engineers. [Chapter 10]

21. Don't try bridging communication between multiple business stakeholders, strive to build alignment among them. [Chapter 11]

22. Product and tech are complementary to each other. One should not report to the other. [Chapter 13]

23. Prioritization without involving product teams leads to frustration and lack of commitment. [Chapter 14]

24. Collaboration beats documentation. [Chapter 14]

25. Help others see what you see. [Chapter 14]

26. Becoming your customer can reveal unforeseen value drivers. [Chapter 15]

27. Overconfidence will inevitably lead to tragic results. [Chapter 15]

28. Strive to uncover unknowns instead of confirming your biases. [Chapter 15]

29. Experimenting with multiple solutions for the same value driver lets you learn what's most valuable to your customers. [Chapter 15]

30. Ensure that you assess the value of your current features for your users. Naturally, some features become obsolete, and it's wise to remove them. [Chapter 16]

31. Create room to treat failures as learning opportunities. [Chapter 16]

Bibliography

Bland, David J., and Alexander Osterwalder. *Testing Business Ideas: A Field Guide for Rapid Experimentation.* Wiley, 2019.

Bryar, Colin, and Bill Carr. *Working Backwards: Insights, Stories, and Secrets from Inside Amazon.* St. Martin's Press, 2021.

Cagan, Marty. *Inspired: How to Create Tech Products Customers Love,* 2nd ed. Wiley, 2018.

Catmull, Ed. *Creativity, Inc.: Overcoming the Unseen Forces That Stand in the Way of True Inspiration.* Bantam, 2014.

Cote, Catherine. "Growth Mindset vs. Fixed Mindset: What's the Difference?" March 10, 2022. https://online.hbs.edu/blog/post/growth-mindset-vs-fixed-mindset.

Croll, Alistair, and Benjamin Yoskovitz. *Lean Analytics: Use Data to Build a Better Startup Faster.* O'Reilly Media, 2013.

Dalio, Ray. *Principles: Life and Work.* Avid Reader Press/Simon & Schuster, 2017.

Dalmijn, Maarten. *Driving Value with Sprint Goals: Humble Plans, Exceptional Results.* Addison-Wesley, 2024.

Dweck, Carol S. *Mindset: The New Psychology of Success,* updated ed. Random House, 2007.

Fried, Jason, and David Heinemeier, *ReWork: Change the Way You Work Forever.* Vermilion, 2010.

Maslow, Abrahm H. *Toward a Psychology of Being.* Wilder Publications, 2018.

Mauborgne, Renée, and W. Chan Kim. *Blue Ocean Strategy: How to Create Uncontested Market Space and Make the Competition Irrelevant,* expanded ed. Harvard Business Review Press, 2015.

Maurya, Ash. *Running Lean: Iterate from Plan A to a Plan That Works,* 3rd ed. O'Reilly Media, 2022.

Moore, Geoffrey A. *Crossing the Chasm: Marketing and Selling Disruptive Products to Mainstream Customers,* 3rd ed. Harper Business, 2014.

Olsen, Dan. *The Lean Product Playbook: How to Innovate with Minimum Viable Products and Rapid Customer Feedback.* Wiley, 2015.

Osterwalder, Alexander, and Yves Pigneur. *Business Model Generation: A Handbook for Visionaries, Game Changers, and Challengers.* Wiley, 2010.

Osterwalder, Alexander, Yves Pigneur, et al. *Value Proposition Design: How to Create Products and Services Customers Want.* Wiley, 2014.

Osterwalder, Alexander, Yves Pigneur, et al. *The Invincible Company: How to Constantly Reinvent Your Organization with Inspiration from the World's Best Business Models.* Wiley, 2020.

Patton, Jeff, with Peter Economy. *User Story Mapping: Discover the Whole Story, Build the Right Product.* O'Reilly and Associates, 2014.

Ries, Eric. *The Lean Startup: How Today's Entrepreneurs Use Continuous Innovation to Create Radically Successful Businesses.* Crown, 2017.

Rogers, Everett M. *Diffusion of Innovations*, 5th ed. Free Press, 2003.

Sinek, Simon. *Start with Why.* Portfolio, 2009.

Torres, Teresa. *Continuous Discovery Habits: Discover Products That Create Customer Value and Business Value.* Product Talk, 2021.

Vernon, R., and L. T. Wells. "International Trade and International Investment in the Product Life Cycle." *Quarterly Journal of Economics* 81, no. 2 (1966): 190–207.

Index

Register Your Product at informit.com/register

Access additional benefits and save up to 65%* on your next purchase

- Automatically receive a coupon for 35% off books, eBooks, and web editions and 65% off video courses, valid for 30 days. Look for your code in your InformIT cart or the Manage Codes section of your account page.

- Download available product updates.

- Access bonus material if available.**

- Check the box to hear from us and receive exclusive offers on new editions and related products.

InformIT—The Trusted Technology Learning Source

InformIT is the online home of information technology brands at Pearson, the world's leading learning company. At informit.com, you can

- Shop our books, eBooks, and video training. Most eBooks are DRM-Free and include PDF and EPUB files.

- Take advantage of our special offers and promotions (informit.com/promotions).

- Sign up for special offers and content newsletter (informit.com/newsletters).

- Access thousands of free chapters and video lessons.

- Enjoy free ground shipping on U.S. orders.*

* Offers subject to change.

** Registration benefits vary by product. Benefits will be listed on your account page under Registered Products.

Connect with InformIT—Visit informit.com/community

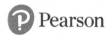

Addison-Wesley • Adobe Press • Cisco Press • Microsoft Press • Oracle Press • Peachpit Press • Pearson IT Certification • Que